Dorothy Carey

Dorothy Carey

The Tragic and Untold Story of Mrs. William Carey

James R. Beck

BAKER BOOK HOUSE
Grand Rapids, Michigan 49516

Printed in the United States of America

Library of Congress Cataloging in Publication Data

Beck, James R.
    Dorothy Carey : the tragic and untold story of Mrs. William Carey / James R.
Beck.
        p.   cm.
    Includes bibliographical references and index.
    ISBN 0-8010-1030-6
    1. Carey, Dorothy, 1756–1807. 2. Carey, William, 1761–1834. 3. Missionar-
ies —England—Biography. 4. Baptists—England—Biography. 5. Missionaries—
India —Biography. 6. Baptists—India—Biography. 7. Mentally ill—India—Biogra-
phy. I. Title.
BV3269'.C3B37   1992
266'.61'092—dc20
[B]   92-28468

Printed Sources for Illustrations

Carey, S. Pearce. *William Carey, D.D., Fellow of Linnaean Society.* London: Hodder and Stoughton, 1923. Illustrations #3, 4, 7, 8, 10, 11, 12, 15.

Leigh, Denis. *The Historical Development of British Psychiatry.* Vol. 1, *18th and 19th Century.* New York: Pergamon Press, 1961. Illustration #14.

Taylor, John, ed. *Biographical and Literary Notices of William Carey, D.D.* . . . Comprising Extracts from Church Books, Autograph Mss., and Other Records. . . . Northampton: Dryden Press, 1886. Illustration #13.

Carey centenary pamphlet, 1892. Copy in Central Library of Northampton, England. Illustrations #5, 6, 9.

The maps were rendered by Ross O'Dell.

Cover artwork: Canterbury Manor Collection,
Pattern #6992, Hoffman California Fabrics.
Reproduced with permission.

To all those husbands, wives, and children who,
like Dorothy, have suffered from the ravages of
mental illness while serving in the
missionary cause of Christ and
his Great Commission.

Contents

Foreword

William Carey is deservedly acclaimed as one of the great men of Baptist mission work, but the spotlight has never been very much played upon Dorothy, his first wife. For many decades it was shameful to admit that there was a mentally ill person within the family circle, but attitudes have changed in recent times with the growth of knowledge about such illness. In this study of Dorothy Carey, James Beck has tried to set the record straight and also to suggest quite firmly that the troubles afflicting William and Dorothy are still liable to be present today among those who undertake work on the mission field.

Indeed, *Dorothy Carey* is a valuable addition to the library that has already been built up regarding William Carey and his work. It is thoroughly researched and most readable. From time to time the story reaches a peak. One example is Dr. Thomas's letter of January 11, 1796, to the staunch Andrew Fuller, a matter of particular interest to me as I well recall my uncle, Rev. S. P. Carey, advising that the mental instability of Dorothy be not much referred to. Yet another high point is reached when the author discusses in some detail the final decision of Dorothy to go with William to India—though her change of mind may have been brought about as a result of some "pressure."

A multitude of books has been written about the early days of Baptist missions in foreign parts, but I think readers will find that this volume breaks new ground and adds a lot to our comprehension of the issues involved in the time of Carey, and to a considerable extent even today. James Beck has used his professional knowledge, his command of the English language, and his thorough research to compile a most fascinating and instructive book about Dorothy Carey.

Michael Carey (Great-great grandson of William and Dorothy Carey)
Little Cowarne
Herefordshire, England

Acknowledgments

The author wishes to express grateful appreciation to the following for permission to quote from copyrighted material:

To Mrs. Susan J. Mills, Archivist at the Angus Library, Regent's Park College, Oxford, for granting permission to quote from documents owned by that library.

To M. Y. Ashcroft, Archivist at the North Yorkshire County Record Office, Northallerton, and to the depositors of the manuscripts for permission to quote from materials held in that collection.

To the Oriental and India Office Collections of the British Library for permission to quote from materials in their custody.

To Miss R. Watson, Archivist at the Northamptonshire Record Office, and to the vicar and Parochial Church Council of Piddington for permission to quote from and reproduce materials held at Wootton Hall Park, Northampton.

To the Baptist Missionary Society of Didcot, United Kingdom, for permission to consult and select my own quotations from their archive material, which is housed in the Angus Library at Regent's Park College, Oxford, United Kingdom.

Introduction

Scene: Village of Mudnabatti, Bengal, India
Date: Friday, February 6, 1795

Suddenly it hit her. William was gone again. She was trying to get twenty-one-month-old Jabez dressed for the day when it dawned on her. Dorothy had been careful to watch her husband, and now he had escaped again. She could kick herself for letting him get out the front door.

The members of the Carey household scurried about today just like they did every Friday. It was wash day. The servants heated water and gathered laundry from different rooms in the sturdy brick house. Over the last seven months Dorothy had worked hard to train these servants so that laundry day would go smoothly. She felt pride at her success.

But this particular day was not starting out well at all. She finished dressing Jabez and called out for Will. Now seven years old, Will was the most pensive of her three boys. Dorothy worried about him because he still seemed morose and preoccupied with his brother Peter's death four months earlier. Will responded, "I'm on the back veranda." Dorothy quickly asked Will to watch baby Jabez.

"I've got to go down to the factory to find your father. I won't be long. Please be good."

Now all she had to do was locate Felix and she could be on her way. Her first hunch was correct. He was out by the front pond trying to poke around with a long stick to get a crocodile to surface.

"I've told you a dozen times, Felix. Get away from the edge of that pond!"

"Why doesn't Felix understand how dangerous that can be?" she thought as she insisted that her ten-year-old come back into the house. She despaired of getting her husband to build a safety fence around the pond.

She told all three boys to stay together and that she would be back shortly. One of the servant girls who was learning a little English seemed to understand Dorothy's hurried instructions as Dorothy flew out the front door.

She wasn't sure just where William had gone, but he probably went to the factory even though he had agreed to stay home today. Dorothy was still fuming about her argument with her husband the night before. Never before had they argued so long with such little agreement.

Anger fueled her fast-paced steps through the village. The half-mile walk to the factory didn't seem far today. People along the way, still unused to seeing a white woman, stared all the more intently. But Dorothy was too angry to notice.

She was more and more sure in recent weeks that William was having affairs. He was spending less and less time with her and the boys. His only excuse was work. Work, work, work! That was all he cared about. And he wouldn't admit he'd been unfaithful.

"I'll just have to catch him at it," she thought as she made the last turn to the river where the indigo factory was located.

There he was! Talking to that English lady who was visiting the area. "I've caught him!"

William had mentioned that Mr. Udney planned to send a new investor and his wife to visit the Mudnabatti factory. Dorothy was sure this woman was William's latest paramour.

William was pointing out the ponds and drying pits where his workers were processing indigo plants. His English guests, Mr. and Mrs. Harold Whitney, and the Bengali plant superintendent were surprised when Dorothy came screaming into their conversation.

"William, get home right now! You're not going to get away with it this time!"

William was chagrined. Dorothy had accused him of improprieties with women before, but this was the first time she had torn through the streets of the village to accuse him in public.

"Dorothy, I'm just visiting with the Whitneys who are here from Bristol. Let me introduce you to them."

"You scoundrel, I won't let you humiliate me any longer! Come back home!"

Dorothy grabbed William's arm and began to drag him away from the factory gates. William was mortified that his guests and the plant superintendent were witnessing this scene. He did his best to excuse himself so that he could take Dorothy home.

The two of them spent the rest of the day arguing. Nothing William said would calm Dorothy. And no charge by Dorothy could bring William to confess. They came to the very same impasse they had experienced the night before. William did not know what to do.

Finally, an uncanny calm returned to the household that evening. The boys were all asleep. Dorothy went off to bed. William pulled down his journal from the shelf above his desk and used the last light from the lantern to make the following entry:

> 6 February 1795. I sometimes walk in my garden and try to pray to God, and if I pray at all, it is in the solitude of a walk. I thought my soul a little drawn out today, but soon gross darkness returned; spoke a word or two to a Mahomedan upon the things of God but I feel as bad as they.

The scene described above is a reconstruction; the journal entry, however, is real. We do not know with confidence just what prompted William Carey's outburst of agony in his journal on February 6, 1795. But all the evidence points to his wife's emerging mental illness as the precipitator of his distress. Scenes similar to the one described above apparently happened repeatedly during the early months of 1795.

The name "Dorothy Plackett" does not have high recognition value. Only when we add her married name, "Carey," do we begin to associate her with the famous William Carey. She never wrote a book, never founded a society, and never achieved any of the other accomplishments that usually bring fame or notoriety. But she did marry William, and that brings her to the story of this book.

At first glance the insane wife of the great William Carey might not seem like an important person to us. After all, Carey seemed to succeed in spite of her illness. Why should we bother learning about her? Because every person is worth understanding.

Shame continues to surround those who struggle with psychological disturbance. In spite of advances in the mental health field and the large number of Christians working in this area, we continue to stigmatize ourselves and others if we become entangled with mental illness. Why do we treat ourselves and our heroes and heroines in this manner? Why does it surprise us that we are as subject to all the forms of human suffering as is anyone else?

Much of the shame may stem from the lingering suspicion that mental illness strikes those who are weak, or who lack character, or who have some hidden quirk of moral failure. These views of mental illness are actually old, nineteenth-century views that we cannot seem to dispel. In actuality, struggles with emotional problems strike the strong, the brilliant, the righteous, and the gifted as frequently as they affect anyone else. We can no longer say that the presence of mental illness automatically indicates constitutional weakness, immorality, or defect.

Two features of Dorothy Carey's life might repel us. First, the story is a sad one, a story without a "happy" ending. These stories are hard for us; we sometimes prefer to read tales of gladness, overcoming, and glorious climax. Yet we all know that life does not always have a "happy" ending, or at least one we can see this side of heaven. We can learn much from the lives of our foremothers and forefathers in the faith whose lives did not always end on heroic heights of victory.

The other aspect of Dorothy's story that can prove difficult for us 200 years later is that her life raises a host of questions, some of which may be unanswerable. Questions without answers are frustrating. But if we do not ask the hard questions, all the answers we do have may be worth very little. By at least asking the tough questions about missions and God's will, we should be ready for answers that God may wish us to hear.

Dorothy Carey made a great sacrifice, and this book chronicles the gift that she gave to Christ, to the church, and to us. Perhaps her sacrifice was not a voluntary one, but it was a sacrifice nonetheless. She has a host of descendants around the world today who are very aware of her life and story. Their courage in giving her due honor is an encouraging example to the rest of us to do the same.

William Carey was a nineteen-year-old shoemaker's apprentice when Dorothy Plackett agreed to his proposal of marriage. Neither she nor he had any idea at the time they began life together that he would someday become the premiere statesman of the modern missionary movement. Marriage soon propelled Dorothy toward missions and missions hurtled her toward mental illness.

Many books tell the story of William Carey. In most of these accounts, Dorothy "flits through his story like a pale and unhappy shadow."[1] The purpose of this book is to tell the story of William and Dorothy once again, but this time to recount the events of their lives together with special attention to how they must have affected Dorothy.

We will focus on William and his relationship to his wife and children, and on Dorothy as she encountered William's bold and radical idea of going to India. Perhaps this approach to the Carey story will help cast some light and understanding on Dorothy, an otherwise shadowy figure from the past.

William is famous for some remarkable accomplishments in many fields. Dorothy, if we know anything about her, is chiefly known as a wife who did not share her husband's vision and who went insane on the mission field. Her life with a great person was hard. Perhaps it always is.

Dorothy may have been the first to struggle on the mission field with emotional disturbance, but she certainly was not the only one to go through these kinds of trials. Early evangelical missionaries to the South Seas struggled with intemperance, some even with alcoholism.[2] Missionaries like Adoniram Judson struggled with severe depression; some wives (such as Margaret Simpson) were very reluctant to go or even refused to go; still other missionary marriages such as that of the Livingstons and the Studds were strained by long separations when the husbands were overseas.[3]

Biographers have not known what to make of Dorothy's experience. Mental illness is puzzling enough in and of itself. But in Dorothy's case, the issues are even more complicated because her tragic experience in India is almost the reverse of William's glorious experience there. As a result a wide range of opinions about her appear in the Carey literature. Some of these evaluations are none too flattering.

Just Who Was Dorothy?

Ogilvie called her a "dull commonplace woman" who was "deplorably unsuited" to be William's wife.[4] One of Dorothy's female biographers said, "It was an unlucky marriage, for she was a dull, ignorant woman, with no feeling for her husband's high aims or superior powers."[5] Wright labeled her an "illiterate, weak-minded woman, who never had the slightest sympathy with his undertakings and was utterly unsuited for his companionship."[6] These are but a few of the many overstatements and misstatements made about Dorothy. No evidence exists that they are true or even representative of her. The conclusion that she was not an intelligent person apparently comes from the fact that she could not sign her own name at the time of her marriage. But her illiteracy was far more related to the absence of a village school than it was to her intelligence or ability. She might have been a highly capable woman. We simply do not know. Seldom do these authors mention that she learned to read and write during her marriage; presumably William was her teacher.

In addition, authors often have portrayed her reluctance and initial refusal to go to India with William as but one example of her problems:

> Previous to her residence in India symptoms of her mental malady which so seriously developed in her later life had not been wanting. Her reluctance in the first instance, to accompany her husband may have been in some measure due to this affliction.[7]

Several biographers state that she had a predisposition to mental illness.[8] The implication is that while she was totally insane in India, she was partially disturbed even when living in England. Again, no evidence exists for these assertions. As we shall see, what facts do exist point to the very opposite conclusion.

The most telling indictment, however, comes from those who maintain that William's marriage to Dorothy was a mistake. "He assuredly led a wise life afterwards and he assuredly did a foolish thing when he married the melancholic sister of his former employer."[9] "Carey's wife was never anything but a clog to him. She hindered his going and in India she merely cumbered his life."[10] She was a "dead weight" to Carey.[11] Some of the most biting criticism of Dorothy comes from what otherwise is one of the best nineteenth-century biographies of Carey. George Smith says, "Never had minister, missionary, or scholar a less sympathetic mate," and to the last she remained "a peasant woman with a reproachful tongue."[12]

How can we explain this harsh treatment of Dorothy by early writers? Perhaps part of their criticism stems from nineteenth-century views of women, especially wives who disagreed with their husbands. Wives were to comply, to be supportive, and not to voice contrary opinions. Dorothy did not fit this stereotype of a wife very well. She clearly told William that she did not want to go with him. These harsh words from biographers may reflect the well-known prejudice that people have toward the mentally ill. Kind and humane treatment of emotionally disturbed persons is relatively recent. These cruel words about Dorothy may simply represent such inappropriate and unjustified attitudes toward the mentally disturbed.[13]

Meanwhile many of these same authors have subjected William to a similar but opposite disservice: overpraise. Sometimes we cannot tell which does us more harm: harsh criticism or bloated praise. Some of the praise is general overstatement: "Mr. Carey had probably the greatest facility for acquiring foreign languages ever possessed by any human being."[14] John Clark Marshman said that "The extreme consideration and tenderness which invariably marked his conduct towards her, place the meekness and magnanimity of his character in the strongest light."[15] "No word of complaint escaped him."[16] But of course he complained. Carey himself says in his journal at the beginning of Dorothy's emotional retreat from reality, "I don't love to be always complaining— yet I always complain."[17] So to suggest that Dorothy's problems never bothered Carey, that he never uttered one word of complaint, or that he never lost patience with her is to place him in an untenable position. He was as human as she. We can honor and remember him well without having to make ourselves believe he was perfect in all that he ever said or did.

Having reviewed the misstatements made about both Dorothy and William by their biographers, we must be quick to add that these same authors could also be very understanding of the tremendous difficulties this couple faced. Eustace Carey gave us a remarkably balanced view of the Careys even though he was writing very soon after the events and was the nephew of William:

> The reader is already apprised that Mr. Carey was proceeding to embark for India without his wife. All persuasions to induce Mrs. Carey to accompany him, at present, were utterly vain. To resign her eldest son, Felix, was the utmost to which her consent could be obtained. His mind was irrevocably fixed upon the mission, whatever pain, or perplexity, or odium the pursuit of it might involve.[18]

John Clark Marshman could also demonstrate some empathy with Dorothy's plight:

> A voyage to India at that period was considered, even in educated circles, a far more formidable undertaking than at the present time. It was regarded in the light of a perpetual banishment from home; and it is scarcely a matter of surprise that Mrs. Carey, who had never been beyond the limits of the county in which she was born, should have shrunk from

the prospect of accompanying her husband to so distant a country with four children on a project in which she had no sympathy.[19]

Samuel Pearce Carey, a great-grandson of Dorothy and William, wrote in 1923 a major study of their lives. In the preface of the eighth edition he said:

> I have most rejoiced to rescue the name of the mother of all his children from the cruel wrongs which have been done to her. Biographers without exception have echoed her dispraise. Now that the facts will be known, feeling will rebound in her favour. She will be unanimously defended in her first-felt inability to accompany Carey to Bengal, and will be acclaimed for *her eventual going at a single day's notice,* and will then be deeply compassionated for the price she tragically paid. Carey would wish me to lay this wreath upon her grave.[20]

S. P. Carey's hopes for the improvement of his great-grandmother's reputation have not come true. We could simply ignore nineteenth-century distortions of her if it were not for the fact that they continue to influence current writers. A 1988 play written for use by churches in their missionary education program tells the stories of several famous missionaries including the Careys. The narrator says, "William Carey had many challenges. Not the least of these was Dorothy, his wife, who could be quite testy when things didn't go her way." The narrator, who then becomes William Carey and steps into the play as an actor, says, "Well, I guess I'd better get there before she tears the town apart. (Puts on coat) Come along and join me. (Pause) By the way, from this point on, you'll know me as William" (Dorothy's voice overshadows his as she yells).[21]

A radio dramatization broadcast in 1990 contains similar distortions regarding Dorothy. After William has asked for Mr. Plackett's permission to marry Dorothy, the dramatization proceeds as follows:

WC: "Have I your blessing Sir?"

DP: "Oh indeed you have and most heartily, Mr. Carey. Only there's something, something I should tell you."

WC: "Well please go ahead."

DP: "It's about Dolly. I don't know if you made note of it, Mr. Carey, but, but Dolly is a might nervous, sometimes a bit touchy about things. Perhaps you've noticed."

WC: "Why no, she's never been that way with me."

DP: "Of course, you've only known my daughter a short time."

WC: "Yes, that's true but . . ."

DP: "You see, the thing you don't know is Dolly's mother, my late wife, before she passed away suffered for many years with a mental affliction."

WC: "A mental affliction? You mean she was . . ."

DP: "Yes, Mr. Carey, my wife went insane. Oh, she was never dangerous or violent, you understand but . . ."

WC: "Oh, I see. And you think that Dolly might . . ."

DP: "Oh no! Not that, Mr. Carey. Please, God, that will never be. It's just, well you must be patient and understanding with Dolly."

WC: "Aye, that I'll do, Mr. Placket, for I love Dolly very dearly and I want to be a good husband to her."

DP: "I know you will be Mr. Carey, or should I say Pastor Carey."

Later in that same episode the narrator says:

Much as Will Carey loved Dolly Placket, he soon began to realize that many of the things her father said about her were true. Normally, she was as sweet and gentle as any woman alive. But at times Will was disturbed to notice queer traces of a strange mental disease that had afflicted her mother. Her actions were odd and unaccountable. She would make plans or promises and then either forget or ignore them. Occasionally she would burst into violent anger over some unimportant trifle or even over nothing at all.[22]

All of the above events—the warnings from Mr. Plackett, the mental illness of Dorothy's mother, Dorothy's erratic behavior in England, and the early death of her mother—are pure fiction.[23] Tragically, these distortions needlessly color the Christian public's perception of Dorothy.

In 1834, Christopher Anderson, the great Scottish preacher who was a staunch supporter of Carey's work in India, wrote about such inaccuracies: "So it has begun to be in regard to Dr. Carey, and more, no doubt, are forthcoming. Every man will like to tell his own tale, and what with wrong hearing and wrong rehearsing, they will, I doubt not, make strange work of it."[24] Some biographical comments have been strange indeed.

William's Role in Dorothy's Story

Even though our focus in this book is Dorothy's story, we will be looking a great deal at William also, especially his personality and his family relationships. Readers must realize that this account does not give a full coverage of William's life. We can only mention in passing his accomplishments in missions, printing, linguistics, and journalism.

Dorothy's story of mental illness does not have a culprit. If we could blame William or John Thomas for the tragedy, we would have a simplistic but very unrealistic solution. We cannot even blame Dorothy's background or personality makeup for her distress. If we can locate any answers at all, they will be complex ones without any single culprit. Our goal in this book is not to assign blame; our purpose is to understand Dorothy as best we can.

While William will not be identified as the culprit in her story, we will discuss some of the features of his personality that equipped him well to handle her emotional crisis as well as some features in his makeup that worked against him as he tried to cope with her retreat from reality. Our purpose is not to debunk a hero. Carey is a giant among our forefathers in the faith, and no one book is going to destroy that. But we do need to strip away some of the myth that has accumulated around Carey suggesting that he was somehow righteously detached from any involvements with Dorothy's insanity.[25]

Understanding Dorothy's condition requires that we learn about three persons very important to Dorothy's story even though they do not normally play a major role in understanding William. We will look at Dr. Thomas Arnold of Leicester, a friend of William and a leading psychiatrist in England at the time. Dr. John Thomas, who accompanied William on his first attempt at sailing and who later convinced Dorothy to go to India, will also be a focus of our attention. Finally, we will look at the life of Felix Carey, William and Dorothy's oldest son who had an episode of emotional disturbance of his own seven years after his mother's death. We will need to explore the possibility of the similarity between Dorothy's struggles and those of her son.

The story of Dorothy's insanity is an important one because her struggles and the related issues that William faced prefigure many of the struggles faced by missionaries today. How should we educate the children of missionaries overseas? What is a missionary call? Does God call individuals, couples, or families? How much cultural affiliation with nationals is optimally good? Can a missionary be too closely bonded with the host culture? How should we care for the mental health needs of overseas personnel? How can we promote good adaptation patterns and thereby minimize cultural adjustment traumas? All of these issues are as present in our current considerations as they were in the lives of William and Dorothy 200 years ago.

By telling the story of Dorothy's mental illness we can remind all other missionaries who have similar dark and difficult episodes that they are not alone. All too often a missionary struggling under the load of emotional distress can feel like the world's first missionary "casualty." To the contrary, all who wrestle with psychological distress in the course of serving Christ overseas follow in Dorothy's train.

Dorothy's story is also important because it helps us understand the role women have played in the missionary movement.

> More recently the history of women has received increasing attention. Historians have long neglected many aspects of this subject, assuming that the history of women was covered adequately in general histories. But younger scholars have demonstrated that this is not at all the case.[26]

And so one of the greatest of all modern missionary stories (William) includes one of the most tragic (Dorothy). While he was making an almost unparalleled contribution, she was making the greatest of sacrifices. Death might have been easier for her. She was making life miserable for him, and he was making life miserable for her. In the Carey home, then, we find a microcosm of the best and worst of missions: giftedness, fear, great accomplishment, insanity, God's blessings, and withheld answers to prayer.

We will now look at Dorothy's story, taking up the challenge of H. L. McBeth who wrote, "Somewhere in missionary history a word of compassion should be written for Dorothy Carey, who paid a high price for Baptist missions and never knew why."[27]

Part One

Life in England

1

The Early Years

On January 25, 1756, Dorothy Plackett was christened in the parish church of Piddington in Northamptonshire.[1] Dorothy was the seventh child and the fifth daughter born to Daniel and Lucy. Later a son and another daughter were born into this not-so-little farming family. Two of the sons may not have survived infancy, but we do know that at least five of the Plackett children lived long enough to be married.

Dorothy Plackett's Family

Father: Daniel Plackett: baptized July 17, 1720
Mother: Lucy

Children: Elizabeth: baptized April 29, 1744
married Thomas Old, October 22, 1769
William: baptized July 13, 1746
Phoebe: baptized April 10, 1748
married Thomas Shrosberry July 25, 1785
buried May 14, 1788
Jane: baptized May 24, 1750
Lucy: baptized May 7, 1752
married Joseph Timms
Robert: baptized July 28, 1754
buried (?) January 12, 1755
Dorothy: baptized January 25, 1756
married William Carey June 10, 1781

buried December 9, 1807
Richard: baptized August 27, 1758
buried (?) April 1, 1759
Catherine: baptized May 5, 1763
married Charles Short in 1795

Notes: Most of this data is found in the Piddington parish registers of christenings, marriages, and burials, Northampton County Record Office [NCRO]. The marriage of Lucy to Joseph Timms is recorded in John Taylor, *Biographical and Literary Notices of William Carey, D.D.* (Northampton: Dryden Press, 1886), p. 27.

Piddington cum Hackleton

The village of Piddington is situated about five miles southeast of Northampton, the central city of Northamptonshire. Thus Dorothy grew up in a village closer to a "big city" than did William, whose home village was located farther to the south.

Piddington shared, and still shares, much in common with many English villages. Ancient settlements strung out along a central road consisted of houses or cottages, a public house (pub), and a church. The parish church in Piddington, as in all other villages of England, served as the locale for all baptisms, marriages, and burials. And in earlier centuries, when laws required villagers to attend Sunday services or have a good reason why they couldn't, the church was in many ways the center of life in the village. The wealthiest parish resident was often the Lord of the Manor, with perhaps a few other landowners. The vast majority of villagers, though, were peasant workers, most of whom were involved in agriculture. The parish register was the one leveling force among all residents: Baptism, marriage, and burial would be entered in precise order of occurrence next to rich or poor with little distinction made by class.

Outside of the parish register, though, life was much more segregated into the class structure: a few rich at the top, some artisans or craftsmen in the middle, and the vast majority of residents at the bottom eking out a living. The Placketts probably were at the top of this third and lowest class.

Northamptonshire was a pleasant place to live. Located almost exactly in the center of England, it was known as a shire with very little waste or scrub land.[2] The shire is only about seventy miles long and twenty to forty miles wide—relatively small for an English shire.[3] Some hills rise to the west, but the eastern sections of the shire where

Dorothy grew up slope into arable lands well drained by rivers. The major river is the Nene in which William was baptized in 1783. Today the shire retains much of its rural character because the Industrial Revolution with its machines and steam engines did not have the same impact on Northampton as it had on other English shires.

Much of the shire was still covered with royal forests as late as 1300. Today a portion of that mixed wood forest remains for public use; known as Salcey Forest, it lies close to Piddington on the way to William's home village of Paulerspury. The shire was home to poets John Dryden (1631–1700) and John Clare (1793–1864), who spent his last year in an asylum in nearby Northampton.[4]

Farming was the biggest occupation in Northamptonshire. In 1777 when Dorothy was a young adult, 51 percent of the males worked on the land. Worsted weaving was the next biggest occupation.[5] Edmund Carey, William's father, was a worsted weaver before becoming village schoolmaster in Paulerspury.

Piddington is located on a slight rise above the neighboring hamlet of Hackleton. The two are separated by a small brook; and even though Piddington should have been more important because it contained the parish church, Hackleton had a practical advantage because it was situated on a major road leading out of Northampton. In the years when Dorothy lived in the parish, Piddington enjoyed the status of village but Hackleton was only a hamlet.[6] The Plackett clan lived in both areas, and Dorothy and William likewise lived in both sections of the parish during their early married years.

The Plackett Clan

The Placketts were a large family in Piddington. Dorothy's grandparents, Daniel and Elizabeth, are the first of the family to appear in the parish. They had eight children, seven of whom appear to have survived infancy. At least four of these Plackett children remained in Piddington to rear their own families. Among these four families were Dorothy's parents, Daniel and Lucy. In the 1750s, the decade of Dorothy's birth, the curate of the Piddington church christened seventeen Plackett babies! Dorothy grew up surrounded by a sizable number of cousins, aunts, uncles, and relatives even more distant. We do not know how all the Placketts supported themselves, but we can guess that most of them were engaged in agricultural pursuits. Since no wills survive for any of these Placketts we can also assume that they did not likely own any land or houses—a major reason for making a will in those years.

Several extant parish documents give us some information about Dorothy's father Daniel.[7] Among these documents is a lease signed by Daniel on October 17, 1753, three years before Dorothy was born. The document identifies Daniel as a yeoman. In a strict sense the title of yeoman was reserved for a man holding a small landed estate, but was more loosely used of a commoner or countryman who had some respectable standing in the community. A yeoman was a status below that of a gentleman. In Daniel Plackett's case the title probably indicates that he had leased some land previously. The lease, granted by Mr. William Wake for ninety-eight years, consisted of a house "lately erected by Placket" and a piece of ground. So in 1753 with five children and several yet to come, Daniel and Lucy settled into a new cottage.

On two different occasions, in 1754 and in 1764, Mr. Plackett placed mortgages (£10 sterling each) on this leasehold cottage. Perhaps he used the funds for capital improvements, perhaps to deal with farm losses. Presumably both mortgages were paid off. No mention of them is made in 1792 when Daniel assigned the unused portion of his lease to Mr. William Smith of Piddington. At seventy-two years of age, Dorothy's father probably felt eligible for retirement![8]

In 1765 when Dorothy was nine years of age, a tragedy occurred that undoubtedly shocked the entire parish. Although parish registers of burials rarely give causes of death, the Piddington register has the following notice written after listing the burials of three teenagers on August 13, 1765:

> The three last above mentioned were drowned in a canal belonging to the Rt. Honorable the Earl of Halifax on Sunday the Eleventh day of Aug 1765 having gone there to bathe themselves and walking abreast dropped into a sand pit and were drowned.[9]

Among the dead were William Old, sixteen years old, a brother of Thomas Old who was later to marry Dorothy's sister, Elizabeth (1769). Perhaps the teenage boys did not know how to swim and were overwhelmed when they stepped into a deep hole. The curate added to the register a three-line verse in Latin lamenting the brevity of life. No doubt young Dorothy and all the children of the parish were deeply affected by this tragedy.

Illiteracy

Before her marriage, Dorothy could not read or write. We know this because she signed her name with a mark in the marriage register when she married William. Her illiteracy is often the most highlighted fact about Dorothy when biographers are telling the story of William. This inability to read or write is all the more stark when compared to William's great abilities with language. In fact most of his great accomplishments involved the use of language: the writing of his *Enquiry,* his translations of the Bible, his innovations in the printing of Asian languages, his pioneering of journalism in Bengal, and his contributions to Bengali prose. Dorothy's illiteracy at the time of her marriage is a major contrast to William's linguistic accomplishments.

The result of this one-sided comparison is that we can pick up unnecessarily negative ideas about Dorothy. Illiteracy in our day is a sign either of massive public school failure, some serious learning disabilities, a deficit in intelligence, or dropping out of school prematurely. We have grown so accustomed to universal education that it is hard for us to imagine a society in which such was not the case. In addition the word "illiterate" is now an insult, a pejorative term we use for someone we dislike or want to defame. The phrase "He's illiterate" is likely to trigger the response, "Oh, I see . . ."

To evaluate Dorothy's illiteracy at the time of her marriage in a way that is fair to her, we should compare her with her female contemporaries from the village of Piddington. We can quite easily do this comparison by looking at the register of marriages for the parish.[10] In the five years immediately preceding Dorothy's marriage and the five years immediately following, eighty-three weddings took place in the Piddington church. At the time of each wedding, the officiant would obtain the signatures of the bride, the groom, and the two witnesses. If one or more of these four persons could not write a signature, the person would make a mark, usually an "x," and the curate or vicar would add the phrase "The mark of _____." Presumably, the ability to sign one's name is related to the ability to read or write in general, since one of the first things children learn to write is their own name.

Of these eighty-three weddings, ten of them included either a bride or a groom from another parish. Thus we will eliminate these ten weddings from our analysis since the educational opportunities in other parishes are not our immediate concern here.

Eleven out of the remaining seventy-three wedding parties (or 15 percent) were composed of four people who could each sign his or her name. The remaining 85 percent of the wedding parties contained at least one person who made a mark. In 46 percent of the cases both bride and groom made marks instead of signing their names. And of the brides who came from the parish of Piddington, only 26 percent of them were able to sign their names. Forty percent of the grooms from Piddington were able to sign their names. These literacy rates for Piddington compare fairly well with social historian R. W. Malcolmson's estimates:

> The best that can be offered at the moment is an inferential statement that, given what is known about the levels of literacy in England, perhaps about half of the sons of labouring families received some sort of elementary school education, and probably not more than one-third of the daughters.[11]

The education most children did receive was minimal. Malcolmson estimates that in the 1750s 63 percent of the women and 40 percent of the men were unable to sign their names in marriage registers.[12] So when we compare Dorothy to the other women of her parish of about the same age, she is not at all an exception but part of the rule. In mid-eighteenth-century rural England, illiteracy was not a rare characteristic of women, especially in villages such as Piddington that had no school.

Why would a village lack such a basic necessity as a school? Universal education was not yet in place in England, and schools were not automatically a part of the community. Schools, like charity work, existed in villages where some wealthy benefactor or benefactress had made provision for one with a bequest or legacy. Before 1770, when Dorothy was of school age, only thirty-nine free or charity schools existed in rural Northamptonshire.[13] Thus only a minority of the parishes had a school available.[14] As late as 1825, fifty-five years after Dorothy's childhood, the parish of Piddington still did not have a school for either boys or girls. A school does appear in Piddington by 1849 since a gazetteer of that year lists a schoolmaster and a schoolmistress as residents of Piddington.[15]

So Dorothy's illiteracy had little to do with her own abilities but much to do with the lack of available educational opportunities. Dorothy did learn to read and write during her marriage to William. Presumably William was her teacher. Dorothy's sister Catherine also became literate, probably in the same manner.

Social Conditions

What were the social conditions at that time in rural England for a family like Dorothy's? Malcolmson estimates that 80 percent of England were laboring people in the eighteenth century. With only 5 percent of the population in the upper class, only a few belonged to what we now call the middle class.[16] Probably 80 percent of the English people had never seen London even though 10 to 12 percent of the total population lived there. In 1700 75 percent of the population was linked to agriculture. So far Dorothy's family fits well with this profile: a laboring (or somewhat better) family, working in agriculture, and very much linked to a local area. William's family varied somewhat from this pattern because his father was first a weaver and then later a schoolmaster.

Malcolmson writes:

> The experience of childhood in the families of labouring people is, unfortunately, almost entirely unknown to us. We have virtually no evidence concerning the treatment of babies, the practices of childrearing, the familial sentiments involved in parent-child relations, and the expectations that children had of their parents and parents of their children.[17]

We do know with some certainty, however, that infant mortality rates were high, and that almost every family had to face the agony of burying infants or young children. Around 1750 about one out of every five babies died. In the first half of the eighteenth century, even the children of noble families had less than a 75 percent chance of surviving until the age of five. "It is probably safe to estimate that, among labouring families throughout the country at large, approximately 30 percent of their children died before the age of five."[18] Most of these deaths were due to infectious diseases for which little treatment was available. Some authors speculate that parents coped with this tragic reality of life by deferring strong attachments with their children until the children survived at least until the age of two. The theory is more believable of fathers than of mothers, however. "Careful family planning made little sense in a world of such pronounced biological uncertainties."[19]

How do these facts about the rearing of children compare to Dorothy's experience? We know that she and William buried three out of the seven children born to them. Her mother apparently had to bury two of her nine children. It appears that only one out of her fifteen cousins in Piddington failed to survive infancy.[20] The extended family seems to have suffered less in this regard than did Dorothy and William and less than national averages.

Mobility was surprisingly common in the eighteenth century, but it was very local mobility. "For a majority of people the parish of their death was different from the parish of their birth. . . . At least 80 percent of the migrants moved less than fifteen miles" and most never lived more than a day's walk of their natal village.[21] In this regard Dorothy is a major exception to the rule. She became one of the few women of rural England to sail halfway around the globe to India.

The Newcomer in Town

In a small parish like Piddington cum Hackleton newcomers were probably quite conspicuous. William Carey, born in 1761 in Paulerspury, Northamptonshire, moved to Hackleton as a teenager. "Clarke Nichols has a new apprentice, somebody named Will from down south," might have been the gossip running through the village.

We have very little information about young Carey during his teen years. His sister Mary (or Polly) wrote down her recollections of her brother William many decades after their youth.[22] But even more interesting is a letter written by Rev. J. B. Vincent from the manse in Paulerspury, Carey's home village. The document is dated June 13, 1784, well before William became a person of fame:

> William Carey as a lad of 14 or 15 was looked upon as a *heavy, half-intelligent* youth from whom *little* or *nothing* was expected, most awkward and useless at any agricultural *work*. . . . His parents said he seemed to be always awake, at whatever time of the night they might speak to him.[23]

Vincent's desultory language smacks of sour grapes; perhaps the vicar was upset that William had left the Anglican communion and had become a dissenter. Nevertheless the letter suggests that William was an ordinary lad and not unusually noteworthy at this time of his life.

Carey himself wrote a description of his teenage years in an 1804 letter to Andrew Fuller. Carey asked that his comments not be printed until after his death so as not "to bring any public scandal" upon the gospel.

> My companions were at this time such as could only serve to debase the mind, and lead me into the depth of that gross conduct which prevails among the lower classes in the most neglected villages: so that I had sunk into the most awful profligacy of conduct.[24]

Most likely these statements represent a sort of Calvinistic overkill on depravity themes that was a very fashionable expression of piety at the time. William probably was just a very normal teenager.[25]

William Carey was sixteen years of age when his father saw an advertisement placed in the Northampton newspaper by cordwainer (shoemaker) Clarke Nichols of Hackleton.[26] Nichols's most recent apprentice had run away and he was anxious for a new recruit. William's first choice for a career had been to work outdoors. His uncle Peter Carey had recently returned from Canada where he had been a soldier fighting the French, and he and William loved to romp in the nearby woods. But Carey suffered from ultrasensitive skin, resulting from a cutaneous, scorbutic disorder. So outdoor work was out of the question.

Perhaps Edmund Carey sensed that an apprenticeship in weaving, his own occupation before becoming a schoolmaster, was not the thing of the future. Edmund proved right because worsted weaving soon went into sharp decline, and shoemaking was destined to become its replacement as a cottage industry.[27]

In the social conditions of the day, most parents were unable to accumulate any wealth they could later leave to their children as an inheritance.

> Consequently, the main objective of parents was to provide for their children suitable positions of employment: positions from which they could advance in life, in anticipation of future prospects, and by means of which they could support, or help to support, themselves on their way to full adulthood.[28]

Only a small minority of children, most all of whom were males, were actually apprenticed outside of their families. But William was to be just such an apprentice. Most apprentices started at thirteen or fourteen years of age and finished by the time they were twenty.[29] William's experience fit this pattern precisely. In very formal arrangements the father of an apprentice would pay the master worker a fee for taking on his son as a trainee. But if such formalities occurred between Edmund Carey and Clarke Nichols (who does not appear to have been a registered cordwainer or shoemaker), records of the transaction have not survived. William Carey began his apprenticeship sometime in 1777 at the age of sixteen.

The other apprentice in the Nichols cottage shop in Hackleton was John Warr, a convinced dissenter. All of Carey's experience up to this point in his life had been with the established Anglican Church. But John Warr's shop talk began to influence William. When King George III called for a national day of fasting and prayer on February 10, 1779, because the war in America was going poorly for the British, Warr convinced Carey to accompany him to the Hackleton Meeting House.[30] Carey heard a stirring message that day from dissenter Thomas Chater, not necessarily about the war in America, but about the gospel of Jesus as the evangelicals of the day understood it. Carey became a convinced dissenter at this time in his life, and the day is the closest date to a point of conversion that he was later able to give.

Dissent was not an easy road to travel in the England of 1779. Non-Anglicans could not become members of Parliament, educate their sons at a university, or enter certain preffessions. Therefore many of the dissenters were poor and of the lower classes.[31] Northamptonshire had a long tradition of dissent from the established church. Early nonconformists included the fourteenth-century Lollards. Quakers and Puritans were also strong in the shire in subsequent centuries. In the eighteenth century, the Baptists took a lead in the dissenting movement.[32]

After his conversion to the dissenting persuasion, Carey intensified his friendship with John Warr. On April 17, 1780, William signed as a witness at John's marriage to Ruth Pearson in the Piddington parish church.[33] John and William were able to witness of their faith in Christ to their master Clarke Nichols. Nichols made his own profession of faith shortly before his death in 1779.[34]

William Carey was almost immediately apprenticed to Thomas Old of Hackleton, a relative of Clarke Nichols by marriage. In the words of Polly Carey, William's sister,

> At the time of his master's death, brother was not master of his business, and was then put to a Mr. Old, of Hackleton, who agreed to pay his former master's widow so much for his time. This was not a necessary step, as the apprentice is free on the death of his master; but his father felt so much for the widow's loss, that he inclined to the side of mercy rather than add to her distress.[35]

Polly's words are somewhat unclear at this point, but perhaps Edmund Carey and Thomas Old had some negotiations about making this gesture of kindness toward the newly widowed Frances Nichols.

A Prospect for Marriage

We do not know how Dorothy Plackett met young William Carey. Perhaps they met when her father took her with him to services at the Hackleton Meeting House. We do know that Daniel Plackett was active with that group of believers. Or perhaps Dorothy met William when she visited her oldest sister Elizabeth, wife of Thomas Old. We can guess that they met at least by October 1779, when Carey began his apprenticeship with Mr. Old. William and Dorothy were married June 10, 1781.

When they married William was nineteen, almost twenty, and Dorothy was twenty-five. The age gap was not an unusual one for William; his mother was five years older than his father. But we can ask the question whether Carey was financially prepared to take on these new responsibilities. Malcolmson tells us that an apprentice might finish his apprenticeship and then "work as a journeyman for a while, saving some money and perhaps hoping to get a workshop of his own before deciding to marry."[36] The decision to marry was most often made if the young couple had found a place to live. Craftsmen also needed money for furnishing the house and for tools necessary for work. Perhaps Carey had been given some or all of Nichols's shoemaking equipment. Surely William must have assessed his ability to pay for a small cottage, and so the decision to marry may have been a very natural one for him to make, even though he was not quite twenty years of age.

Carey obviously knew about Dorothy's inability to read or write, but we can assume that he did not see this fact as a problem. Perhaps he was excited about the opportunity he had to teach her, and perhaps she was just as eager to learn.

The vows that Dorothy and William made to each other on their wedding day in the parish church of St. John the Baptist in Piddington were similar to the formal vows sometimes still used today.[37] Marriage was created, said the vicar, "for the mutual society, help, and comfort, that the one ought to have of the other, both in prosperity and adversity." "Wilt thou, William, love her, comfort her, honour and keep her in sickness and in health . . . ?" "Wilt thou, Dorothy, obey him, serve him, love, honour, and keep him in sickness and in health . . . ?" They both answered positively. And then they vowed to each other their love "for better for worse, for richer for poorer, in sickness and in health, till death us do part."

They could not know what these promises would later require of them.

2

The Pastor's Wife

On May 19, 1781, three weeks before William and Dorothy were married in Piddington, members of the nearby Hackleton Meeting House organized themselves into a church.[1] For fourteen years they had met together for worship as dissenters, but formal organization did not occur until 1781. The new church was congregational in format but was not a Baptist congregation. This group of believers had just emerged from some very difficult years. The congregation had mortgaged their building for £40, and could not pay it off when the mortgage was called in 1775. In addition to this financial struggle, the small assembly of dissenters had to face opposition from Lady Elizabeth Mercer who had evicted several of the congregation from their homes because of their participation in the meeting house. As a result of these struggles, attendance plummeted until 1781 when the group took on new life.[2] Among the nine charter members when the church was organized were William Carey and Daniel Plackett (Dorothy's father).[3] Thus the beginnings of the Carey marriage coincide almost exactly with the beginnings of their involvement in this new Hackleton church.

We do not know a great deal about Dorothy's personal faith at this time in her life. However, we can be certain of at least two facets of her spiritual development in these early years. First, her father and presumably his entire family had been involved as dissenters for quite a while even before the formal organization of this new church. Second, we know that William's newfound faith was very important to him, and we can assume he was careful to make sure that his new bride shared his religious convictions. In any event their new marriage was closely entwined with the faith and practice of the new congregational church in Hackleton.

Life in Hackleton, 1781–85

Dorothy was not the wife of a pastor immediately. William was primarily a shoemaker in the first years of their marriage. Northamptonshire was to become a famous center in England for the production of shoes. Prior to 1857, most shoe production in England was done by hand. Workers labored in their own cottages or perhaps in a small room attached to the house. They would gather raw materials for their work from a central location, and later would return the finished products to the same place. The system was quite efficient and economically viable until the advent of large machines that made handwork an expensive luxury. After the Industrial Revolution had placed machines for the manufacturing of shoes and boots in the Northamptonshire area, only the most luxurious of footwear came from the benches of skilled shoe-makers.[4]

Shoemakers, more properly called cordwainers, took leather pieces and fashioned them into uppers, insoles, heels, and sidelinings. The careful handstitching process also included welts, felts, toe bits, and stiffeners. The boot or shoe was not a simple item to make. This cottage industry greatly profited from large contracts for army boots that the government began to issue as early as the mid-seventeenth century. Many cordwainers kept birds in their workshops and were more literate than many of the other crafts groups in England.[5] Certainly Carey was more literate than most of his contemporary craftsmen neighbors, but we do not know that he kept birds in his workshop even though he was very fond of them. Another stereotype of cordwainers was that an unusual number of them went on to become writers, poets, or philosophers. Included in the number of former shoemakers are George Fox, Thomas Hardy, Robert Morrison of China, Hans Christian Anderson, and John Greenleaf Whittier.[6] Quite an impressive group! If the stereotype is at all true, the reason for such a respectable track record may be the countless hours the cordwainer spent alone at the bench fashioning boots and shoes. The shoemaker had lots of time to think and contemplate. We can be quite sure that Carey's active mind developed many of his preaching and missionary ideas during just such long hours engaged in sewing leather.

Wives of cordwainers eventually joined in the manufacturing process, often sewing the uppers in between "excursions to the kitchen to see how the dinner is cooking, or superintending the mysteries of the family wash."[7] But this development did not occur until the middle of the nineteenth century. So Dorothy's involvements in shoemaking as a new bride were probably very limited.

At some point in their first year of marriage William preached his first sermon in the Hackleton church.[8] Lay preachers were quite common among Baptists of the day. Dorothy and her father must have been proud. Because preachers, lay or ordained, were a rare commodity at that time, word must have spread quickly that William Carey of Hackleton was a budding preacher of the gospel. The church in Earls Barton, a nearby village, soon asked him to preach for them. He began preaching there every other week in June 1782. This neighboring village was a walk of about seven-and-one-half miles from Hackleton. Carey probably walked through Brafield-on-the-Green and Cogenhoe to get to Earls Barton. He would have had a major task getting across the waterways of the Nene on his way to church Sunday morning. In good weather the two-hour walk (one way) was probably a delight, but inclement weather could no doubt make the walk less than pleasant. The long trek must have given William ample time to work out the sermon in his mind and even to practice giving it once or twice!

Did Dorothy ever take the Sunday morning walk with her young preacher husband? We do not know, but if she did it wasn't for long since she gave birth sometime in 1782 to their first child, a daughter.[9] They named her Ann after William's grandmother and sister.

At about the same time William developed ague, a malaria-like fever characterized by successive chills and sweats. At twenty-two years of age William went prematurely bald, and the family always blamed the ague for this condition. William soon began wearing a wig that some called ill-fitting. Carey was only 5'4" tall, and the wig was less than flattering.[10]

For the first year or so of their marriage the Careys lived in a Hackleton cottage described by Polly Carey as "small and neat."[11] But finances were tight. During William's bout with ague he sent for his mother to come help manage the family. Carey's mother was shocked at the abject conditions in which Dorothy and William were living. William's brother gave the young family some money, and friends back home in the village of Paulerspury collected money to help William and Dorothy find a better place to live.[12] With this money they moved to a slightly better house in Piddington. In this new house two-year-old Ann died from a fever. William and Dorothy probably buried Ann in a now unmarked grave in the cemetery adjacent to the Hackleton Meeting House. And so the young family had to struggle with the most agonizing kind of loss any family can know, the death of a child.

Poverty continued to haunt them. In June 1782, Carey attended a meeting of the local Baptist association in Olney, a few miles distant from Hackleton:

> I, not possessed of a penny, that I recollect, went to Olney. I fasted all day because I could not purchase a dinner; but towards evening, Mr. Chater, in company with some friends from Earls Barton saw me, and asked me to go with them, where I remember I got a glass of wine.[13]

Shoemaking was not a surefire way to get rich. At best it provided the barest of income. And the church in Earls Barton was unable to pay him much for his preaching services.

Another economic blow occurred on the last day of 1783: Thomas Old died on New Year's Eve and was buried in Piddington on January 3, 1784. Carey had worked with Mr. Old for over four years. Carey had probably progressed beyond the level of an apprentice in the craft of shoemaking, but the business had clearly belonged to Mr. Old during this time.[14]

William and Dorothy inherited Old's shoemaking business in exchange for helping oversee the bereaved family. Because Elizabeth Old owned her own cottage and received income from invested assets, the financial burden on William and Dorothy was probably not as great as most biographies suggest. The burden was, however, a heavy moral and emotional obligation. Dorothy and William had been married only two-and-one-half years. And now her sister, a niece, and three nephews were under their informal care. Slowly moving into the teenage years of one's own children can be one thing; inheriting two teenagers of someone else can be quite another matter! No record survives in Piddington records to tell us how long the widow Elizabeth lived. Perhaps she moved to another parish where she married again or lived alone until her death.

Now William had his own business. He got off to a shaky start when some customers of Thomas Old took the occasion of his death as an excuse to back out of some orders for goods.[15] Carey's nephew Eustace wrote that the financial management of the business was not William's strong suit. Even though Carey was very capable at the mechanical aspects of shoemaking, he was "confessedly very incompetent" at the more mundane task of managing the finances.[16]

Spiritually the Carey family continued to develop and change during these years. As William increased his contact with Baptists in the area, he became more attracted to their stand on the value of believer's baptism. Dorothy and he must have had long conversations about the matter because in 1782 they chose not to have their daughter Ann baptized in the Piddington parish church. Such a decision is not a small one for two people who themselves had been baptized as infants. The decision was one of great faith. The death of Ann would have stretched their convictions to a new limit. Burying an unbaptized child would be extremely traumatic for dissenting parents uncommitted in their faith. William and Dorothy must have had their personal position on this matter fairly well worked out by the time Ann died in 1784. The death of an unbaptized child would challenge dissenting parents to express strong faith in the caring qualities of the God whom they worshiped.

When William first began to have an interest in the subject of baptism he enquired about the matter with Rev. John Ryland, Sr., pastor of the College Lane Church in nearby Northampton. Ryland gave Carey a pamphlet on the subject and turned him over to his son John Ryland, Jr., who served as an associate pastor at the College Lane Church.[17] At 6 A.M. on Sunday morning, October 5, 1783, John Ryland, Jr., baptized Carey in the River Nene in Northampton.[18] In an 1812 speech Ryland described the scene:

> October 5th, 1783, I baptized in the River Nene, a little beyond Dr. Doddridge's meeting-house at Northampton, a poor journeyman shoemaker, little thinking that before nine years had elapsed, he would prove the first instrument of forming a society for sending missionaries from England to preach the gospel to the heathen. Such, however, as the event has proved, was the purpose of the Most High; who selected for this work not the son of one of our most learned ministers, nor of one of the most opulent of our dissenting gentlemen, but the son of a parish clerk, at Paulerspury, Northamptonshire.[19]

The Hackleton church did not have a strong position on baptism. The baptism early that Sunday morning was somewhat unusual because

Carey's baptism was not accompanied by membership in the College Lane Church. Carey continued to be a member of the Hackleton church. How much did Dorothy participate in William's decision to be immersed? They obviously talked about it. Dorothy probably did not walk into Northampton at 5 A.M. that Sunday to witness the early riverside service. Responsibilities caring for baby Ann would have precluded that. But she undoubtedly realized that William's decision to be immersed was momentous and important. She was not ready to take such a large step herself, however.

Just who were these Baptists with whom William and Dorothy became increasingly affiliated? They were quite strong in the Northamptonshire area and had an unusual number of very able and qualified leaders.[20] Much of their subsequent fame stems from a major doctrinal shift they were making at the very time William Carey was affiliating with them. Earlier in the eighteenth century English Baptists had driven themselves into a theological cul-de-sac. They were enamored with Calvinism, but their overuse of the doctrine of providence had paralyzed them in the areas of evangelism and missions. If God is indeed sovereign, and if he has chosen those whom he will save, they will be saved without human intervention or effort. The resulting passivity had locked them into an untenable position. They were not growing and God's blessing seemed distant.

A key figure in moving the English Baptists out of their doctrinal stagnation was Andrew Fuller. When Fuller lived in Soham, Cambridgeshire, he rebuked a fellow church member who was often drunk. The chastised inebriate defended himself by saying that he could not help himself; God had willed him to have this problem, and he could not be held accountable. The Soham pastor was dismissed in the ensuing squabble, and Fuller was propelled into a re-examination of his hyper-Calvinism.[21] In 1785 Fuller published *The Gospel Worthy of All Acceptation*. The book triggered a profound shift toward a more evangelistic Baptist faith. Fuller deserves credit for paving the way toward a missionary vision among English Baptists even though Fuller himself said that "The origin of the mission is to be found in the workings of Brother Carey's mind."[22]

Another feature of these nonconforming Baptists centers on their capacity to offer great opportunities to people like William Carey. They did not have ironclad rules about training for their ministers, and they were very much connected with the poorer classes of England.

Amongst the early Dissenters it was the Baptists who offered an exceptional scope and encouragement to laymen of low social and economic position. . . . Great opportunity was offered the ordinary member. Their power of survival and expansion . . . may probably be taken as evidence of their importance in providing social training and developing individual initiative amongst the poorer classes.[23]

Carey eventually greatly benefited from these qualities of English Baptist life.

Life in Moulton, 1785–89

Dorothy must have realized that her husband's reputation as a lay preacher was spreading when the Baptist church in nearby Moulton asked him to serve as their pastor. Moulton was a village on the northern edge of Northampton. Dorothy and William, still childless, moved there on Lady Day (March 25) 1785. They moved into a cottage made for a shoemaker; inside the front door was a trough built into the wall for soaking leather.[24] The flat was immediately adjacent to the Moulton church building and cemetery. Walking to work became a much simpler proposition than trekking from Hackleton to distant Earls Barton.

Now William and Dorothy were beginning a new phase of their lives. Dorothy was twenty-nine and William was twenty-four when they began their work in Moulton. He was moving away from shoemaking as his primary career focus, but he was not moving away from the ravages of poverty. The church in Moulton paid him £10 per year, not a living wage. The Baptist association headquartered in London added an additional sum of £5 per year to what the church could afford to pay.[25] But these two sources of income combined did not protect the Carey family from having to file special documents of the poor.

The Poor Law in effect in late eighteenth-century England was originally passed by Parliament in 1597–98 and again in 1601 in the days of Queen Elizabeth I. The law attempted to give each parish responsibility for its own poor. The Churchwarden, an officer in the parish, oversaw the program. Each parish had to maintain and house the aged, sick, disabled, blind, and poor from its own parish funds. The church was to provide work for as many able-bodied persons in the above groups as it could. Well-bodied beggars were to be jailed.[26]

The law looked better on parchment than it worked in real life. For example, some parishes in England resorted to makework in order to comply with the law. "In desperation they hired some paupers to collect stones from arable land, and others to throw stones back so as to guarantee employment the next day."[27] Another problem emerged when a poor family, such as the Careys, attempted to move from one parish to another. The new parish was not at all eager to welcome a family that might soon become dependent on meager parish funds for survival. In 1662 the Act of Settlement allowed any parish to move on, within forty days, any newcomers who appeared likely to become a burden to the parish.

> A new kind of serfdom was thus imposed on the poor. They were compelled to remain in their village or town, not because they were forbidden to leave, but because no other parish would accept responsibility for them. In an effort to overcome this, certificates were often issued to migrant workmen by the parish accepting liability in the matter of settlement.[28]

This law snagged Dorothy and William in a bureaucratic snare. They had to file for just such a certificate when they moved to Moulton, even though he had employment with the church there. Three overseers in Paulerspury, the village of William's birth where he had not lived for the last eight years, had to sign an affidavit that the parish of Paulerspury would accept William and Dorothy back into its borders if indeed they should become paupers while living in Moulton. After William's father attested to the certificate and two magistrates signed it, the officials of Moulton allowed the young, and probably intimidated, couple to settle into their new home in Moulton. "Carey and his family never managed to live in anything but poverty almost up to the day of his leaving for India in 1793."[29]

English society tolerated poverty in part because many viewed social inequalities as ordained by God. Otherwise why were there commands in the Bible to both servants and masters? People also justified these harsh conditions because the poor, although struggling with material matters, could enjoy much greater spiritual benefits because they had fewer material concerns than did the wealthy.[30]

William and Dorothy did the best they could. In a letter to his father and mother from Moulton, William wrote:

> We have been favoured by the God of Providence lately, in a singular manner. A few days ago I received 5 guineas from the Fund, and in a

week or two I expect from the same quarter, books to the amount of
5 guineas more. My friends have made me a present of a coat, a waistcoat
of Velvet and other articles to the amount of near a guinea more, all of
which were unexpected helps in Providence.[31]

When William and Dorothy first arrived in Moulton they were
excited about the possibility of starting a school. William had observed
his father as a schoolmaster, and the Moulton schoolmaster had recently
moved away, leaving quite a need in the village. Carey's school pros-
pered at first but soon the former schoolmaster returned and siphoned
off many of William's students, who understandably wanted to go back
to their former teacher.

> He therefore turned again to shoemaking, this time as a journeyman
> for a government contractor who supplied boots for the army and navy.
> For making the boots, delivering them to his employer at Kettering and
> collecting a fresh supply of leather, he received about 10 shillings (50
> pence) a fortnight.[32]

The contractor was Thomas Gotch who was later to become an important patron of William's missionary dreams.

We know that Dorothy was involved to a certain extent in the development of William's thinking about the needs of a lost and dying
world. She couldn't avoid it. William mounted a large map of the world
on the wall of one of the small rooms in their house. Andrew Fuller
tells us what the wall looked like:

> I remember on going into the room where he employed himself at his
> business, I saw hanging up against the wall a very large map, consisting
> of several sheets of paper pasted together by himself, on which he had
> drawn, with a pen, a place for every nation in the known world, and
> entered into it whatever he met with in reading, relative to its population,
> religions, etc. The substance of this was afterwards published in his
> "enquiry."[33]

Carey also constructed a small leather globe representing the earth
with the various continents traced on the surface.[34] Both the wall map
and the globe must have triggered conversations between William and
Dorothy. His growing knowledge of the world and its spiritual needs
could hardly have been secrets that he never shared with his wife.

The Moulton church did not immediately ordain their new pastor. Baptists of the day were cautious and did not move quickly in areas of church membership or the ordination of pastors. William's church membership in the non-Baptist church at Hackleton was not a strong recommendation for him as a new pastor at Moulton Baptist Church. Upon the advice of his pastor friends, William applied for membership with the Baptist church in Olney, a village in the eastern part of the county. Then once he had strong connections with a recognized Baptist church, plans could proceed with his formal ordination and installation at Moulton.

The Olney church was large and significant in the association.[35] The following extracts from the church book at Olney trace their evaluations of this young pastor named William Carey.

> June 17, 1785. A request from William Carey of Moulton in Northamptonshire was taken into consideration. . . . He bears a very good moral character. He is desirous of being sent out from some reputable & orderly church of Christ, into the work of the Ministry. The principal Question debated was "In what manner shall we receive him?" By a letter from the people at Hackleton, or on a profession of faith &c.? The final resolution of it was left to another Church Meeting.

> July 14, 1785. W. Carey appeared before the Church, and having given a satisfactory account of the work of God upon his soul, he was admitted a member. . . . He was invited by the Church to preach in public once next Lord's Day.

> July 17, 1785. W. Carey . . . preached this Evening. After which it was resolved, that he should be allowed to go on preaching at those places where he has been for some time employed; & that he should engage again on suitable occasions for sometime before us, in order that farther trial may be made of his ministerial Gifts.

> June 16, 1786. The case of Bro. Carey was considered and an unanimous satisfaction with his ministerial abilities being expressed, a vote was passed to call him to the Ministry at a proper time.[36]

Although Dorothy had married a capable man, he was not such a superstar that he dazzled everyone who met him. The Olney church took one whole year to recognize Carey's call. He was growing and maturing in his abilities to minister, and time was very helpful in this process. We do not know if Dorothy was able to travel to Olney with him for any of these events, but she probably was present in Moulton when, on May 3, 1787, William was received from Olney as a member in the church he had been pastoring for nearly two years. His ordination to the pastorate at Moulton occurred on August 1, 1787, with John Ryland, Jr., John Sutcliffe, and Andrew Fuller participating.[37] From a sociological standpoint, William and Dorothy were experiencing social emancipation.[38] From a spiritual standpoint, God's blessing was evident in their lives and ministry.

An important event in Dorothy's years in Moulton occurred when she was baptized and accepted into church membership in October 1787. We do not know if Dorothy had just recently made a decision to be immersed or if she had made her decision earlier. Perhaps they had postponed her baptism until she was not pregnant or until her husband could baptize her as a fully installed and ordained pastor of the church. Regardless, she must have given testimony to her personal faith in Christ to the church before her immersion. Was this event just perfunctory for Dorothy? Or was her baptism a serious spiritual step? We do not know. Given Carey's growing Baptist convictions and the seriousness with which he regarded church membership, we can be quite sure that he attempted to make Dorothy's baptism a serious and well-intentioned milestone for her.

Three children arrived in the Carey family during their five years in Moulton: Felix, 1785; William, 1788?; and Peter, 1789. No one needs to wonder what consumed Dorothy's time and energy as she cared for this growing family. Undoubtedly she, like every other parent in Moulton, shuddered during 1788 when an epidemic of smallpox ravaged the community. Ten people were buried on one single day, June 16, 1788. The parish register notes, "In the course of this year the Small-Pox prevailed in general throughout the County" and the parish underwent "an almost general inoculation."[39]

William had continued to serve the small Earls Barton church in addition to serving the Moulton church. But he soon had to sever the connection with Earls Barton. "The little that they collect for me does not pay for the clothes which I wear out in serving them."[40] Meanwhile the church in Moulton began to prosper under his leadership. The ten previous years without a pastor had taken to their toll on the little Baptist congregation. They were glad for the renewal God was bringing them. Carey attempted to solidify this spiritual growth by instituting a new church covenant to which all ongoing members would have to subscribe in order to keep their church membership in good standing. Dorothy Carey's name appears under William's when this new covenant is put into place, but the handwriting is clearly William's.[41] Perhaps Dorothy had not yet learned to sign her own name or perhaps she was home that day with a sick child.

Soon the Moulton congregation faced the same problem all growing churches meet: the provision of more space. On April 23, 1787, the church prepared a circular letter asking sister churches in the surrounding areas to help them. The letter was co-signed by several neighboring Baptist pastors:

> We are a very poor Congregation of the Baptist Denomination, who assemble for Divine Worship at Moulton, near Northampton, and are possessed of a small old Meeting-House, which is exceedingly out of Repair, and one Side Wall is become so ruinous, that we are justly apprehensive it will be dangerous to meet there much longer. Besides, it has pleased God, since our present Minister came among us, to awaken a considerable Number of Persons to a serious Concern for the Salvation of their Souls . . . so that for two Years past we have not had Room sufficient to contain them. . . . We are all so poor, that, upon attempting a Collection among ourselves, we could raise but a few Shillings above Two Pounds.[42]

Carey personally took the letter on fund-raising trips to Coventry and Birmingham.[43] Some funds came in, but the church had to borrow additional money. "The increase of our congregation and the ruinous state of our Meeting House rendered it necessary to pull it down and rebuild and Enlarge it, which we have accomplished, tho' we still have a very Considerable Debt upon us."[44]

Soon another church was recruiting Pastor William and his family. The Harvey Lane Church in Leicester, county seat of the shire immediately north of Northamptonshire, wanted him as its pastor. On April 2, 1789, the Moulton church wrote

> Our beloved Pastor who had been in Considerable straits for want of Maintenance informed us that the Church at Leicester had given him an invitation . . . on which account we appointed to meet every Monday Evening for Prayer on that affair.[45]

Prayer did not stop the process. On May 7 Pastor Carey informed the church that he and his family were moving to Leicester to assume a new pastorate.

Harvey Lane Baptist Church, 1789–93

The Careys began their ministry in Leicester on Midsummer Day, June 22, 1789. Following the usual custom, Carey was not ordained to the ministry at Harvey Lane until his time of probation as a pastor had elapsed. On Tuesday, May 24, 1791, almost two years after he had started, this second ordination took place in a service conducted by his friends John Sutcliffe of Olney, John Ryland, Jr., of Northampton, and Andrew Fuller of Kettering.[46]

The family settled into a house across the road from the church. In a letter to his father, William said that they had a good house commanding a view of the countryside. In spite of the taxes and levies, he felt it was an inexpensive house.[47] The cottage must have been a convenient and enjoyable house for Dorothy and William. Gardiner wrote, "I have seen him at work in his leathern apron, his books beside him, and his beautiful flowers in the windows."[48] Unfortunately, Carey's salary at Harvey Lane was no greater than his salary had been at Moulton.[49] Carey supplemented the salary by again teaching school. His oldest son Felix was now one of his pupils.

Very soon the Leicester church also began to prosper under Carey's pastoral leadership.

> At a church meeting Septr. 1789 as our Hearers increased so that we had not room for them to sit conveniently it was agreed to Build a Front Gallery, which was done by Feby. 1790. This with the alterations of some of the Pews below cost about Ninety eight Pounds. After we had applied to several Churches for assistance to defray this expense, in Vain it was agreed to subscribe weekly among ourselves to pay off 60 pounds which remained; this was done by the Minister & many of the Members.[50]

In addition to the changes occurring in the facilities of the Harvey Lane Church, Carey also worked on the spiritual health of the congregation. Again he supervised the reworking of the church covenant. The new document was based on an earlier 1760 covenant, but it omitted an emphasis on particular election, the feature of Calvinism that had locked these Baptists into evangelistic inactivity. The new covenant added that "All rational creatures are under indespensable obligation to obey the law of God."[51] Other changes included issues of order and discipline, the importance of supporting the minister, and a democratic format for church votes.

Tragedy again struck the Carey family. Their second daughter Lucy, who was born in Leicester, died in her second year. They had named this child after Dorothy's mother, Lucy Plackett. Again, a daughter had survived the hazardous months of infancy only to die as a toddler. They buried her in a small graveyard adjacent to the church building. William's sister Polly was later to recall their grief:

> This was a painful stroke both to parents and children. They all seemed so fond of her. He used to mention the death of this child in every letter for some time, yet with a degree of resignation and submission to the Divine will. We were convinced, however, that he was touched in a tender point.[52]

Two other features of the time the Careys spent in Leicester are important to our understanding of Dorothy's story. First, William's work schedule was incredibly heavy. Apparently William's father had complained that his son was not writing letters home very frequently. The following extended passage is Carey's justification for his dilatory correspondence habits:

> I hope to amend for the future. But if I send you an account of the partitions of my day you will see that you must not expect frequent letters. On Monday I confine myself to the study of the learned languages, and oblige myself to translate something. On Tuesday to the study of science, history, composition, etc. On Wednesday I preach a lecture and have been for more than twelve months on the Book of Revelation. On Thursday I visit my friends. Friday and Saturday are spent in preparing for the Lord's Day and Lord's Day preaching the Word of God. Once a fortnight I preach three times at home, and once a fortnight I go to a neighboring village in the evening. My school begins at 9 in the morning, and continues to 4 in winter and 5 in summer. I have acted for twelve months as Secretary to the Committee of Dissenters, and am now to be regularly appointed to that office with a salary. Add to this occasional journeys, ministers meetings, etc. and you will rather wonder that I have any time, than that I have so little.[53]

Carey is obviously somewhat defensive in this passage, and perhaps we should thus allow for a little overstatement. But even with that allowance, he was an incredibly busy husband and father. His thirst for knowledge, his inquisitive mind, and his dedication above and beyond his pastoral job description were commendable. Are we being fair to him when we ask what time he had for his wife and four children? In a sense such a question is very much a twentieth-century query. Even though we tend to feel we have a scriptural obligation to spend time with each other as family members, our forefathers and foremothers did not envision the issue in exactly the same way. We can be sure that Carey was a very busy man, and he may or may not have given much attention to his family. Yet we can also agree with Drewery who wrote about Dorothy, "She must have felt at times very much alone."[54]

The second feature of their life at Leicester that is important for our understanding of Dorothy's story is the friendships that William formed in Leicester. We have already noted how Carey was attempting to loosen the rigid boundaries of the hyper-Calvinism of English Baptists. He also displayed remarkable openness to persons of other faith traditions as he made friends in the city. One friend was a Quaker, Richard Phillips, a radical newspaper editor and publisher. Phillips was known for his sympathies with the American Revolution and with Thomas Paine. A radical friend indeed! Another friendship Carey made in Leicester was with Robert Brewin, a wealthy Unitarian with a garden of rare plants. Brewin and Carey shared botanical interests, and Carey was a frequent guest in Brewin's elaborate garden. Carey was later to establish his own fame as a botanist once he got to India. Thomas Robinson and William Ludlam, both Anglican clergymen, also joined the circle of Carey's friends.[55]

A final significant friendship Carey made in Leicester was with a physician, Thomas Arnold. Today we would call Arnold a psychiatrist although this medical specialty had not yet established itself in the 1790s. Carey had no way of knowing that Dorothy would slip into a psychotic state later in India. Nor did Carey probably realize that Arnold was one of England's most progressive researchers into the nature and treatment of insanity. Carey formed the friendship more because of Arnold's generous offer to let Carey use his personal library. Carey loved books and apparently relished the opportunity to read books he had borrowed from Arnold.[56]

Arnold was a physician at the Leicester Infirmary when it opened in 1771. He later was instrumental in the planning of a wing in that hospital for the treatment of the mentally ill.[57] He also managed a private asylum in Leicester called Belle Grove.[58] Arnold's father had also operated a private mental hospital along with his responsibilities as a lay preacher at the main Baptist Chapel in Leicester.[59] Hence Thomas Arnold probably had sympathies for the dissenters' cause even though he himself was an Anglican.

We do not know if the friendship between Carey and Arnold went beyond their mutual interest in books. Could Arnold have invited Carey to visit his asylum? Could Carey have made a pastoral call on a Harvey Lane Church member who might have been confined there? Did Carey ask questions about Arnold's work with the insane? Could he have known that Arnold was a pioneer in the development of British psychiatry, later to be mentioned in almost every history book on the subject?

In 1782 Arnold published the first of two volumes on the nature of insanity; volume 2 appeared in 1786.[60] We can be almost certain that Arnold gave Carey a copy of at least volume 1 since Carey and John Thomas refer to that volume later in India. Carey must have valued the book enough to take it with him on the sea voyage. Volume 1 was a detailed classification of the various types of mental illness, and it anticipated several major advances in diagnostic understanding.[61] Arnold was one of the first to attempt a classification system based primarily on symptoms, now the favored approach to differential diagnostics.[62] The book gained notice throughout the medical community and eventually came to the attention of King George III, who himself struggled with mental illness.[63]

We do not know if Dorothy ever met Thomas Arnold. Was Arnold's friendship with Carey a providential preparation for what the Careys were later to face? We do not know. But the Careys' years in Leicester were rich ones indeed.

3

William's Decision to Go

The burning missionary vision that propelled William into fame as the founder of the modern missionary movement took shape during the first twelve years of his marriage. We are unable to chronicle the development of his ideas with exact precision. But we do know about some of the books and authors that were influential in this process. His reading and study must have started in the Hackleton–Piddington years. We know that Carey was thrilled to find a New Testament commentary on the shelves of his master shoemaker, Thomas Old. His thirst for knowledge led him eventually to learn New Testament Greek, Hebrew, and Latin.[1]

He learned Dutch by studying an old volume given him by a village woman. Carey's friend John Ryland later received a book of sermons from Holland that included a dissertation on the gospel. He sent the tract to Carey, who translated it.[2] Carey's translation has survived and was found earlier this century in the vestry of the College Street Church in Northampton. While some have questioned Carey's ability to learn so many languages well, we can judge the quality of his linguistic abilities by examining this Dutch translation.

> The deciphering of the Dutch script can have been no small feat, and though there are evidences that Carey was occasionally somewhat baffled as to the sense, there is no doubt at all from the translation both of the letter and the so-called pamphlet that he had a very competent knowledge of the language. These are not school boy exercises.[3]

In addition to studying language, Carey avidly read the *Northampton Mercury*.[4] He borrowed books. He most likely used the library at the Guild Hall in Leicester, only three minutes' walk from his cottage.[5] All of these sources served as storehouses of information as Carey developed his burden to take the gospel to the heathen.

How much did Dorothy know about all the ideas swirling in William's head? We wish we knew. We are faced with two basic options at this point in understanding Dorothy's story. Either William never talked with his family about all the exciting discoveries he was making, or he shared what he was learning to some degree with Dorothy and the older boys. We can make better sense of the story by assuming that Carey shared at least some things than to assume that he shared nothing. We have no evidence that he would attempt to take his family overseas without ever having tried to convince them of the wisdom of the venture. Just how much he shared of what he was learning we do not know. But the wall map, the leather globe, and all the books that came and went from the cottage must have triggered family discussions. What was Dorothy's reaction to these new ideas? Again, we do not know.

Books Around the Cottage

In the various sources available to us, Carey makes mention of several books and authors that greatly influenced him. They form a fascinating set of sources that help us reconstruct what was in Carey's thinking as his missionary vision was taking shape. We can merely guess how much of the following material William may have shared with Dorothy.

Help to Zion's Travellers

Rev. Thomas Skinner gave Carey a copy of Robert Hall, Sr.'s book, *Help to Zion's Travellers*. This personal copy was found among Carey's possessions in India after his death in 1837.[6] The copy is well used with Carey's own notes written in the margins. The book eventually found its way back from India to Bristol College in England, where it now resides.[7] "I do not remember ever to read any book with such raptures as I did that," wrote Carey.[8]

Help to Zion's Travellers had its origins in an association meeting sermon Robert Hall, Sr. of Arnsby preached at the 1779 Baptist Association meetings in Northampton. The message was well received and Hall's colleagues persuaded him to use the message as the substance of a book. Hall attempted to address, both in the sermon and in the book, those issues that impeded seekers in coming to Christ.[9] Based on Isaiah 57:14, the book first dealt with doctrinal objections to faith in Christ. Hall wrote about the deity of Jesus, the changing or unchanging love of Jehovah, election, and the atonement. Then he moved to issues that had arisen out of the hyper-Calvinism of the day: Can the unconverted pray? Which comes first, faith or repentance? How prevalent is sin in the human heart? Can I believe in God's promises when all I see around me are dark and afflictive providences?

In the final section on practical religion Hall talked about hypocrites and pernicious and censorious Christians. How should we react to the lukewarmness of older believers? What is the role of the law in the life of the believer? Who can possibly meet God's high standards for his followers? These topics evidently dealt with the very issues stirring in Carey's mind when he first read the book as a young preacher. Hall was thus a very influential person in helping Carey move toward a Baptist faith that was not locked into a passive Calvinism. Perhaps William discussed some of these issues with Dorothy as she was making her spiritual pilgrimage toward a Baptist commitment.

Captain Cook

One of the most talked about public figures in the England of Carey's day was Captain James Cook. Cook did not stimulate Carey's theological quests, nor did the stories of exciting voyages around the globe aid in Carey's exegesis of the Great Commission. But Cook's accomplishments did give Carey great inspiration for applying the Great Commission. Carey knew that Christ commanded us to go into "all nations"; Cook taught him more about what "all nations" could mean.

Carey said that an important book in the formation of his missionary ideas was the *Last Voyage of Captain Cook*.[10] No such exact title appears in the vast Cook literature.[11] Thus we are not able to pinpoint exactly which account of the exciting life of Captain Cook Carey read. Perhaps the best guess is the suggestion made by Walker that Carey had access to the *Journal of Captain Cook's Last Voyage*. This book was issued by the *Northampton Mercury* in twenty-four weekly parts, each costing a shilling. This serial edition appeared in 1785, and if Carey could not afford them he surely could have borrowed them.

James Cook (1721–79) was one of England's greatest circumnavigators. He was the son of a Scottish farmhand but rose to become a household name in all of Britain. Perhaps Carey identified with Cook's rise from obscurity to prominence. Cook is most famous for his three journeys to the Pacific Ocean (1768–71; 1772–75; 1776–79).

Cook is also known for major improvements in navigation. Cook used the discoveries of others to solve the longstanding problem of calculating longitude accurately.[12] "He peacefully changed the map of the world more than any other single man in history."[13] Cook was killed in an unfortunate confrontation in Hawaii. His crew returned to England, but before the survivors left the Pacific all of their logs were seized in an attempt to control accounts of the third and last voyage of Cook. The attempt by the Admiralty to prevent unauthorized versions was only partially successful.[14] What Carey read about Cook's last voyage was probably part official, part unofficial.

Cook was not a religious man.

> So far as I can see, he had no religion and no politics. He mentions Providence once or twice. As for the world, the flesh, and the devil, that trio of embarrassments to all good men, he probably had his own definition of them, as no doubt most good men have. The world was to be explored.[15]

Nor did Cook urge the Christians of England to take Christianity to the South Seas.

Perhaps Carey shared some of the Cook saga with Dorothy. Several features of the life of Cook may well have made a lasting impression on William and perhaps on Dorothy. For example, Cook was very concerned with health. A major blot on the entire age of discovery had been scurvy. This disease took the lives of many sailors and was obviously a barrier to those considering a long sea voyage to some farflung outpost of the Empire. We now know that scurvy develops from a lack of Vitamin C. As early as 1753 a Polish Lutheran pastor had written a treatise on scurvy that correctly prescribed the cure for scurvy: a diet of fresh vegetables and fruit.[16] But most sea captains had a difficult time forcing new diets on crusty old cooks and sailors. James Cook did not have trouble enforcing dietary changes. Cook assembled "the most extensive array of . . . anti-scorbutics, some to prove more useful than others, but all (and More) to be forced down the reluctant seamen's rum-sodden throats."[17] Cook was very successful in maintaining good health among his crew members. Carey must have noticed the importance of diet on sea voyages.

Cook also encountered serious problems with disease whenever his crews went ashore in the tropics. In Java one time his crew contracted malaria and dysentery. Illness was on the rampage among the men and many died.[18] If Carey had shared this little tidbit of information about the tropics with Dorothy, she might well have become reluctant about moving to a tropical climate. Also, Cook was at sea for half of his married life. Perhaps that example encouraged the Careys later to consider a separation while William first set out for India alone.

The Moravians

When Carey was making his last-minute pleas for the establishment of a new missionary society, he referred to the success of the Moravians in sending out missionaries. He made reference to the latest edition of the Moravian *Periodical Accounts*. We do not know if Carey subscribed to this magazine or if he borrowed issues from Moravian friends in the area.[19] A review of the issues in volume 1 (1790–92) reveals a host of stories that he and Dorothy may have read together. Many of the missionary principles that later appeared in Carey's *Enquiry* may have originally been inspired by Moravian accomplishments.

The Moravians centered their motivation on God's grace. They were thus able to endure hardship and suffering and even death itself. They had no objection to sending as missionaries those without a "learned education" or those of "mean extraction" as long as they were endowed with the Holy Spirit.[20] Missionaries were to live frugally, supported by voluntary giving. Undoubtedly Carey formed some of his plans for the Baptist Missionary Society from Moravian examples.

Carey may well have read Zeisberger's account of his wife's illness among the Indians of North America: "My wife was confined to her bed for four weeks with an inflammatory fever, so that her recovery seemed doubtful."[21] The missionaries in Greenland wrote about smallpox, "which threatened the destruction of the Greenland nation."[22] Letters from Tobago told of surviving a hurricane that sailed rafters through the air as if they were kites.[23] A missionary wrote: "With a heart deeply affected, I must inform you, that it has pleased the Lord to take my dear wife home to eternal rest. . . . Her illness was a fever which lasted seven days."[24] A missionary in Barbados died of dysentery, the very disease that would later plague Carey's family.[25] Three missionaries sailed from Copenhagen for India and arrived seventeen months later![26] On September 12, 1791, a group of missionaries working among the Indians of Detroit buried a baby, "the fifth child we have buried here."[27]

Carey's reading of the Moravian experience must have been sobering. While he learned of their commitment and commendable faithfulness to the Great Commission, he also learned a great deal about the price they had to pay for their obedience. Did he discuss these hazards with Dorothy? If he did, the stories would dampen anyone's enthusiasm. If he didn't, perhaps he knew that Dorothy would be discouraged if she knew the true cost of missionary service.

John Eliot and David Brainerd

The missionary efforts of Eliot and Brainerd were also influential in the life of Carey. We do not know exactly which books about John Eliot's life Carey may have read.[28] But most accounts of Eliot's work discussed the difficulties he had determining which conversions were genuine, the distress of disciplining errant converts, and the discouragement of a lack of converts. Sometimes Eliot met with forceful refusals when he entered a new town. On other occasions he rejoiced when Indians renounced their false gods and followed the God of the Bible. The confessions of faith by several Massachusetts Indians printed in *Tears of Repentance* must have challenged Carey's growing interest in taking the gospel to the heathen.

We know that Carey possessed the *Life and Diary of David Brainerd* by Jonathan Edwards.[29] Edwards was a popular author among English Baptists; no doubt he helped popularize the life of Brainerd in England. The first converts baptized by Brainerd were his interpreter and his wife. Brainerd was alternately very impressed with how attentive his hearers could be and very discouraged when other listeners were inattentive. He noted that their inattention "so sunk my spirits I could scarce go on with my work."[30] Brainerd was repulsed by idolatrous sacrifice yet thrilled when Indians believed at the very time he had given up all hope: "It is good to follow the path of duty though in the midst of darkness and discouragement."[31] He wrote about opposition from gainsayers of his work. He expressed frustration about the number of languages spoken by the Indians of New England and about the many burdensome interruptions. All of these themes later appear in Carey's own journal of his first twenty-four months in India. Brainerd was clearly an important model for Carey.

Brainerd died at Northampton in New England at the age of thirty on October 9, 1747. Edwards, a perceptive biographer, made the following observation:[32]

There is one thing in Mr. Brainerd . . . that may be called an imperfec-
tion . . . and that is, that he was one who by his constitution and natural
temper was so prone to *melancholy* and dejection of spirit.[33]

Edwards was very interested in depression and had devoted a great
deal of attention to the subject in his work on the religious affections.
In Brainerd's final illness he read Edwards's account of melancholy
and was helped by it. Edwards felt that Brainerd had a second fault, a
weakness in being excessive in labor. Brainerd admitted to such a fault
and in fact warned his brother about the dangers of overwork.

Carey was later to write extensively about his depression and discouragement. Carey was also overcommitted at various times to his
work. Did Carey realize his similarity of temperament with Brainerd?
Did he and Dorothy ever discuss it as a problem in their relationship?
We cannot know the answers to these questions.

The Carey cottage indeed saw the presence of some very influential books. Dorothy and William must have talked together about some
of them. According to S. P. Carey, Carey was never heard publicly praying without praying for the people of Cook's islands.[34] Surely Dorothy
must have heard his prayers.

His Growing Vision

In 1788 Carey made a trip to Birmingham to recruit funds for the
Moulton church building project. While there he met businessman
Thomas Potts, who was thrilled with Carey's conviction that Chris-
tians should take the gospel to the heathen of the world. Potts urged
Carey to write a pamphlet that would set out his ideas. Carey felt intim-
idated by the prospect of writing and initially approached Ryland, Sut-
cliffe, and Fuller to write the pamphlet. All of them said no and urged
Carey to do it himself.[35]

Meanwhile Baptist churches in the Northampton area had been
engaged in a unique prayer effort. In 1747 Jonathan Edwards published a plea for concerted prayer on the part of God's people. Edwards
urged believers to assemble in their homes at a stated time of the month
and join in concerted prayer for the work of God in their midst. This
idea was a new one for the churches of New England. Edwards urged
them to follow this practice on a regular basis for seven years beginning in November 1756. Edwards urged the seven-year goal on his
people on the basis of material about the vials in the Book of Revelation.

John Sutcliffe, pastor of the Baptist church in Olney, arranged for this 1747 book to be republished in England in 1789.[36] In the association meetings at Nottingham in 1784 the Baptists had committed themselves to pray the first Monday of every month, and Edwards's suggestions no doubt encouraged them in this endeavor. To counter a general malaise among the churches, the Baptist leaders challenged the churches with a major prayer goal:

> Let the whole interest of the Redeemer be affectionately remembered, and the spread of the gospel to the most distant parts of the habitable globe be the object of your most fervent request.[37]

Carey was not present at the meeting when the call to prayer was first issued in 1784, since his baptism had taken place only nine months before.[38] But as he increasingly affiliated with the Baptists of the Northamptonshire association, he found them to be a praying people. These people were asking God to move in their midst so that the gospel could be spread throughout the world. They prayed for more than seven years before they saw their first answer to prayer. Eight years elapsed between the time of the first call to prayer and the formation of the first Baptist missionary society in 1792. And then it was nine more years until missionaries in India baptized their first convert (1801).[39] God clearly answered the prayers of his people. Carey's growing missionary convictions were but one example of such answers to prayer.

In 1786 the association of churches met in Northampton. John Ryland, Sr., pastor of the College Lane Baptist Church of that city, asked the gathered ministers for possible subjects for discussion at future meetings. Carey, a relative newcomer and a pastor for only about one year, proposed a topic that had been burning in his heart:

> Whether the command given to the apostles to teach all nations was not binding on all succeeding ministers to the end of the world, seeing that the accompanying promise was of equal extent.[40]

Those of us who have lived our entire lives within the modern missionary era have difficulty envisioning a time when the Great Commission did not seem to say what we know it to say: that Christians should take the gospel to all who have not yet heard it. But in the late eighteenth century the normal manner of reading Matthew 28:19–20 was very different: The command was given to the apostles, and they fulfilled it; the command did not reach beyond those early years of the church. Accompanying this approach to Matthew 28 was a hyper-Calvinism that expressed great confidence in the God of providence to save all those he wished to save. Human instruments were quite unimportant in the grand scheme of things. God would accomplish his will in his time and in his way.

Carey was a good enough exegete to notice, however, that the promise in those verses ("And surely I am with you always, to the very end of the age") was parallel to the command. If the command had expired, then the promise had expired also. Not surprisingly, however, most people preferred to keep the promise and dismiss the command. And on that day in Northampton young Pastor William was confronting the church with its inconsistency.

Carey's suggestion of a discussion topic did not go over well. Tradition says that Ryland immediately said:

> Young man, sit down, sit down. You're an enthusiast. When God pleases to convert the heathen, he'll do it without consulting you or me. Besides there must first be another pentecostal gift of tongues.[41]

John Ryland, Jr., denied that his father had been so abrupt and rude. No doubt the rebuff had become embellished with frequent retellings over the years. Carey did later write that the rebuff was indeed a rebuff even though Ryland's exact wording is now lost to us. Dorothy was not likely in attendance when her husband received the rebuke. Undoubtedly, though, the discouraged William shared his disappointment with her when he returned home.

Carey continued to wrestle with the Great Commission. He could not easily dismiss it. When Thomas Potts of Birmingham had encouraged him to publish his ideas in a pamphlet, he promised to pay £10 toward its cost.[42] Carey wrote the first draft while pastoring in Moulton, but delayed in getting the book published. Carey's procrastination caught up with him at the association meetings at Clipstone in the spring of 1791.

The sermons preached at those meetings in Clipstone by Sutcliffe and Fuller showed that the Spirit was moving these English Baptists to rethink the Great Commission. These speakers stirred the people toward a missionary vision.

For Carey the next logical step was the formation of a society that would begin to send missionaries out to all the world. The decades of hyper-Calvinism were coming to an end for the Northampton Baptists. The gospel had to be preached to all the world. When Carey made a formal proposal that just such action be taken by the assembled ministers, the vote instead was for Carey to publish his pamphlet and to present it at the next association meeting. Now he had no choice but to complete the editing of his apology for missions.[43]

Carey's *Enquiry*

The full title of Carey's pamphlet suggests a much longer book than it turned out to be:

> *An Enquiry into the Obligations of Christians to Use Means for the Conversion of the Heathens, in Which the Religious State of the Different Nations of the World, the Success of Former Undertakings, and the Practicability of Further Undertakings are Considered.*

No wonder books of that day did not need a table of contents. The title told all!

Carey's book ushered in the "missionary movement in modern history."[44] Carey was the first Anglo-Saxon Protestant in America or Great Britain to propose taking the gospel to all peoples.[45] The language of the book is clear, unadorned English. Carey avoided the obtuse and embellished style of the day. His plain language may have been too modern in its style of expression to gain great popularity in the 1790s.[46] While Carey's simple writing style may not have appealed to the people of his day, the book is amazingly readable in our day. Very few original copies have survived, although subsequent facsimile and edited editions have appeared several times during the last 200 years (1818, 1892, 1934, 1961, 1988).

The publishers and booksellers who got involved in 1792 with Carey's *Enquiry* formed quite a radical lot! The book was advertised in the *Leicester Herald* on May 12, 1792. The publisher of that paper was on trial just eight months later for circulating Thomas Paine's *Rights of Man*.[47] The London booksellers who handled the *Enquiry* also specialized in antislavery and nonconformist titles.[48]

How did Carey craft his arguments in his attempt to change the views of his contemporaries? In the first section Carey asked the question: Is the Great Commission still binding? Some twenty years later Carey said that this section was a delayed answer to the rebuff he had received years earlier from Ryland. Objections to taking the gospel overseas were numerous: We have enough work to do in our own country; the apostles have no successors; God will accomplish the conversion of the heathen if he wills it. Carey argued that if we are not going to go we should also stop baptizing since both commands (in participial form) are part of a unified whole in Matthew 28. Jesus has never repealed the Great Commission. The so-called insurmountable barriers to missions (travel, language, climate) have all been conquered by English traders, the Moravians, and Roman Catholics. "Why can not we do the same?" he asked.

Section 2 surveyed the Book of Acts. Carey reviewed the apostolic missionary journeys, both canonical and traditional. He traced how faithful missionaries eventually brought the gospel to Britain, implying that even his readers would not yet be believers if all previous generations of Christians had treated the Great Commission as the English Baptists were treating it. He referred to Eliot and Brainerd of New England who took the gospel to native Americans. And he mentioned the king of Denmark who had expressed a missionary interest in India. This same king was later to enable the English Baptists to gain a foothold in India.

Section 3 set out in tabular form Carey's evaluation of the state of the world in relation to the gospel. "The following tables will exhibit a more comprehensive view of what I propose, than anything I can offer on the subject."[49] These displays of data foreshadowed modern missiologists such as Patrick Johnstone who have in more recent years assembled similar material about the state of Christianity in the world at large.

For each of the major countries in the world at that time, Carey gave its length and breadth in miles, its population, and its major religion. He had collected this information from any and every source to which he had access. He first had written all the information on the wall map in their Moulton cottage, later transferring it to his pamphlet. Dorothy may have become very familiar with some of this information by the time it found its way into book form.

Carey listed separately islands that were as small as eight by two miles and with populations as few as 100. Perhaps his reading of Cook's explorations of South Sea islands triggered this fascination with islands. Of India beyond the Ganges he wrote that it was 2,000 miles long and 1,000 miles wide, with 50 million residents. He listed the religion of India as Mahometan and Pagan. If he did not know the population of a particular country he calculated an approximate figure based on a certain number of people per square mile.

It must undoubtedly strike every considerate mind, what a vast proportion of the sons of Adam there are, who yet remain in the most deplorable state of heathen darkness, without any means of knowing the true God, except what are afforded by the works of nature; and utterly destitute of the knowledge of the gospel of Christ, or of any means of obtaining it.[50]

Carey observed that those who did not have the Bible were subject to tragic conditions such as cannibalism and human sacrifice; but they were as capable of belief as others, he argued. Their "depravity" probably stemmed from some early affront and was not proof of "inhuman and blood-thirsty dispositions."[51]

Section 4 examined the impediments to taking the gospel to the heathen. Carey undoubtedly had heard these objections voiced by many of his colleagues. Perhaps some of them had also been expressed by Dorothy in family conversations around the Moulton cottage wall map. The first obstacle was distance. Carey argued that recent advances in the science of the mariner had removed this barrier.[52] A second impediment was the barbarous and savage manner of living of the heathen. "This can be no objection to any, except those whose love of ease renders them unwilling to expose themselves to inconveniences for the good of others."[53]

We will later see that Carey's definition of convenience was quite different from Dorothy's. On this point Carey was uncharacteristically uncharitable. He stated that men of commerce were more than willing to set aside convenience for the purpose of making money, although he was later to be very critical of their high standard of living in Calcutta. The apostles, Brainerd, and Eliot did not wait until people were civilized before they went out. Why should we wait any longer?

A third objection was the danger involved in going overseas. But, Carey argued, Paul and Barnabas were not afraid of being killed. John Mark's timidity earned him censure. Besides, much of the violence seen overseas was the result of impudent sailors (perhaps a reference to Carey's views of why Captain James Cook was murdered by Hawaiians). A fourth objection involved the difficulty of obtaining the necessities of life. Carey wrote that the minister is not his own; he is a servant of God. He must not focus on his own pleasure or convenience.

At this point in the *Enquiry,* Carey addressed issues that clearly would affect his own family. We cannot imagine that he would not understand the implication of what he was writing for Dorothy and his sons. Ministers of the gospel should not look for luxury, he wrote.

The slights, and hatred of men, and even pretended friends, gloomy prisons, and tortures, the society of barbarians of uncouth speech, miserable accommodations in wretched wildernesses, hunger, and thirst, nakedness, weariness, and painfulness, hard work, and but little worldly encouragement, should rather be the objects of their expectation.[54]

We can imagine a subdued reaction from Dorothy to this passage.

Carey urged that two married men go together and "to prevent their time from being employed in procuring necessaries, two, or more, other persons, with their wives and families" might also go.[55] The colony would be self-supporting from their farming, fishing, and fowling.

The fifth and final objection had to do with language acquisition. Carey was very confident that any language on earth could be learned in a year or two. His own experience with language had already demonstrated that fact. No second Pentecost was needed, only hard work. Missionaries would learn the language best by mingling with the people.

The pamphlet concludes with a plea for ongoing, united prayer. Carey suggested the formation of a society that would send missionaries out with the support of the tithes of God's people. He, along with other Baptists, had ceased to use West India sugar "because of the iniquitous manner in which it is obtained."[56] Why not use the money thus saved for missions? he asked.

In simple but powerful terms Carey challenged the churches of Britain to obey Christ's command.

It was the 18C Carey who, more than any other man, gave to the modern missionary movement its geographical perspective. . . . All his contemporaries knew St. Matthew's Gospel and St. Mark's Gospel. It was William Carey who saw the "interdependence" of the Gospels and the voyages of Captain Cook *and* the obligations of the missionary enterprise, and who not only saw but insisted upon the relevance of this interdependence for Christian practice.[57]

Action at Last

Carey's *Enquiry* was in print by the time these Baptists next assembled in Nottingham for their May 1792 association meetings. Carey was given the assignment of preaching at the 10 A.M. service. He preached about his vision for missions based on Isaiah 54. The sermon has been called his "deathless" sermon because its effects have never ceased. In this sermon he coined the phrase "Expect great things from God, attempt great things for God." The assembled ministers voted to prepare a plan of action to be presented at the next meeting in Kettering. On October 2, 1792, the society later known as the Baptist Missionary Society began its official life. Carey volunteered all profits from the sale of the *Enquiry* to the new mission. The initial collection of £13 did little to suggest the massive outpouring of funds that would eventually come from the people of Great Britain and North America toward the cause of missions as outlined by Carey.

On November 27, 1792, William wrote a letter from Leicester to his father:

> Polly tells me that you are afraid lest I should go as a missionary. I have only to say to that, that I am at the Lord's disposal, but I have very little expectation of going myself, though I have had a very considerable offer, if I would go to Sierra Leone in Africa. I however don't think I shall go.[58]

Nonetheless, Carey soon volunteered to be the society's first missionary. He had obviously been thinking about himself in the role of a missionary for some time. He originally thought that the island of Otaheite (present-day Tahiti) should be their first mission field.[59] But when they heard that a Dr. John Thomas had recently returned from Bengal and was looking for someone to return with him as a missionary, the society turned its attention toward India. On January 9, 1793, at Kettering, Carey and Thomas officially became the society's first missionaries.

In spite of his father's fears and his wife's reluctance, William had made his decision. And the decision was to go.

4

Dorothy's Decision to Stay

Every researcher who works on the story of Dorothy Plackett Carey dreams of stumbling upon Dorothy's diary. We would know so much more if we could open those dusty pages and read her thoughts, dreams, and fears. "Tonight Will mentioned to us for the first time that he wants to go as a missionary to the South Seas. . . . I felt a rush of different feelings." But we must not linger with our fantasies; no such diary exists.

As we attempt to understand Dorothy's decision to stay in England rather than to go overseas, we are quite handicapped by this lack of direct information from her. We do not know if she was reading books that aided in her decision. We do not even know the extent to which she could read. We do not have reconstructions of conversations she had with friends and family as she tried to sort out all the ramifications of her husband's growing dreams. She left us nothing that would let us see the inner workings of her decision-making process.

We do have several accounts from those around her that give us some clues. The best we can do is to handle these scattered hints and allusions carefully in an attempt to reconstruct her decision. We are confident that she had clearly decided to stay, that she was able to verbalize her decision with clarity to all who interacted with her about the matter, and that she stuck by her decision for many months until the very last minute. She must have had numerous conversations with

William and others about going or staying. Only the very last talk with
John Thomas led to a change of mind.

Dr. John Thomas

The role of Thomas in Dorothy's eventual decision to go, in the
choice of Bengal as the first mission field, and in the events of the
Careys' first few months in India is a major one. In spite of his importance in the story, Thomas remains somewhat of an enigma, a mysterious figure about whom we would like to know much more than we
do. Culross said of Thomas that he was fickle, capricious, moody, at
times ecstatic, "never able to guide his affairs with discretion," yet full
of zeal for the gospel.[1] Such an evaluation of Thomas is typical among
his biographers and is supported by what we know of his involvement
with the Baptist missionaries in India.

The major biographer of Thomas is C. B. Lewis who said that
Thomas's "mental constitution was not evenly balanced, but was pecu-
liarly liable to disturbance"; he could be "impulsive and imprudent,"
and "the even path of tranquil steady trust and obedience was very
hard, nay, was impossible to tread."[2] Ironically, Thomas was the person
who later evaluated Dorothy's mental illness, yet he himself became
subject to erratic emotional states that eventually necessitated his hospitalization in a mental institution.

The exact nature of Thomas's emotional problems is difficult to
assess. His symptoms were many and varied. His ability to manage
money or to do effective financial planning was impaired. He was constantly in debt; creditors hounded his trail both in England and in
India. He apparently had some problems with gambling.[3] He could
be very persuasive in speech as, we will later see, he was with Dorothy
on May 24, 1793. Perhaps Thomas struggled with a personality disorder that was characterized by some sociopathic tendencies. At times
he seemed to function very well; at other times he was unstable. At
some point he began to manifest some internal disintegration of personality that would suggest an even more serious disorder.[4]

John Thomas trained for the medical profession in Gloucestershire
probably in the early 1780s.[5] His medical skills qualified him for the
position of surgeon on the *Earl of Oxford*, which first took him to Bengal in 1783.[6] He stayed in India for some time and attempted to find
others who shared his religious interests. We know he returned to England at some point. On July 14, 1786, he returned to India, again as

surgeon on the *Oxford*. He soon established a friendship with Charles Grant who was later to become an important official of the East India Company. Grant was impressed with the religious zeal of Thomas and arranged for him to become a missionary in Malda, Bengal. There Thomas met George Udney, a company official who shared Thomas's evangelical faith. Thomas immediately began to learn Bengali.

> John Thomas was the first in the Christian evangelical history of Bengal to conceive the idea of learning the language of Bengal and applying that knowledge to the propagation of Christianity.[7]

Thomas began some Bible translation work (Mark, Matthew, and James). He was hopeful that his translation assistant, Rama Rama Vasu, would become a convert. Some strain developed in the friendship between Grant and Thomas over issues of financial responsibility. When Thomas was unable to raise sufficient money to underwrite his translation projects, he returned to England to seek funds and a colleague.

Mutual friends of Carey and Thomas in London put them in correspondence with each other. Carey was initially interested in pursuing the possibility of Bengal because of Thomas's head start on the language. The society commissioned Andrew Fuller to investigate the matter. Fuller's positive report on Thomas paved the way for Bengal, India, to become the first mission field of the new society. When Thomas arrived at the society meeting in Kettering on January 9, 1793, he brought with him a letter from two Brahmin inquirers in India. They had written a joint letter requesting preachers to come to India who would be "such as will forward translation."[8] When Carey heard the word "translation," he was certain that India was the place for him.

Andrew Fuller

The society faced a dilemma. Carey, described by Fuller as one of "the ablest and best ministers in our part of the country," was the logical person to serve as the society's first missionary.[9] No one had a clearer or better articulated vision for this enterprise than did Carey. But at some point Carey had told officials of the society that his wife did not want to go. They had no written policy on such an eventuality. The society did not even have an application form or an interviewing procedure for candidates! The entire enterprise was a brand new experience for all of them.

Andrew Fuller soon addressed the problem directly. On January 16, 1793, just seven days after the appointment of Carey as their first missionary, he wrote the following letter to John Ryland:

> I have this day been to Olney, to converse with Brother Sutcliff, to request him to go with me to Leicester . . . to conciliate the church there, and sound Mrs. Carey's mind, whether she will go and take the family, that we may know for what number of passengers to provide, and to apply for to the Directors of the East India Company. . . . If his family should go, they must have, I think, £100 or £150 a year, between them all for the present. If not we must guarantee the family, as well as support him in the mission.[10]

This letter of Fuller may be one of our most important insights into Dorothy's situation in January 1793. Carey had obviously told Fuller about Dorothy's reluctance to go. But Fuller hinted in this letter to Ryland that he was not quite sure yet if in fact Dorothy would refuse to go. Perhaps Carey himself was unsure just what Dorothy would say to someone from outside the family. Perhaps Dorothy had never discussed the matter with anyone but her husband. The second remarkable feature of this letter is that Fuller seems to be giving Dorothy a free rein to make her own decision. He did not appear to go to Leicester to talk her into going. Nor did he decide for her that she should stay at home this first time around. Fuller treated Dorothy as a responsible woman who had a monumental decision to make.

Andrew Fuller's involvement with Dorothy at this point in the story is important because of his own experience with mental illness. In 1792 Fuller's wife died shortly after giving birth to a child. For the entire summer of 1792 his wife had been emotionally unstable, or to use Fuller's term, "deprived of her senses."[11] Her psychotic state and tragic death left Fuller a widower with young children. We can safely assume that Fuller was keenly aware of the hazards of mental illness and the devastation it can cause in family relationships. If Dorothy had been mentally unstable during her years as a pastor's wife, or if she had exhibited any predisposition toward mental illness, would Fuller have treated her as he did in the above letter? Again, Fuller treated Dorothy here as a sane woman perfectly capable of making a decision. Fuller was prepared for either eventuality: If she agreed to go, plans were ready; if she decided to stay, the society would adjust its plans.

Fuller's treatment of Dorothy in January 1793 is the strongest evidence we have about her mental health before the Careys left for India. If anyone should have expressed reservations at this point about the suitability of her going overseas, Fuller would be the person. He had just recently discovered all too personally what the price of mental instability could be. Fuller was the ideal mission administrator in this situation.

When Fuller and Sutcliffe visited with Dorothy, she presumably told them her decision: "I do not want to go." Dorothy was not alone in her hesitancy about this mission project. About one-third of the Harvey Lane Church in Leicester initially resisted the idea.[12] Many of these church members were spiritual children of Carey's ministry in their midst, and they did not want to lose him. The church members eventually changed their minds; Dorothy did not. The Leicester church was later to include some of Carey's strongest supporters:

> How noble has the church at Leicester acted. They loved Carey, as they loved their own souls; yet not a murmuring word was heard; and when any censure him for leaving them and his family, they will vindicate him with the greatest fervour. They had more a mind to go with him, than to persuade him to stay with them.[13]

The Baptist ministers of London also had some hesitancies about the program. Churches there eventually became more active supporters; but they, like Dorothy, were not at all sure about the practicality of this endeavor when it was still in the planning stages.

Reasons for Staying

Why did Dorothy decide to stay? The question is a fascinating one even though we may be unable to find a definitive answer. Several possibilities emerge. Perhaps one of the following is correct. Or perhaps some combination forms the best set of reasons for her clear decision to stay in England while her husband went to India.

She Knew Too Little

The most frequently suggested reason for Dorothy's refusal to go is that the proposed venture contained too much of the unknown. She did not have the benefit of even a minimal exposure to a school education. She surely did not know much about the globe as it had been explored by Columbus, Drake, Magellan, and Cook. Perhaps she knew

nothing about Islam or Hinduism. She may never have heard someone speak a foreign language. She knew nothing about foreign foods.
Perhaps she asked herself, "Why give up all that is familiar to me for the
unknown?"

The following passage, written over 130 years ago by Marshman,
typifies this explanation for Dorothy's refusal to go with William:

> A new difficulty, however, now arose. When the subject of proceeding to
> India was mentioned to Mrs. Carey, she declared that she would never
> consent to quit her native land. A voyage to India at that period was
> considered, even in educated circles, a far more formidable undertak-
> ing than at the present time. It was regarded in the light of a perpetual
> banishment from home.[14]

Marshman's argument is that *even* educated persons viewed a trip to
India as a sentence of banishment. The request William was making
of Dorothy was simply beyond her capacities to comprehend, let alone
agree to. She did her best, but her best was simply not equal to the
massive undertaking. Perhaps she simply knew too little.

Manson-Bahr and Apted discuss the difficulties of living in the tropics:

> It is probably true that expatriate residents in the tropics or in develop-
> ing countries who suffer from disorders of the mind would do so if they
> lived in their own countries, but that certain environmental factors tend
> to exacerbate these conditions. Expatriate men have usually chosen to live
> abroad for economic reasons, or for the adventure of seeing the world.
> To this extent they take the advantages and disadvantages willingly. This
> does not always hold with their wives, many of whom do not realize
> the conditions of life they are about to enter and sooner or later begin to
> wish they were settled at home.[15]

She Knew Too Much

On the other hand, perhaps we should consider the exact opposite as
a possible explanation for Dorothy's refusal. Maybe she knew too much.
Perhaps Carey did indeed share information with her. Maybe she knew
of the stark struggles of the Moravians. Perhaps she prayed for that
group of Moravians who were seventeen months in transit to India.
Maybe she heard too much about Captain Cook's experiences: scurvy,
tropical diseases, hostile South Sea islanders.

She may also have known that the East India Company was very
hostile toward missionaries at the very time when the society was con-

sidering going there.[16] In fact, in that very year, 1793, Wilberforce was to introduce into the House of Parliament a resolution calling for the religious advancement of the inhabitants of India. English evangelicals had hoped that such a resolution would force the East India Company to allow missionaries into the country. The company lobbied hard against the bill. "In the eighteenth century it had been a settled principle of the company's government in no way to meddle with the religious and social customs of the Indians."[17] Nonetheless, the resolution won approval in Parliament. Proponents failed, however, in their efforts to get the policy added to the governing charter of the East India Company.[18] Wilberforce and others would have to wait an additional twenty years before they would be successful in this effort.[19] So at the time Dorothy was deciding whether or not to go with William, the venture was illegal, especially if traveling on a company vessel. Perhaps Dorothy knew.

Perhaps Dorothy knew too that France had declared war on England just a few days after that small group of Baptists had appointed her husband as a missionary. Any sea voyage during wartime was dangerous. Perhaps Dorothy remembered hearing a passage that outlined the oppressive discouragement associated with pioneer missions:

> And yet my health is so impaired, and my spirits wasted with my labours . . . so that I become fit for nothing at all, entirely unable sometimes to prosecute any business for days together.[20]

Dorothy may have known too much.

She Was Pregnant

The reason for her refusal to go may not be as esoteric as the above discussion would suggest. We know she was pregnant when Fuller and Ryland came to visit her—five months pregnant to be precise. This pregnancy was her sixth, and she knew exactly what to expect. A sea voyage may not have been a pleasant thought if she had just recently emerged from the nausea of early pregnancy. Was she willing to give birth aboard a sailing vessel? "If the departure took place as planned on 3rd April, her baby would be born at sea and the only woman in attendance so far as she was aware would be Mrs. Thomas whom she had not even met."[21]

Or if they went later, did she want to set out for India with a nursing baby? Her other three sons were eight, five, and four years of age, no doubt an active tribe of normal boys. The thought of such a major change in their living situation may have overwhelmed her and led to her decision to stay.

She Feared the Loss of Family

As we have already seen, the Plackett clan was a large one in Northamptonshire. In 1793 Dorothy lived in the county to the north, but she was probably able to see them on occasion. At least she could easily keep up on family news and events. William's uncle Peter had gone off to Canada and returned safely so the Carey family had some experience with international travel. But not so with the Placketts. Dorothy's family had continued to be active in the Hackleton church. In 1792 Daniel Plackett was a deacon in that church.[22] No doubt leaving her family would be hard on Dorothy, just as it is for any who go to serve Christ overseas in missionary service.

She Was a Fearful Person

Dorothy did exhibit fear on several occasions. We have not encountered any evidence that Dorothy was an emotionally unstable person during her years in England, yet she could still have been an easily frightened woman or perhaps a fearful person. Many otherwise well-adjusted people will experience hesitancy at the new or unknown and fear change in general. Perhaps Dorothy was such a person. Normal fears may have kept her from agreeing to go.

In her role as wife of a cordwainer and pastor, Dorothy frequently had to be alone, had to manage the children when William was on trips, and had to deal with customers when her busy husband was away. So we cannot attribute too much timidity or fearfulness or hesitancy to her. But normal fears may have nonetheless been present. In this regard, Dorothy may be similar to the host of Christians who have decided they are not cut out for missionary service. Only a minority of us choose to go; the vast majority, like Dorothy, choose to stay.

She Thought It Unwise

When Edmund Carey first heard the news that his son William was going to India as a missionary, his reported reaction was "Is William mad?"[23] Edmund Carey was later to become a more active supporter of his son in India, but his initial reaction was disbelief. Could Dorothy have responded in the same manner? Could the impracticalities of the venture have seemed so insurmountable as to make the proposed journey seem unwise to her?

If any pattern for overseas work existed at all, the standard was for the husband to go alone at first. Such was the experience of John Thomas who had been to India two times without his wife. Most military personnel and company officers went to India alone, without families. Even 100 years later the pattern for half of all women who went as missionary wives was to go in the first year of their marriage. For most missionary wives, marriage "confirmed a vocational and religious decision along with a romantic one."[24] Dorothy knew nothing of William's plans when she married William; he himself didn't know at that point. Now they had been married twelve years and had three children with one on the way. The proposed new vocation for the family may have seemed simply unwise.

She Was Out of God's Will

Many of us have an easier time determining God's will for others than we do for ourselves. We could conclude that Dorothy was quite obviously wrong in her decision to stay, and that if she had been in tune with God's will for her and her family she would have gladly consented to go with her husband. The chain of logic would run as follows: (1) God obviously blessed William Carey's pioneer missionary work in India; (2) thus God had called William to India; (3) his wife should have also responded to God's call and gone with him willingly.

But is God's will always that easy for us to determine, even after the fact? Yes, God richly blessed Carey's missionary efforts in India. Yes, William repeatedly testified to a powerful burden for the heathen overseas, and he went in obedience to that call. But was it also God's will that Dorothy accompany William on his first trip out? We do not know. She strongly felt that she should stay, not go. When she finally did agree to go to India with William, can we find evidence that God richly blessed her there? Could Dorothy's refusal to go have been her understanding of God's will for her and her children?

Rather than drawing conclusions about who was in God's will and who was not, we should invest our energy in understanding the dilemmas faced by all the main characters in this story: William, Dorothy, the children, the mission administrators, and the constituency of the mission society. Each of them faced some very difficult decisions. No easy answers appeared in handwriting on the wall. All simply had to act and respond as best they knew how. And the decisions each were making did not always fit together in perfect harmony.

In summary, we do not know exactly why Dorothy decided to stay. To be fair to her, however, we must admit that the available evidence points to her decision to stay as being a sane and sensible choice rather than an insane and sinful one. Her decision to stay may have been a better decision than her later hasty decision to go with her husband proved to be.

Changing Plans

From January 9 until March 26, 1793, the Carey family seriously considered at least four different plans for their future. In the course of these eleven weeks, both William and Dorothy must have agonized over what to do. We are unable to reconstruct these planning steps precisely, but the general outline appears to be as follows.

Plan 1: All Go

When William first volunteered to go as a missionary he must have suspected that Dorothy was not willing to go with him. But at some point they must have discussed the option of everyone going together. To this plan Dorothy said no. Perhaps she hoped that her refusal to go would change William's plans. Instead, her refusal merely triggered the next suggested alternative.

Plan 2: William Go Alone

Carey was probably very aware that most men who went to India went without their families.[25] John Thomas had already followed this exact plan two times. Andrew Fuller had anticipated this alternative when he first went to visit Dorothy. The society was prepared to support William in India and his family in England. So William's next alternative was to go alone. Letters from William during this period to his friends seem to reflect Plan 2.

My wife appears rather more reconciled than she was to my going.[26]

My heart is much set upon the undertaking. I much desired to take Felix with me, but it seems the will of God to strip me of all earthly comforts. I find satisfaction, however, in reflecting that I am prompted by a sense of duty, and a desire for God's glory, and that I am in His hands. I have never wavered about the duty itself, but I feel much leaving my family and people.[27]

My wife and family will stay behind at present, and will have sufficient support in my absence; or should they choose to follow me, their expense will be borne.[28]

Plan 3: William and Felix Go

The letter quoted above implies that William posed an alternative to Dorothy. Perhaps she had already agreed that William should go alone. Or perhaps she did not agree to Plan 2 until Plan 3 was suggested. Maybe she felt that she could handle three small children alone better than she could handle all four. Or perhaps eight-year-old Felix suggested himself that he accompany his father to India. Regardless of who originally suggested the idea of Felix going, Dorothy must surely have consented to the plan.

Andrew Fuller reflected on all of these changes of plans in his memoir:

When he had made up his mind to engage in missionary labours, he expected Mrs. Carey and his family to accompany him; but to this she was for a long time utterly averse. This was a heavy trial to him, and to the society, who could not but foresee that though men are allowed to leave their wives and families for a time in mercantile and military expeditions; yet, in religion, there would not only be a great outcry against it from worldly men, but even many religious people, who had thought but little on the subject, would join in the general censure. He determined, however, to go; and if Mrs. Carey could not be persuaded to accompany him, he would take his eldest son with him, and have the rest of his family under the care of the society. She might afterwards be persuaded to follow him; or, if not, he could but return after having made the trial, and ascertained in some measure the practicability of the undertaking.[29]

Plan 4: When to Return

Now that they had decided that William and Felix should go and Dorothy, William, Jr., Peter, and the unborn child should stay, the only remaining issue was to discuss when William should return to England. We do not know exactly what was in Carey's mind. J. B. Myers suggests, with no supporting evidence, that William was prepared for a lifelong separation.[30] Fuller, in a letter to Thomas Stevens, said, "His church mourns, but no one murmurs; he goes, and returns again in three or four years on account of his family."[31] Fuller was prepared for Carey to return and again ask Dorothy if she was willing to go. If she decided at that point to stay, Fuller hints that he was prepared to abandon the whole missionary enterprise.

Eustace Carey suggested that Carey's intent was to return to England after he had prepared a home for the family, "hoping that he might then persuade Mrs. Carey to return with him, as it might seem to her less perilous, than it was to adventure at first, when the path was untrodden."[32]

What then did Carey have in mind? He probably intended to return to England to take his family back with him to India. However, in light of Carey's determination to keep at the task in India and his later unwillingness to return to England, no one would have been surprised if he had asked some of the later arriving missionaries to bring Dorothy and the children out with them. Thus William would not have had to sail back to England.

The Move to Hackleton

The plans now called for Dorothy and the two boys to move back to a cottage in Hackleton. Dorothy's youngest sister Catherine (Kitty) would live with her and the children. Dorothy first visited relatives in Lamport and Brixworth.[33] William made a trip north to Yorkshire to raise funds. He was also able to visit his brother Thomas for the last time. A church member in Leicester arranged to purchase a load of wheat for his bakery from a supplier in Northampton so that the empty wagon could inexpensively carry the Careys' belongings back to Hackleton. Carey's last Sunday at the Leicester church was March 17, 1793. Dorothy, William, and the three boys then moved back to Hackleton and said goodbye to each other on March 26, 1793, not knowing when they would see each other again.

William and Felix Sail

On April 4, 1793, William and Felix set out for India on the *Earl of Oxford,* the same ship on which John Thomas had previously served as surgeon. Carey had tried without success to obtain permits from the East India Company to enter India. He had been able to visit with company director Charles Grant, but Grant had lost his enthusiasm for John Thomas and was not anxious to see him return to India. Through friends in Olney, William was able to see the famous John Newton in London. Tradition says that Carey asked Newton what he should do if, after arrival in India, the company should send him back to England. "Conclude that your Lord has nothing there for you to accomplish. If he have, no power on earth can prevent you."[34] John Newton in turn introduced Carey and Thomas to William Wilberforce, who later became their staunch defender in Parliament.[35]

Finally Captain White agreed to take them to Calcutta without the required permits.[36] The captain was thus assuming some risk, and Carey was participating in a less-than-straightforward approach to entering company territory. The penalty for unauthorized entry into India, though not always enforced, was forced return and confiscation of goods.[37] Included in the group with William and Felix were John Thomas, his wife, daughter, and two cousins, Samuel and Sarah Powell.[38]

The ship sailed to the Solent, opposite the Isle of Wight, where the *Oxford* had to wait for a convoy to form before proceeding any farther. Here they experienced a six-week delay. William and Felix rented a room in Ryde on the Isle of Wight while waiting for the convoy to form. From Ryde, William wrote to his sisters that the trip from London to the Solent had gone well. Carey did not become seasick although Felix had one bad day. The ship had 250 people on board, 100 of whom were soldiers. Carey was hoping for a chance to preach to the group. "I have heard from my wife and the children are well. May God bless them all."[39] He asked his sisters not to address letters to Rev. William Carey since the East India Company "do not know of our being ministers. They would not have permitted us to go if they had."[40] To his father he wrote that Felix "has not the smallest inclination whatever to go back. . . . I have heard from my wife since I have been here. She is not yet brought to bed—but her and the children are well."[41]

Dorothy asked in her letter to William about Mrs. Thomas and about Carey's own state of mind. Perhaps she was wondering if he was still as committed to his plans. William wrote:

> You wish to know in what state my mind is. I answer, much as it was when I left you. If I had all the world I would freely give it to have you and my dear children with me, but the sense of duty is so strong as to overpower all other considerations. I could not turn back without guilt on my soul. . . . Tell my dear children, I love them dearly and pray for them constantly. Be assured I love you most affectionately.[42]

Did Dorothy possibly ask him in the letter referred to here to return home? We do not know.

Meanwhile, back at Hackleton Dorothy gave birth to Jabez, their fourth son.[43] William was not present but Dorothy likely had many of her family members with her to help. The name "Jabez" comes from 1 Chronicles 4:9–10. The Carey and Plackett families had not recently used the name, so something about the following text must have inspired Dorothy to use the name for this child:

> Jabez was more honorable than his brothers. His mother had named him Jabez, saying, "I gave birth to him in pain." Jabez cried out to the God of Israel, "Oh, that you would bless me and enlarge my territory. Let your hand be with me, and keep me from harm so that I will be free from pain." And God granted his request.

Perhaps his birth had been particularly painful, or she was attracted to this verse because the mother named her son. William was not involved in naming this child because he later enquired what Dorothy had named him.

Toward the end of the six weeks, the captain received an anonymous note signed "Verax." The note warned the captain that he had on board his ship someone who should not be allowed to go on to India. The captain assumed the note was alluding to John Thomas, and so he asked both Thomas and Carey to disembark. Perhaps Thomas's reputation had preceded him. Carey took Felix off the ship with him, of course. Mrs. Thomas, her daughter, the Powells, and presumably the servant Andrew stayed on board. Thomas and Carey were able to get £150 refunded but had to leave on the ship the utensils and supplies they had planned to sell upon arrival in Calcutta to finance their first year there. To have taken them off board would have involved customs duties.

This turn of events devastated both Carey and Thomas. Thomas made a quick trip to London in an attempt to get his bad credit record cleared but had no success. Thomas was aware of the outstanding debts that had apparently prompted "Verax" to warn the ship captain. He had returned from his previous trip to India with goods he hoped would cover his obligations in England. However, the sale of these goods netted only enough to pay about two-thirds of the debt.[44] Meanwhile, Thomas ignored his creditors thinking they would be satisfied with partial payment and would understand that he had little money in reserve. But when the creditors heard that he was booked on an expensive trip to India, they had trouble believing that Thomas was penniless.

Now the entire missionary experiment seemed in jeopardy. Carey and Thomas watched the *Oxford* sail without them, their hopes dashed on the rocks of credit problems. Carey began to think of demanding permits from the East India Company or, if that strategy failed, of traveling overland to India.

John Thomas was at his best in this crisis. He immediately enquired about foreign ships that might be sailing soon to India and learned of a Danish ship scheduled to arrive at Dover in five days. And the ship had room for three or more! Money was a problem, though, because they had only enough for William and Felix on the more expensive Danish ship. Carey wanted to return home to see if his wife would consent to go. He dashed off a letter to her saying that they would be in Hackleton on the next night's coach. They checked their luggage in Portsmouth.

A Most Significant Breakfast

Carey, Thomas, and Felix took the overnight coach to Northampton where they arrived at 5 A.M. They walked to Hackleton and arrived in time for breakfast. Dorothy and William saw each other again under the most unforeseen of circumstances. Felix was able to visit with his brothers, and William met three-week-old Jabez for the first time. In the space of one or two hours Dorothy changed her mind and consented to go. Carey did not leave us with a detailed reconstruction of how she changed her mind. Our two best sources are Polly Carey and John Thomas.

Polly, William's sister, wrote her account many years later. She was not an eyewitness to the momentous breakfast so her information was secondhand:

> Providence so ordered it that they came back. He had only Felix with him then. He said, when they went in, he pleaded by silence and tears; while Mr. Thomas pleaded by arguments, till his wife consented to go. No time was then lost in getting ready, lest she should change her mind, or the vessel sail without them.[45]

John Thomas's account of that morning gives us more detail from an eyewitness vantage point.

That night, therefore, we set off, and breakfasted with Mrs. Carey the next morning. She refused to go with us, which gave Mr. Carey much grief. I reasoned with her a long time to no purpose. I had entreated the Lord in prayer to make known his will, and not to suffer either of us to fight against him, by persuading her to go on the one hand, or stay on the other. This expression moved her, but her determination not to go was apparently fixed.[46]

As persuasive as John Thomas apparently could be, he did not succeed the first time around in changing Dorothy's mind. But her hesitancy in their initial conversation that morning may have encouraged him to try again.

We now set off for Mr. Ryland, of Northampton, to ask for money; and on our way thither I found Mr. Carey's hope of his wife all gone. I proposed to go back once more; but he overruled it, saying it was of no use. At last I said, "I will go back." "Well, do as you think proper," said he, "but I think we are losing time." I went back, and told Mrs. Carey her going out with us was a matter of such importance, I could not leave her so—her family would be dispersed and divided for ever—she would repent of it as long as she lived. As she tells me since, this last saying, frequently repeated, had such an effect upon her, that she was afraid to stay at home; and afterwards, in a few minutes, determined to go, trusting in the Lord: but this should be on condition of her sister going with her. This was agreed to. We now set off for Northampton like two different men; our steps so much quicker, our hearts so much lighter.[47]

Thomas was persuasive. Just how did he convince Dorothy to change her mind? His own account seems to suggest that he convinced her to go using fear. The essence of Dorothy's decision to go may have been that to stay was too frightening. She felt she had to go with her husband. Her change of mind does not seem to have been based on a reconsideration of her original objections to going, whatever they may have been.

The decision of Dorothy to stay gave way to a decision to go. Her prior decision was in place for several months; she made the latter decision in a matter of minutes. The Careys had fewer than twenty-four hours to pack, sell any possessions they could not take with them, say goodbye to family, and raise more money for the passage—an almost impossible task.[48] Somehow they accomplished it all.

Dorothy's sister Kitty had just celebrated her thirtieth birthday. Dorothy may have reasoned that Kitty would be an invaluable help to her with the children. Kitty's presence would also be a great psychological encouragement and reassurance. Kitty's willingness to go was a pivotal factor in Dorothy's decision to go.

Carey dashed off a letter to Sutcliffe soon after Dorothy said yes.

> I however much wanted to see my wife and try if she would accompany me, which I did and to my great joy and astonishment she consented and is to go with me and all my family and her sister tomorrow morning for London. . . . I must beg of you to dispose of my household furniture which we must leave behind. . . . Being obliged to pack some articles tonight. I cannot add more.[49]

Friends, family, and neighbors must have all pitched in to get the family of six ready. The society had to scramble for funds to pay for the added tickets. One surviving letter of Andrew Fuller, most likely a fund-raising letter, gives us his impressions of these last-minute changes:

> The additional sums of money now wanted is on account of Carey's family going with him. But this is so desirable an object, that nothing should be thot much of to accomplish it. . . . Carey's heart is happy, having his family with him. An objection against the Mission is removed, of its separating a man from his wife. . . . Had not Carey taken his family he must have come home again in a few years. Now there will be no need of that. He will live and die in the midst of 100 millions of heathens for whose salvation I am sure he is ready to sacrifice his life, and a thousand lives if he had them.[50]

As word spread throughout England and Scotland, enthusiasm grew:

> We could scarcely believe that such a number of impediments had, in so short a time, been removed. The fear and trembling which had possessed us at the outset, had insensibly given way to hope and joy.[51]

Supporters of the mission were happy. Thomas was pleased. Carey was excited. How did Dorothy feel? We wish we knew.

Part Two

Life in India

5

The Moving Sick

Sunday, May 25, 1793, was a momentous day. The Carey family, including baby Jabez, left Hackleton in two coaches for Dover accompanied by all their luggage. Travel on Sunday was not a normal practice for Carey, but the importance of the venture overruled Sabbath sensitivities. John Thomas headed for Portsmouth to reclaim luggage; he would eventually rejoin the Careys at Dover. The ship was due in a few days, and they had little time to spare.

All of this hurry and scurry only resulted in waiting and watching. The ship was over two weeks late in arriving! The Careys must have had some unanticipated rest while they waited in Dover. Meanwhile John Thomas had quite a time getting the luggage from Portsmouth to Dover. Most seamen were unwilling to transport him and the luggage, at least for the money Thomas could afford to pay, because of all the French pirates who were reportedly tyrannizing coastal waters. Finally Thomas was able to recruit a fisherman to take the risk. Thomas thought he might be late, but he arrived in ample time after all.

The Voyage

The ship arrived during the night of June 13. Someone awakened the family at 3 A.M. A hastily written note from that early morning has survived:

Dear Father,

We are just going. The boat is just going out, and we are going on
board—Thursday morning at five o'clock—June 14th 1793. We are all
well and in good spirits.

    To Mr. Daniel Placket, Hackleton.[1]

The captain elected not to come into port, so the family boarded a
small shuttle boat. Daylight had barely broken when the family climbed
rope ladders to board the Danish ship, *Kron Princessa Maria.*

The party was pleased to sail on a Danish ship. Now they would
not face any charges of duplicity since British laws banning passage to
India did not apply to foreign ships. In addition, the Danes were neu-
tral in the recently declared war between Britain and France, so the
ship did not face as much danger from French warships as the *Oxford*
might have. Also, the failed plans to sail on the *Oxford* now allowed
all the Careys to sail together, and "the world has lost thereby an objection often raised against his going."[2]

This little party of missionaries was not the first to go to India. Tradition tells us that the apostle Thomas came to India and was later
martyred by a priest of the Kali Temple. We are more certain of the
fourth-century arrival in India of Thomas, bishop of Edessa. Roman
Catholic missionaries also went to India (John Monte Corvino, ca.
1292; Francisco Xavier, 1536). Danish missionaries arrived in Tanquebar on July 9, 1706.[3] Few traces of this missionary effort remained
in Bengal, however, by the time this party set sail. Although not the first
to go to India, Carey and Thomas are among the best known.

As the vessel began its long five-month voyage to Calcutta, Carey
realized that his dream of many years was coming to pass. He was a
participant in the realization of his own plan set forth in the *Enquiry.* In
his first journal entry of the voyage William wrote: "This is an Ebenezer
which I raise to God—and hope to be strengthened whenever I reflect
upon it."[4] The family's excitement was no doubt curtailed by the seasickness that predictably set in, but the kind captain provided them
with soup and wine to weather the adjustment period.

The Carey family enjoyed a commodious cabin. Soon Carey and
Thomas organized a Sunday worship service that met in the cabin.
They even formed a choir. The journey was unusual for that time
because they did not stop at any port along the way. The wind was
favorable as they were going around the Cape of Africa, so the cap-

tain elected not to stop. Carey was disappointed since he had wanted to stop and visit with Dutch missionaries there. Once past the Cape, the ship encountered a severe storm that battered the *Maria* badly. The crew spent eleven days repairing the damage.

Three people died on the voyage: a black woman and child who were ill at the beginning of the trip, and a carpenter who died of pleurisy six days before the ship reached Calcutta.[5]

Carey enjoyed sighting islands and recording longitude and latitude in his journal. Reading about such sea adventures in the life of Captain Cook is one thing. Being able to experience it is quite another. From Carey's standpoint, the voyage went well. "Our infant has thrived more than if it had been on land, and the children are as well satisfied."[6] "The children were complete sailors; and the women were much better than I ever expected."[7] John Thomas wrote:

> Mr. Carey was at one time ill with a complaint in his bowels, which he has been used to at home; but the Lord had mercy on him and me: he is now well, I suppose, as he ever was in his life, and has been for some months.[8]

Carey was busy during the trip learning some Bengali from Thomas, planning future sites for missionary work as they passed various ports on the way, and dreaming dreams for his boys.

> I am very desirous that my children may pursue the same work and now intend to bring up one in the study of Sanskrit, and another of Persian. O may God give them grace, to fit them for the work.[9]

But the trip did not go as well for Dorothy. John Thomas later wrote:

> Poor Mrs. Carey has had many fears and troubles; so that she was like Lot's wife, until we passed the Cape; but ever since, it seems so far to look back to Piddington, that she turns her hopes and wishes to our safe arrival in Bengal. She has had good health all the passage, and her little babe has grown a stout fellow.[10]

Again we hear of fears on Dorothy's part. If her decision to go was fear-based, we should not be surprised that the trip stirred up even more anxious concerns. These fears do not yet sound like phobias, but she was undoubtedly beset with agonizing worries. She had little idea of what was ahead. The fierce storm off the Cape of Africa surely did not help calm Dorothy's anxiety.

Carey must have noticed his wife's growing distress. In a brief journal entry made toward the end of the voyage Carey tells us, "My wife thro mercy is well satisfied with our undertaking, and we are all now in remarkably good health."[11] After the seasickness, after the homesickness, and after the storm, Dorothy and William apparently had some serious conversations. Carey was able to allay her fears, at least for the present. The implication of the entry is that they were all now ready, both physically and emotionally, for their November 11 landing in the Bay of Bengal. The Carey family and John Thomas disembarked from the *Maria* on to a harbor boat rather than going ashore directly from the ship, perhaps to avoid a confrontation with officials.

Calcutta

The first three weeks in Calcutta were not tranquil. Both William and Dorothy reacted badly to the city. The indulgence of the Europeans there offended William. Dorothy contracted a physical ailment in the city that was to persist for many months. The settled state of mind, body, and spirit on September 20 on the *Kron Princessa Maria* did not last long in Calcutta.

Their supporters in England were praying for them. People back home had no idea where the Carey and Thomas families were on November 13, 1793. Yet they felt compelled to observe a day in fasting and prayer for the new missionaries on that particular date, just two days after the ship arrived in the Bay of Bengal.[12] Would the Careys' struggles have been worse if supporters in England were not praying for them?

Mrs. Thomas and the Powells had already arrived in Calcutta and were living in the city. The Careys and John Thomas were able to locate them without too much difficulty. For the first three weeks the families all lived together in the same house. Carey became very nervous, however, because of the high rent. Carey complained that "the great expence into which Mr. T. had inadvertently given of servants etc filled my mind with anxiety and wretchedness."[13] Carey was very aware of limited funds and his responsibilities as a steward of the money donated to the society:[14]

> The success of future missions, also, lies near my heart; and I am fearful lest the great expense of sending out my family should be a check upon

the zeal of the society: how much more if I should now live upon a European plan, and incur greater charge.[15]

In a letter to Andrew Fuller in January 1794, Carey warned of the risk of allowing new missionaries to settle in the city of Calcutta:

> And in a country like this settled by Europeans, the grandeur, the customs, and prejudices of the Europeans are exceedingly dangerous. They are very kind and hospitable, but even to visit them, if a man keeps not a table of his own, would more than ten times exceed the allowance of a Mission—and all their discourse is about the vices of the Natives: so that a missionary must see thousands of people treating him with the greatest kindness but whom he must be entirely different from in his life, his appearance and everything. . . . This is a snare to Mr. T., which will be felt by us both in some measure.[16]

The group was disappointed to discover that Rama Rama Vasu, an earlier convert of John Thomas, had slipped back into his prior religious beliefs. But Carey hired him almost immediately as a language pundit so that work learning the Bengali language begun on the boat could continue. Carey was initially very impressed with the Bengalis. "I like their appearance very much, they appear to be intelligent persons . . . and appeared to be attentive to whatever was said to them."[17] Carey and Thomas also sold the supply of penknives, scissors, and other small trading goods they had brought with them to help finance the first year.[18] The proceeds were less than anticipated, however. Carey's intention, just two weeks after arrival in Calcutta, was to apply for waste or uncultivated land on which he could establish a sugar plantation. He felt the plan was "agreeable" because no slavery was allowed in India.[19]

Dysentery

Dorothy and the oldest Carey child, Felix, fell ill in Calcutta with dysentery.[20] Three days after landing in India Carey wrote to Fuller: "My family is well."[21] But their health was shortlived. The family contracted the "bloody flux," an eighteenth-century phrase referring to dysentery. Although all members of the family no doubt struggled with this condition, Felix and Dorothy had the most prolonged bout with this very common disease of the tropics.

Dysentery has been the major cause for the hospitalization of Europeans in India. Before the discovery of the microscope, the best medical opinion attributed the disease to atmospheric changes "by which the temperature of the surface of the body was apt to become unduly or suddenly depressed."[22] They based this understanding of the disease on observations made at the time of hospital admissions: low body temperature of patients; and wide ranges of diurnal temperature, moist air, and strong winds on days of admission.[23] Because people did not know the true cause of the disorder, victims of the bloody flux were futile in most all of their efforts to avoid the disease.

After the invention of the microscope, researchers found amoeba in dysenteric patients. But because they also found amoeba in nondysenteric patients as well, the role of the amoeba remained unclear. Only later were they able to establish that most cases of dysentery result from amoeba, but not all carriers of the amoeba have dysenteric symptoms.[24] Current medicine is able to differentiate between bacillary dysentery (caused by bacteria and treated with antibiotics) and amoebic dysentery (caused by amoebic infestation and treated with emetine or emetine-like medication). Of the two types of dysentery, Felix and Dorothy most likely had the amoebic variety since bacillary dysentery is normally not chronic.[25]

Treatment in the eighteenth century for the poorly understood disease was understandably irrelevant. Blood-letting, the application of leeches to the abdomen, or the use of mercury compounds were the standard treatments. Fatality rates from such treatment could range as high as 10 percent.[26] We do not know if Dorothy and Felix received any of these "treatments." Dysentery accounted for about one-third of the deaths in the British army in India.[27]

Before the discovery of effective medication to kill the amoeba, patients with amoeba in the intestinal tract would carry the organisms for the rest of their lives. A serious complication was liver abscesses. Thus when patients with amoebic dysentery "got well," the improvement was actually just a remission of symptoms, not the eradication of the amoeba. The host intestine and the invasive organism would simply learn how to live together in a state of physiological truce.[28]

Symptomatic dysentery was to be a part of Dorothy's life for the first twelve months she lived in India. The chronic nature of the disease must have greatly discouraged her. Moving frequently from house to house and town to town could only make her discomfort worse.

Bandel

The Careys stayed in Calcutta for only three weeks. In the words of Carey, Calcutta produced

constant discontent and restlessness of mind. We therefore went on
excursion into the country where we had the offer of either buying or
renting an house at Bandel; We thought at first of purchasing but the
time approaching when we must pay and money not being at hand we
changed our minds, and from that moment my mind was fully determined to go up into the country and build me an hut; and live like the
natives.[29]

So Bandel, a Portuguese community not far from Calcutta, was a
temporary place to live from the very beginning. But the cost was more
affordable. At Bandel the children must have thought they were living in
a zoo! In a letter written at Bandel, Carey describes their surroundings:

Wild beasts are plentiful. Jackals are everywhere. Mrs. Thomas had a
favorite little Dog for which she had been offered 200 rupees carried
off from the door by one while we were at prayer one evening and the
door open—yet they never attack men. Serpents abound. To day I found
the skin of one about six feet long which was just cast off in my garden. We have no tigers nearer than eight or ten miles, and indeed have
no more fear of them than you have in England—upon the whole it is a
charming country.[30]

The above passage sounds like a person whistling in the dark. Dorothy
may or may not have agreed with William's assessment that the place
was no more dangerous than rural England. The boys were no doubt
having a ball. "Here we intend to reside."[31]

But this intent did not last long. Carey soon began to wonder where
they should go next. "They anxiously discussed the advantages of Gour,
Malda, Cutwa, and Nubbea, as suitable localities for their mission."[32]
Carey bought a small boat and began to explore the area. On December 22, 1793, several nationals urged him to settle at Nubbea and on
Christmas Day he was still determined to live entirely "amongst the
natives."[33] Bandel was proving unsuitable to William because he could
not live as he felt missionaries should, "in a state of similarity to that of
the people among whom they labour."[34]

How was Dorothy handling these uncertain days? Not well, as we
will see in their next move. Between Christmas and New Year's Day
John Thomas heard from Captain Christmas of the *Kron Princessa
Maria* that a botanical job was open in Calcutta. All of a sudden new
options flashed through Carey's mind. He loved plants and was already
skilled in botanical pursuits. Maybe a job as superintendent of the com-

pany's botanical gardens would not be such a bad option, even if they would have to live in Calcutta! He rushed to make application for the job only to find that the company had already filled the position. Another disappointment.

While in Calcutta he enquired again about obtaining free land. The initial response was encouraging so the two families moved back to Calcutta. Carey wrote:

> Upon our arrival I found that I had only been trifled with about land, and that no free land could be got now. The Banian (banker) offered me to live in his garden house till some could be got—at which house I now am at Manicktullo.[35]

And so the family moved again, this time to their third house.

Manicktullo

From the beginning of January to February 3, the family lived in cramped quarters in a suburb of Calcutta. The banker was a charitable person who opened his garden house to this sick, penniless family of six. They did not have to pay any rent. "His distress was extreme. The house was small and ill-ventilated; he was a stranger in a strange land, without money or friends; illness was beginning to invade his family."[36]

Carey was busy pursuing two options. Even though the botanical superintendency was no longer available, he had been able to dine with the company official in charge and "there is every reason to believe I may be presented with a place there." Employment there would be a "pleasant and profitable amusement and would take very little of my time; this however I leave with God."[37] The second possibility was applying for free land. Although the prospects were discouraging, Carey still felt some land might be obtainable.

Manicktullo was the Careys' third place of residence in less than two months. Even Carey himself was exasperated: "For these two months past I have seen nothing but a continual moving to and fro."[38] Their unsettled state bothered William, but Dorothy felt pushed to her limit. William's journal entry for January 13, 1794, described her complaints:

> My wife and sister too, who do not see the importance of the mission as I do, are continually exclaiming against me, and as for Mr. T. they think it hard indeed that he should live in a city in an affluent manner, and

they be forced to go into a wilderness and live with out many of what they call necessaries of life (bread in particular).[39]

Ten days earlier, in a letter to Sutcliffe, Carey complained, "If my family were but hearty in the work, I should find a great burden removed."[40]

Two issues were pushing Dorothy to a point of great frustration. Her husband continually talked of going to live in the wilderness. Life was hard enough in Calcutta, Bandel, and Manicktullo. How much harder would the tasks of daily life be in the jungle? She could not understand why Thomas could live and work as a missionary in Calcutta but they could not. The second source of frustration for her must have been radically new kinds of food. Rice was the staple of Indian diets.[41] Suffering from constant diarrhea, she must have longed for more familiar foods such as bread, the staple of English diets. Dorothy was upset; she and William must have had many arguments regarding the family's future.[42]

Dorothy was miserable and sick. And William was just as distressed. After a day of futile searching for funds from John Thomas, he wrote:

> I was much dejected at this. I am in a strange land, alone, no Christian friend, a large family—and nothing to supply their wants. . . . I am dejected, not for my own sake but my family's. . . . In the evening poured out my soul to God; but still my burden continued. The next day had a pleasant time in prayer to God in the morning but afterwards the abusive treatment I receive from her who should be an help to me quite overcame my spirits. I was vexed, grieved, and shocked. I am sorry for her who never was hearty in the undertaking, her health has been much impaired, and her fears are great, tho five parts out of six are groundless. Towards the evening had more calm both within and without. Oh that I may have wisdom from above.[43]

To Sutcliffe, Carey lamented that their time on board the ship in the carnal company of sailors and their time in Calcutta had ruined Dorothy and Kitty's attitudes

> so as to make them unhappy in one of the finest countries of the world, and lonely in the midst of an hundred thousand people. These are burdens and afflictions to me but I bless God that I faint not.[44]

Carey is not at his best here. He seems unable to grasp the magnitude of the adjustments he was asking Dorothy and Kitty to make.

India was a land of great cultural contrast to their homeland. They did not know Bengali. How could they help but feel isolated even though many people lived around them?

On January 17 Carey returned home from a walk to find Dorothy and Kitty calmer than he anticipated.[45] But Dorothy continued to be physically ill and emotionally discontent. Carey's relationship with John Thomas continued to deteriorate, a development that did not help matters at all.[46]

The Sunderbunds

The great Ganges River spreads out into several major rivers as it flows eastward and southward to the Bay of Bengal. The mouth of the river is a vast delta, comprised of low-lying, swampy land. The steamy jungle was crowded in the eighteenth century with many species of animals. This was the Sunderbunds, the next home of the Careys.

The government had sponsored a program beginning in 1781 to reclaim the area. Mr. Henckell had originated a plan to grant plots of land to any person who would work at clearing it.[47] Carey's free land was a part of this government program. An uncle of Rama Rama Vasu, Carey's language pundit who was helping them find an alternative to Manicktullo, was a local ruler in the area to which the Careys were moving.

On January 27, 1794, Carey obtained a boat to carry them forty miles east to Debhatta on the Jebuna River. They spent several days preparing their meager belongings for the journey.[48] On February 3 they loaded the boat and were able to set sail at 8 P.M. in the evening from Baliagaut. They sailed on salt rivers and lakes. Carey described the area through which they were traveling:

> There not being water enough for us to go the nearest way we were necessitated to go through the Sunder Bunds which is a very large impenetrable forest only intersected with large rivers by which our boats went, these forests are some hundreds of miles in extent, and entirely uninhabited by man. They swarm with tygers, leopards, rhinoceroses, deer, buffaloes, etc. I thought I heard the roar of a tyger in the night but am uncertain.[49]

When Carey wrote this entry he obviously did not yet realize that the area he described was exactly the kind of territory in which his free

land was located! Five months later, after the family had moved out
of this jungle, he looked back on the Sunderbunds and gave another
description of it:

> We have no fear of beasts though there are many buffaloes, hogs, and
> tygers in our neighborhood. Tygers seldom attack men but commit
> dreadful devastation among cattle, except those of the Sunderbunds, a
> very large forest near the sea, where there are no cattle; there they
> seize men.[50]

We are curious to know how Dorothy handled this growing awareness
of just why this land was free! On February 6 they arrived at Debhatta.
The company had given them permission to stay in an empty bungalow
there while they constructed their own home. But upon arrival they
discovered that Mr. Charles Short, a salt agent for the company, was
living in the house. Providentially Mr. Short was another good Samari-
tan to the Carey family. He took them in and provided housing for
their entire stay in this area, a total of three-and-one-half months.

Did this area of Bengal have any commendable features? Food was
plentiful. However, the area was politically unstable, and twenty men
had been devoured by tigers in that department in the previous twelve
months.[51] Many of the nationals had deserted the area. Rama Rama
Vasu began to recruit families to return to the area where the Englishman William Carey "would be a father to them and protect them from
wild beasts"[52]—quite a large task for Carey!

Carey began to clear land and build a house. He selected a site across
the river from Mr. Short's house. Each day he would cross the river
with one or more of his boys to work on the plot of land he had chosen. With helpers they cleared the land leaving the coconut, peepul,
tamarind, and sundari fruit trees in place. He started a bamboo and
mat house, hedged a garden plot with plantaino, and planted a garden of lentils, mustard, onion, and peas.[53]

On March 1 a letter arrived from John Thomas that suddenly brought
all of this wilderness-breaking to a halt. Thomas had renewed his
acquaintance with George Udney. Thomas and Udney knew each other
when Thomas had previously lived in India, but they had a falling out at
that time. Just recently Thomas, hearing of a tragedy in the Udney family, contacted Mr. Udney to express his condolences.[54] George Udney
was a civil servant stationed in Malda, 300 miles from Calcutta. As a
commercial resident in that area, he had authority to loan money to

contractors who would agree to develop agriculture and industry in the vicinity. He could also deal privately.[55] Probably in this latter capacity, he made John Thomas a tempting offer. Would Thomas be willing to superintend an indigo manufacturing site at Moypaldiggy? Yes, decided Thomas, if Udney could also offer such a job to his friend William Carey. Udney was building another site at Mudnabatti, and he was most glad to offer Carey that position.

When Carey received news on March 1 of this new possibility, he was in no position to turn it down. Although he was developing a free plot of land that appeared bountiful, the area was obviously dangerous. A salaried job had fallen into his lap! He could finally house his family in a suitable dwelling, and after almost four months could experience some certainty.

> Though I have the great pleasure of hoping that the mission may be abundantly forwarded by having a number of the natives under my direct inspection, and at the same time my family be well provided for, though I have no doubt respecting provision even here, yet a too great part of my time must have necessarily been employed in managing my little farm with my own hands; I shall likewise be joined with my colleague again, and we shall unitedly engage in our work.[56]

Dorothy must have agreed with him that the new job was a good offer.

The abandonment of the plans to live in the Sunderbunds was clearly a wise choice. The house Carey was building was unsuited for Europeans who had just arrived in India since he chose to erect the shelter in "a malarious uncultivated district."[57] "It would have been almost certain death for an unacclimatized European family to take up their dwelling" at that site.[58] "Carey's scheme of evangelizing the swamps of the Soondarbuns was fortunately of short duration" since the area was the "most unpromising and deadly spot in all India."[59] Now with a secular job, Carey and Thomas could both apply for permits that would allow them to stay in East India Company territory. Without the permits the company would have likely forced them out.[60]

From the time Carey received the letter outlining his job offer in Mudnabatti on March 1, 1794, until the arrangements were complete allowing them to move to their new home on May 23, Carey experienced what sounds like a significant depression. The following samples from his journal of the period reveal his downcast mood:[61]

2, 3, 4, March. In this state of uncertainty nothing but suspense and vacancy of mind is experienced.

17 March. Still low and dejected. . . . This unsettles my mind again and makes me careful about this present world perhaps too much.

21 March. The conversion of the heathens is the object which above all others I wish to pursue; yet a long course of unforseen things and changing circumstances have hitherto prevented my making that active effort which I wish.

March 24. Long delay, and unsettledness have filled me with discouragement.

25–28 March. Was it not that my wife is so ill as to be unable to sustain the fatigue of an incommodious voyage to Malda, I would set out at any rate—but as it is I cannot till Mr. Thomas sends me a letter.

8 April. A day of business, hurry, sorrow, and dejection; I seem cast out of the Christian world and unable yet to speak to the heathens to any advantage—a daily disappointment discourages my heart. I not only have no friend to stir me up, or encourage me in the things of God, but every discouragement arising from my distance from Mr. Thomas.

19 April. When I first left England my hope of the conversion was very strong, but among so many obstacles it would entirely die away, unless upheld by God—nothing to exercise it, but many things to obstruct it for now a year and 19 days, which is the space since I left my dear charge at Leicester; since then I have had hurrying up and down; a five month imprisonment with carnal men on board the ship, five more learning the language; my Moonshee not understanding English sufficiently to interpret my preaching—my family my accusers, and hinderers, my colleague separated from me, long delays, and few opportunities for social worship—no woods to retire to like Brainerd for fear of Tygers. . . . no earthly thing to depend upon, or earthly comfort; except food and raiment; well I have God, and his word is sure.

1 May. I have none of those helps and encouragements from my family or friends that many have—they are rather enemies to the work that I have undertaken but though I find it extremely difficult to know how to act with propriety, and sometimes perhaps act indiscreetly, yet I find that support in God which I can find no where else, and perhaps these

trials are designed to put me upon trusting in and seeking happiness
from the Lord alone.

This span of eleven weeks sounds like a very miserable time for Carey.
Dorothy may have had just as unhappy a time, for we can imagine that
their disagreements and arguments continued through this time of waiting. Carey's depression may have been the result of a combination of the
ongoing domestic tension as well as the frustration of not being able
to do what he enjoyed most: work. He also sounds in these passages
like a man who is having to scale down his expectations of how quickly
evangelistic success is going to come his way.

Carey had a few bright spots during this span of time. On four different occasions he records his pleasure at being able to instruct his
family in the things of God on the Sabbath. Two important visitors
came to see Mr. Short, and Carey seemed to enjoy meeting with them.
He relaxed so much at one point that he and his family kept the Sabbath on the wrong day of the week!

William and Felix witnessed some self-torment that must have made
Dorothy cringe when they later told her about what they had seen. At
the gates of Mr. Short's home they watched religious pilgrims with
poles stuck through their sides, with their tongues pierced, and with
hooks in their backs. One of the pilgrims showed his wounds to Felix
and William.[62] Carey had seen religious devotion before, but not to
this magnitude.

Finally all of the arrangements were complete. The salary was certain
and Carey determined in his mind to write the mission society at home
telling them he no longer needed their support.[63] Carey had now
accomplished his dream first set out in the *Enquiry:* to be a self-supporting missionary.

As excited as Carey must have been to set out for Malda, Dorothy
must have been equally downcast. Her sister Kitty had been with her on
the voyage, in Calcutta, Bandel, Manicktullo, and now Debhatta. But
in this last place of residence Kitty had fallen in love with Mr. Short
and had decided to stay and marry him.[64] Dorothy was still ill, but
Kitty apparently felt Dorothy could carry on without her. Dorothy
must have had mixed feelings: happiness for her thirty-one-year-old
sister now anticipating marriage, sadness at having to leave the one
person who had helped her cope thus far in India.

At 3 A.M. on May 23, 1794, the family, minus Kitty, set out on a three-week river voyage to Malda.[65] Carey wrote, "I feel thankful to God for thus providing, and also that now we have a place of our own, tho' not an house but a boat."[66] William used the boat time to work on his translations, but the children must have bothered him.[67]

> 11 June. Had some little enjoyment of God today but travelling with a family is a great hindrance to holy spiritual meditation.

> 12–14 June. Much mercy has followed us all through this journey and considering the very weak state of my wife we have been supported beyond expectation. Travelling in general I have always found unfriendly to the progress of the divine life in my soul, but travelling with a family more particularly so.

On June 15, 1794, they arrived in Malda.

Mudnabatti

The Udneys gladly welcomed the weary traveling party. Talk soon turned to the eventual location of the Careys in Mudnabatti. Carey was to be situated thirty-two miles from John Thomas by land, seventy miles by water. Carey made several trips to the indigo works at Mudnabatti while his family stayed in Malda with the Udneys. On August 4 the entire family traveled to their new home.

> It is now just one year and 14 days since I left England—all which time I have been a sojourner and wandering to and fro, at last however, God has provided me a home. May he also give me piety and gratitude.[68]

> We have a very pleasant and beautiful place, a good brick house, and extensive garden, and every necessary of life in plenty; indeed every article of living is remarkably cheap, about two pence apiece.[69]

Carey's new secular employment involved the production of indigo, a blue dye. The extraction of the dye was a complicated process. Workers grew and harvested the plant on surrounding farms before bringing the crop to the factory. There bundles of the plant fermented in large vats. Next came the beating and aerating of the watery material. The sediment had to be cleaned, boiled, strained, pressed, dried, cut, and prepared for shipping. Indigo manufacturing was complicated, and

Carey had to oversee scores of workers. The industry was liable to economic downturns and natural disasters such as floods.

Carey had time to start a small farm and garden to feed his family.
He bought hogs, cows, and sheep. Dorothy must have felt much more
at home here in Mudnabatti since she had her own house and could
care for her family as she wished. Carey soon hired several helpers for
the house and farm. Danger from wild animals was not as high in this
new locale. "We know where danger is, and avoid it."[70] Near the front
door of their new house was a large pond in which a crocodile lived, but
many people bathed there every day without trouble. Of crocodiles
Carey wrote:

> One of these creatures stole a goose one day, and in half an hour twenty
> people were in the pond to kill him, which they soon did. He was seven
> cubits long and could easily have bit a man's leg off at one snap—but all
> such creatures are more to be dreaded as thieves than as open enemies.[71]

We wonder if Dorothy was as nonchalant about leg-snapping crocodiles
swimming in the frontyard pond!

Dorothy, William, and the boys immediately began to learn much
more about the religion of the people around them. William tried to
hire a poor orphan boy of the shoemaker caste (the lowest of the castes
because they handled the skin of cattle), but the boy would not join the
Carey household for fear of retribution.[72] When construction was complete on the factory, the Hindu workers wanted Carey to make a sacrifice to the goddess Kali; when he refused, they went ahead and sac-
rificed a goat anyway.[73] On a Mohammedan holy day Dorothy and
William found 1,000 people coming to their property. Unbeknownst to
the Careys, their house was built near the site of a saint's burial place.
Most of the pilgrims had not seen a white man and woman before and
they stared at the Careys, trying to determine who was the male and
who was the female.[74] Dorothy, still ill with dysentery at this time, was
surely having an intense enculturation experience!

The Death of Peter

The Carey family arrived in Mudnabatti on August 4, 1794. For
the next seven weeks life was more normal than it had been since their
landing in November. Dorothy and Felix were still sick with the bloody

flux, but the family had their own home and a salary. No longer would they have to survive on the charity of people who would take them in.

On August 25, 1794, Carey wrote, "Except the disorders we had before we came we have had but little sickness here, but every servant we have is ill and perhaps 40 workmen."[75] Soon Carey himself was very ill.

> Have been taken with a violent fever. One of the paroxysms continued for 26 hours without intermission when providentially Mr. Udney came to visit us, not knowing that I was ill, and brought a bottle of bark with him. This was a great providence, as I was growing worse every day, but the use of this medicine by the blessing of God recovered me. But in about ten days I relapsed again and the fever was attended with a violent vomiting and a dysentery. And even now I am very ill, Mr. Thomas says with some of the worst symptoms.[76]

John Thomas with his medical training and George Udney with his long experience living in Bengal must have been a welcome help to the Carey family.

Then Peter fell ill. Peter was an active child described by his father as a "fine engaging boy."[77] Since his birth in Moulton in 1789, five-year-old Peter had lived an exciting life. Even before his father achieved fluency in Bengali, Peter could speak it fluently.[78] His illness lasted for two weeks. Felix had been ill for a long time and the other boys must also have had their sieges of fever and flux. At first Dorothy might not have viewed Peter's illness as anything unusual.

But then he took a turn for the worse. "He had been seized with a fever, and was recovering, but relapsed, and a violent dysentery carried him off."[79] Dorothy had watched as her four boys did well on the sea voyage. They survived Calcutta, Bandel, Manicktullo, and Malda. Felix carried on even though his small body weakened under chronic dysentery. But in Mudnabatti, just when life was taking on some normalcy, Peter died.

Peter's burial was not the first for William and Dorothy. But when they attended to the burial of daughters Ann and Lucy back in England, friends and family were present to help them. On October 11, 1794, no one was there to help. Dorothy, William, and Peter's three surviving brothers would have to attend to the burial by themselves.

The shock of Peter's death was enough to cause great problems for Dorothy, but the events of the next seventy-two hours only made her grief worse. We can follow the events best by listening to Carey's own account:

> On the same day we were obliged to bury him, which was an exceeding difficult thing. I could induce no person to make a coffin, tho' two carpenters are constantly employed by us, at the works. Four Mussulmen, to keep each other in countenance dug a grave. But tho' we had between two and three hundred labourers employed, no man would carry him to the grave. We sent seven or eight miles to get a person to do that office, and I concluded that I and my wife would do it ourselves, when at last our own Matu (a servant kept for the purpose of cleaning the necessary and of the lowest cast) and a boy who had lost cast, were prevailed upon to carry the corpse; and secure the grave from the jackals.[80]

In England a grieving family only needed to contact the appropriate people in the village after a family member died. Finding gravediggers, coffin makers, and pall bearers was not a difficult task even though burying a child was hard enough in and of itself. In India, however, the Carey family was surrounded by a host of Hindus and Mohammedans (called Mussulmen in the above passage). Both religions had numerous taboos about touching corpses, digging graves, and burying the deceased.[81] Carey realized that the hesitancy of even his own employees to help them was not due to any personal disrespect but was related to strong religious practice.[82] Carey knew that the Hindus often "buried" their dead by tossing the corpses into a river so as to minimize contamination by having to touch the body. He knew that the Mohammedans so abhorred touching a corpse that "the bamboos on which they carry their dead to the water or the grave are never touched or burnt but stand in the place and rot."[83]

Knowing the religious reasons for all of the hassles related to Peter's burial did not allay the emotional pain and agony both Dorothy and William faced. No one except the lowest of the low would even consent to carry their beloved Peter to his grave. Years later when Jabez and his wife faced the same problem, he could say to his father, "I have for one felt that kind of anguish of mind which you must have felt my dear father when you had to bury my brother at Mudnabaty."[84]

Pushed to the Limits

Two days later the burial issue erupted again. Dorothy was still ill with her chronic dysentery and William continued to battle his fever.

The four gravediggers who had reluctantly agreed to dig Peter's grave soon found themselves in serious trouble with the local political and religious leader.

> The Mundul (that is the principal person in the village who rents immediately under the Rajah, and lets lands and houses to the people in the place) forbid every person in the village to eat, drink or smoke tobacco with them or their families, so that they were supposed to have lost cast. The poor men even came to me full of distress, and told their story.[85]

These four men had been ostracized by their families and village. They had feared the worst, and now it had come to pass. Carey felt a moral obligation to help them. John Thomas had come to visit the Careys in their grief, and so he was at their house when the four men came to plead for help.

Carey had now reached his limit. The steps he and Thomas next took were very uncharacteristic for William. He was faced with a monumental task: aiding these four men who had just two days prior been of such help to him and Dorothy.

Thomas and Carey immediately summoned some leading Mohammedans. "Did these men do anything wrong?" The answer of all of them was no. They then sent two servants to bring to the Carey house the Mundul who had ostracized the men, "with secret orders to bring him by force if he refused to come."[86] When they confronted the Mundul with his overreaction, the leader consented to smoke with the four gravediggers but refused to lift all of the bans.

> As we knew it to be a piece of spite and trick to get money we therefore placed two guards over him, and told him that he must either eat and drink with the men before the men of his own village, or stay here till we had sent to four men to Dingapore to the judge about the matter. He stuck out however till about dinner time when being hungry he thought fit to alter his terms, and of his own account wrote and signed a paper purporting that the men were innocent and he a guilty person. He then went away and gave them a dinner.[87]

When Carey confirmed from eyewitnesses that the reconciliation ceremony had in fact happened, the matter was finally ended.

The trauma of Peter's death and burial had temporarily pushed William, the kind and meek shoemaker-turned-missionary, to become a somewhat highhanded colonial baron. Thomas and Carey were effective in easing the tension, but their strategies bordered on the side of high risk.

These sad events pushed William to a temporary extreme. But these same events pushed Dorothy to a permanent extremity, as we next shall see.

6

Retreat from Reality

The Udney family showed great sensitivity to the grieving Careys. George Udney was not only a considerate employer but a true Christian gentleman. Soon after the trauma of Peter's death and burial, Mr. Udney suggested that the family take a break from Mudnabatti. Dorothy and the three boys stayed with Mrs. Thomas and Mrs. Udney while William and John Thomas set off on a mission survey trip. Carey had wanted to see Tibet since they were now living closer to it than to Calcutta. Although they did not get as far as the Tibetan border, Thomas and Carey did see an exciting variety of animals, vegetation, and landscape. An army officer advised them not to proceed farther because of low water and extremely high seasonal grass.[1]

The trip seemed to renew their strength. Carey began to improve in health even though his moonshee (language helper) was ill for a three-month period. He was forced to set aside some of his translation goals as everyone tried to get back to good health.

Christmas 1794 was a happy time for the Careys. Dorothy finally enjoyed improved health. On December 5 Carey was able to say that his family was well, the first time since very early in their time in India.[2] The Carey family and other Europeans gathered with the Udneys to celebrate the holidays, and Carey wrote that he and his family were much refreshed.[3] On New Year's Eve the Careys traveled back to Mudnabatti, passing the Thomas family who were on their way to join the Udneys for a New Year's Day celebration.

William faced two unsettling developments. Mr. Udney began to sound less committed to the Mudnabatti factory. The indigo market was never very certain, and weather problems often made the economic future of a plant such as the one Carey was superintending uncertain. The questionable future of the plant could only have eroded some of his recent sense of stability. Added to that, Carey faced school difficulties. He established a school for national children, but the first attempt failed since many parents removed their children when the work season began again.[4] His revised plan was to start two schools for twelve youths in each. He was beginning to realize that he would also have to feed and clothe the children due to the poverty of these families. On top of this, he was a very busy man since the full factory operation required him to supervise the work of 400 to 500 men.[5]

Dorothy's Retreat from Reality

We have observed Dorothy so far in many settings: Hackleton, Moulton, Leicester, and India through five different moves and in six different houses. We have seen her distressed, stubborn, frightened, and plaintive. None of these moods and attitudes comprises mental illness, although each of them no doubt served as a prelude to her retreat from reality in the first few months of 1795. We may have had questions about her sanity before this point in her life, but now we can be certain that she became mentally ill in 1795. She stepped from living in reality into an unreal world some time in January, February, or March 1795. Her physical illness waned at the end of 1794 but her emotional troubles waxed at the beginning of 1795.

Dating Her Insanity

The fine line between Dorothy's relating to reality well and being out of touch with reality is hard to pinpoint. If we had been at Dorothy's side during those three tumultuous months we might not have seen any clear demarcation between sanity and insanity. We can be confident though that by the end of March she was in a psychotic state. She had lost her ability to monitor reality accurately and was living in an unreal mental world.

Even though we cannot be sure of the exact date she lost her reality contact, three pieces of evidence help us narrow our search down to these three months. First, on January 11, 1796, John Thomas wrote that Dorothy had been insane for "about 9 or 10 months past."[6] His estimate of the duration of her illness thus brings us into March 1795. Second, in his journal entry for January 1–15, 1795, Carey wrote: "This time have had bitters (of a family kind) mingled with my soul."[7] Third, the entries in Carey's journal from February 3 to March 15, 1795, are full of remarks that probably reflect his response to Dorothy's accusations. Soon after March 15 his entries revert to ministry-oriented observations. Thus our best estimate of the onset of Dorothy's mental illness is somewhere in the first three months of 1795.

Dorothy's Delusion

The most complete description of Dorothy's symptoms came from the pen of John Thomas. His medical training had most likely equipped him to observe patients carefully. For this reason his account is most likely more complete than would be an account from a lay observer. This January 11, 1796, letter was sent to Andrew Fuller and was probably a planned way of informing the society in England of Dorothy's mental illness.

> Mrs. Carey has given us much trouble and vexation, and has formed such black designs and carried them so far into execution that we have been obliged to go to Heaven for help. Do you know that she has taken it into her head that C(arey) is a great whoremonger; and her jealousy burns like fire unquenchable; and this horrible idea has night and day filled her heart for about 9 or 10 months past; so that if he goes out of his door by day or night, she follows him; and declares in the most solemn manner that she has catched him with his servants, with his friends, with Mrs. Thomas, and that he is guilty every day and every night. . . . She has uttered the most blasphemous and bitter imprecations against him, when Mrs. Thomas and myself were present, seizing him by the hair of his head, and one time at the breakfast table held up a knife and said "Curse you. I could cut your throat." She has even made some attempt on his life. And for some minutes together she will say "You rascal: You d____d rogue! God almighty damn you" etc, etc. too bad to mention and far worse if possible in obscenity than in profaneness. I need not go further to convince you that we have had our troubles. For some ladies have almost hesitated, till, thank God, she accused them of being intimate with her husband and then she was out of her senses. But before it was doubtful. In all other things she talks sensible and she minds nobody nor fears any one but me. If I come into the room and she is raving, she stops. She has been in confinement by my advice. Yet she speaks highly of me as a good man, but deceived in Carey. In this country everything must be known of this sort.[8]

Dorothy was insanely jealous. She was convinced that her husband was repeatedly unfaithful to her, and no one was able to convince her otherwise. We now call such a condition a Delusional Disorder or Paranoid Disorder.[9] These disorders center around a delusion that is erotomanic, grandiose, jealous, persecutory, or somatic. Dorothy obviously struggled under the jealous type. A Delusional or paranoid person can be very clear and lucid in many other areas of life. Their reality distortion in the area of delusion, however, can be profound and unremitting. Dorothy was to remain locked into the delusion of her husband's unfaithfulness for the remaining twelve years of her life.

A question that comes to us as we read John Thomas's description of Dorothy's condition is: "Is John Thomas a reliable observer?" We know that he had some medical training and that he had worked as a surgeon, but we also know that he was not such a stable person himself and that he was later to have his own struggles monitoring reality. How do we evaluate Thomas the evaluator? First, Thomas seems rather stable at this point in his life. Carey himself wrote Andrew Fuller on April 23, 1796, that John Thomas had not been zealous but "always discouraged and discouraging" from his arrival in India until Christmas 1795 but was now stirred up again.[10] Thomas must have been stable in January 1796 when he wrote the above description. Second, Carey's subsequent letters confirm the observations of Thomas. We have considerable reason to believe that Thomas's report is reliable.

Other documents help us fill in some more details. At some point in 1795 John Thomas wrote a letter to Carey. Unfortunately the letter is undated, but most likely the letter refers to an event in the first half of 1795.

I have many things to say and this is my imperfect way of conveying thoughts in comparison of speech. You know Mrs. Carey sent a letter express yesterday to me, and gave a man a rupee to bring it. I was frightened—seriously her false surmises bring on true troubles, that are rising to such a height that I know not what will be the issue of it. . . . You must endeavour to consider it as a disease. The eyes and ears of many are upon you, to whom your conduct is unimpeachable, with respect to all her charges, but if you resent they have ears and others have tongues set on fire. Was I in your case I should be violent; but blessed be God who suits our burdens on our backs. Sometimes I pray earnestly for you, and always feel for you. Think of Job. Think of Jesus. Think of those who were destitute, afflicted, tormented.[11]

At some point Dorothy felt so frustrated that she secretly sent a letter to Thomas, referred to above. This letter has not survived but is our strongest evidence that she had learned how to write. No one was around to help her write the letter. Her hope had been that Thomas would believe her and would help her deal with her "unfaithful" husband. Although the letter greatly concerned Thomas, he seemed to recognize it as evidence of paranoia, not reality.

Never had Carey anticipated such a problem. Both Thomas and Carey must have been stymied as to what steps to take. One of the first decisions they appear to have made was not to write home about the problem. If her delusion should prove temporary, they would all regret any unnecessary alarm to the society and to family at home.[12] Thomas and Carey decided to wait ten months before informing the society. Carey did tell his sisters about Dorothy in an October 5, 1795, letter. Her condition was "known to my friends here, but I have never mentioned it to any one in England before."[13] Carey did not personally tell his close friend Andrew Fuller until June 17, 1796.[14]

Another early decision of Carey was to write to Dr. Arnold, his psychiatrist friend in Leicester. On March 13, 1795, Carey wrote a letter to Thomas Arnold. The letter is totally silent about Dorothy and has the tone of an initial letter. Carey described the geography and climate of Bengal. He related his feelings that disease in the area was more related to cold and dampness than to heat. He described the peril of dysentery and reported to Arnold that Mrs. Carey and Felix were ill with the disease for twelve months, but he mentioned nothing about her evolving emotional problems. The letter concluded with material about eight different species of cats, a serpent brought to a friend that was nineteen feet long, and a description of the people and their religion. Carey seems to be trying to initiate correspondence with Arnold. Perhaps Carey felt that he could not directly ask for help with Dorothy's condition in this first letter, but would do so in later correspondence. We have no evidence that Arnold responded or that Carey wrote other letters to Arnold.

In addition to sending this letter to Arnold, both Carey and Thomas must have reached for Arnold's textbook on emotional disturbance. In Thomas's January 11, 1796, letter to Fuller he says, "but by reading Dr. Arnold on Notional Insanity I concluded. . . ."[15] Carey wrote to Andrew Fuller that Dorothy was afflicted with "the species of insanity described by Dr. Arnold under the name of Ideal Insanity."[16] We can be almost certain that the book was among those Carey had brought to India with him. They could not have found this title in a local library, and we know that the book could not have arrived that quickly by mail. Although Carey probably brought the book with him to India out of respect for his friendship with Arnold, he now found a use for it that he had never anticipated.[17]

John Thomas reacted to the secretive letter from Dorothy by systematically considering three different explanations of her behavior. First, Thomas must have asked himself, "Could these charges possibly be true?" A paranoid person can be very convincing. In the above letter Thomas mentioned that several women were almost convinced that Dorothy was correct until she accused them of sleeping with Carey, at which point they knew she was delusional. Most paranoid delusions have some believability about them, and Dorothy's charges were no exception, but Thomas soon concluded that his friend Carey was not a whoremonger. "But C(arey) is the last man I should think of, I am fully persuaded that he is circumspect and pure in this matter, and what can be said more of any man?"[18] Carey himself knew of his innocence, but he also was aware that others would inevitably ask whether the charges were true. To his sisters Carey wrote: "Jealousy is the great evil that haunts her mind. Tho blessed by God, I never was so far from temptation to any evil of that kind in my life."[19]

After ruling out truth as the explanation of Dorothy's charges, Thomas next considered demonic activity. "I have listened to all her words, and for a long time was in doubt whether she was actually possessed of a devil or insane."[20] Demon activity, evil spirits, and other manifestations of the demonic existed in eighteenth-century India. In a long journal entry during their period of waiting in Debhatta, Carey had recorded a local belief.

> In this country there is, he (the monshee) informs me, something similar to the scriptural demoniac. They call the spirits of bad men departed *boot,* and say that oftentimes when a woman walks near the woods the *boot* comes from some trees and possesses her upon which she becomes in a manner insane.[21]

The passage goes on to explain how learned men go about expelling the demon with a combination of chants and violent thrashing of a figure of the woman drawn on the ground.

They say that the *boot* causes the woman to pronounce his words, in a whining tone; what this singular thing may be I cannot tell. . . . I am determined to investigate it, if true, it is like the Indian powowing, a striking proof of the power which the devil exercises even over the bodies of people in countries wholly under his dominion and must be a compleat answer to all objections which Socinians or others make to the scripture account of demoniacs.[22]

When Dorothy began to lose her grip on reality, William may have wondered: "Has Dorothy walked through the woods lately?" As awful as demon possession is, a cure exists for the condition: exorcism. But Carey as well as Thomas must soon have abandoned any speculation of demonic involvement since Dorothy's situation was quite different from *boot* possession.

The third explanation was insanity. Thomas came to such a conclusion. Carey was somewhat reluctant at first to admit to himself and to others that his wife was insane. "My poor wife . . . is looked upon as insane to a great degree here by both natives and Europeans. I believe there may be something of that, and perhaps much."[23] But both Thomas and Carey seemed to have relied on Thomas Arnold's volume to help them understand Dorothy's plight. Arnold saw the ravings of an insane person as similar to the excitement of a poet who was losing contact with actual life.[24]

Arnold attempted to divide all psychopathology into two major categories: ideal insanity and notional insanity. The former is "that state of mind in which a person imagines he sees, hears, or otherwise perceives . . . persons or things" that have no external existence. Notional insanity consists of erroneous perceptions about objects that actually do exist in the external world.[25] Arnold was attempting to use hallucinations and delusions as the major differentials of mental illness. However, current psychiatric opinion contends that these two major symptoms of psychotic states are not discrete enough to serve as diagnostic watersheds. Besides, Arnold's descriptions of the distinction between ideal and notional insanity are not precise enough to be useful.[26]

A jealous delusion such as Dorothy exhibited was an example of pathetic insanity in Arnold's system. A normal emotion or passion, jealousy in this case, begins to predominate and obscure all the other passions. Arnold felt that violence often accompanied these conditions, and that some "disease" such as a fever or confinement in childbirth might trigger it. Thus Thomas wrote to Carey, "If she is pregnant, my opinion is, she will wax worse and worse till delivery and then most likely she will return to her former senses."[27] Arnold felt these pathetic conditions began by natural temper, by suspicious circumstance, or by simple indulgence in the passion.

Strategies

The next question Carey and Thomas faced was the issue of what to do with Dorothy. A simple delusion that remained inside the walls of their brick house in Mudnabatti would be less problematic, but Dorothy was attempting to convince everyone that her perceptions were correct. She began to follow Carey in an effort either to catch him at his unfaithfulness or to prevent it from happening.

Carey was always aware of the principal reason for his residence in India: the sharing of the gospel with the heathen. He wanted desperately to send home word of the first convert.[28] He was learning the language as well as he could so that he could preach and translate. He preached when he could. He attempted to argue for the moral superiority of Christianity, and how Christ could liberate Hindus and Moslems from the tragedies of paganism. But how could he evangelize with his wife following him through the streets accusing him in the vilest of language of adultery? Carey and Thomas felt compelled to take some action.[29]

The first intervention was a vain attempt to reason with Dorothy:

> Mr. Udney, Mrs. Udney, Mrs. Thomas, Mr. Powell and I have reasoned with her for hours together, but, say what we would it had no manner of effect. We told her we would neither eat or drink with him till this matter was cleared up, if she could produce one questionable circumstance that looked suspicious, which she has now failed to do. She has no use of her reason on this subject, though quite reasonable in every other.[30]

Reasoning did not help.

The second intervention was a passive one. In Thomas's undated letter to Carey he suggested that if she was pregnant, they should wait to see what might happen when she gave birth. In his book on insanity, Arnold connected psychopathology with sexuality, pregnancy, and childbirth. Arnold "was prominent as a member of the school of thought which laid great emphases on sexuality as a cause."[31] We do know that their last son Jonathan was born in January or February 1796.[32] Assuming a normal length pregnancy, we can place the beginning of this pregnancy in April or May 1795. But Carey's journal entries, which we will later explore, seem to indicate that Dorothy was seriously disturbed before April 1795.

We can be fairly certain that Dorothy was in her paranoid state during this entire pregnancy. We cannot be certain whether the pregnancy was wanted or unwanted. Often physicians would recommend that a mentally ill woman have a child. This advice stemmed from the belief that mental health could be either adversely or positively influenced by childbirth.[33] In a January 11, 1796, letter to Andrew Fuller, John Thomas wrote, "She is just ready to lie in, and then I hope she will be better."[34] Their hope was futile. Dorothy's delusion did not fade when Jonathan came into the world.

A third strategy involved sharing the mail that finally arrived from England. The Careys left Hackleton on May 25, 1793. They received their first mail from England on May 9, 1795.[35] For almost two years they had no contact with the family or friends they had left behind. Dorothy's emotional state must have worsened under such isolation. When the letters came Carey must have eagerly read to her the news of the Placketts, the Careys, and their friends in Moulton, Leicester, and Hackleton. Maybe the news would revive her sagging sense of reality. The second batch of mail arrived in September. Still no remission of symptoms. Renewed contact with home had occurred too late.

Their final intervention was to confine her. No details have survived as to how they arranged this confinement.[36] Perhaps servants kept her in her room, allowing only the children to come and go. "She has been in confinement by my advice."[37] The confinement was in keeping with what Thomas Arnold advised in his books. Arnold's asylum in Leicester faced the perennial issue of how to deal with violent patients.[38] Arnold's theory was on the verge of a new emphasis—listening to the complaints of patients in an attempt to understand them better—but his technique of restraint lagged behind his theoretical commitments about the origin of mental illness.[39] Thomas's suggestion of confinement was thus in keeping with the best psychiatric advice of the day.

Carey was a mild-mannered person who must have dreaded the decision to confine his wife.[40] At times she would be at liberty.

I have been obliged to confine her some time back to prevent murder which was attempted. But she now shows no disposition to commit such violence, and is at liberty.[41]

The tragedy of Dorothy's mental illness was that Carey would have to decide over and over again to confine her, every time she decompensated or seemed on the brink of violence. He felt very much alone.

Carey's Only Friend: The Journal

Carey poured out the agony of his soul in his journal. The following entries give us a graphic picture of the intense misery of these first few months of Dorothy's insanity. We only wish we had her impressions of these same days and weeks. As we read these journal extracts, almost 200 years old now, we must remember their almost certain context: Dorothy's unceasing accusations that William was sexually unfaithful to her.

3 Feb 1795. This is indeed the Valley of the Shadow of Death to me; expect that my soul is much more insensible than John Bunyan's Pilgrim; O what would I give for a kind sympathetic friend such as I had in England to whom I might open my heart.

5 Feb 1795. O what a load is a barren heart, I feel a little forlorn pleasure in thinking over the time that is past and drown some of my heaviness by writing to my friends in England.

6 Feb 1795. I sometimes walk in my garden and try to pray to God, and if I pray at all, it is in the solitude of a walk. I thought my soul a little drawn out today, but soon gross darkness returned; spoke a word or two to a Mahomedan upon the things of God but I feel as bad as they.

7 Feb 1795. Oh that this day could be consigned to oblivion, what a mixture of impatience, carelessness, forgetfulness of God, pride, and peevishness have I felt this day. God forgive me.

17 Feb 1795. I have to complain of abundance of pride; which I find it necessary to oppose. And the more as my wife is always blaming me for putting myself on a level with the natives. I have much to conflict with on this score both without and within. I need the united prayers of all the people of God, and O that I had but the spirit to pray more for myself.

9–10 March 1795. Much to complain of, such another dead soul I think scarcely exists in the world. I can only compare myself to one banished from all his friends, and wandering in an irksome solitude.

12–24 Mar 1795. Mine is a lonesome life indeed.

15 Mar 1795. I have been very unhappy. . . . My soul was overwhelmed with depression.

14 June 1795. I have had very sore trials in my own family from a quarter which I forbear to mention. Have greater need for faith and patience than ever I had and I bless God that I have not been altogether without supplies of these graces from God tho alas I have much to complain of from within.[42]

This last passage was part of the last entry in Carey's journal. Carey abandoned journal writing at this point in favor of writing letters home.

A letter to Carey from Andrew Fuller, secretary of the society in England, conveyed some predictable understanding:

Yesterday I saw a copy of a letter lately rec'd from you to your sister Hobson. Mr. James Hobson shewed it to me. It will not be shewn except to a few particular friends who will pray for you. I have gone through the same things which you have to endure except in the one particular which must be very grievous to you. I hope and trust however that God will support you as he has supported me.[43]

Ripple Effect

As Carey and Thomas began to adjust to Dorothy's unremitting mental illness, several effects occurred. First, they had long wanted to organize a church in Mudnabatti. Although they had no converts, several Europeans in the area met together for worship and the formation of a church seemed logical. However, Dorothy's condition complicated their plans. Thomas wrote:

If any person has hearkened to her for a moment, it was merely in consideration of her being a religious character, and her making such solemn protestations of things utterly false and groundless. But long before we formed ourselves into a church we all agreed that it was impossible to consider her as a member or as a religious character now.[44]

As early as June 14, 1795, they discussed the formation of a Baptist church in Mudnabatti. The actual organization did not occur, however, until December. The delay was probably due, in part, to Dorothy's situation. She was not listed as a charter member, nor was Mrs. Thomas who may have deferred joining out of respect for Dorothy.

Another awkward situation occurred in June 1796. Rama Rama Vasu, Carey's language pundit, was proven guilty of adultery and embezzlement. Carey had to dismiss him. The pundit's adultery occurred with a widow who had a self-induced miscarriage. Having to enforce Christian moral standards in a mission setting is a difficult task; but Carey faced an even greater problem since everyone knew, including Rama Rama, that Dorothy continued to be convinced that William himself was guilty of adultery. Both Thomas and Carey must have taken extra care to carry out the discipline of the pundit given the awkwardness of Carey's domestic situation.

Carey worried a great deal about his children.

> Her misery and rage is extreme; Europeans have repeatedly talked to her, but in vain; and what may be the end of all God alone knows. Bless God all the dirt which she throws is such as cannot stick; but it is the ruin of my children to hear such continual accusations.[45]

It must have been a very difficult situation for the Carey boys, who were ten, seven, and six years of age at that time.

Possible Causes

What caused Dorothy's psychotic retreat? This question arouses our curiosity just as Carey and Thomas must have wondered about the issue. Cause is often very difficult to identify in the development of mental illnesses. A wide divergence of opinion exists in the field of psychology about which factors are more determinative: early childhood events, the immediate surroundings, heredity, or learned experience. In Dorothy's life story we can identify six possible contributing factors. Only God knows exactly which of the following is correct or in what combination they may have triggered Dorothy's retreat from reality.

Nutritional Deficiency

Any woman who gives birth to seven children in the space of fourteen years is physiologically taxed. Dorothy was not only giving birth with regularity during these years, but she was trying to adapt to tropical living with its new diet and climatic conditions. She was also struggling with dysentery, probably of the amoebic variety, for the first twelve months of her time in India. She enjoyed only a few weeks of improvement from the enervating dysentery symptoms before her delusional disorder set in.

Before the advent of medication to kill the amoeba in a dysentery patient, physicians were not able to predict which persons would be able to throw off the symptoms and which people would not be able to. The factors that determined who could withstand it had to do with subjective items such as constitution, general health and fitness, and emotional resilience. Dorothy and Felix may have struggled such a long time with the dysentery because these factors were deficient or low.

If chronic dysentery was causing nutritional deficiency the telltale indicator would be weight loss.[46] Once that process started the patient might eventually die since fewer and fewer internal resources to fight off the condition would be available. We do not have any indication that Dorothy was losing weight during this ordeal. In fact she was probably maintaining her weight even though symptoms of the disease continued. Her long life in India (fourteen years), at a time when many European women only survived six to eighteen months, indicates a strong constitution rather than the opposite. So in spite of her chronic battle with the disorder, Dorothy may not have been suffering from a nutritional deficiency. Also, we do not have evidence that paranoia is related to such deficiencies.[47]

Nevertheless the long battle with dysenteric symptoms could have left her exhausted, discouraged, and worried. Thus the general tenor of her physical and emotional health was probably impaired. In such a weakened psychological state, a person could be more susceptible to an emotional retreat from reality. In Dorothy's case the ongoing dysentery could have intensified her resentment at being forced to come to India, and could have fueled her anger at William for participating in that decision. A reservoir of anger that she could not effectively resolve may have served as the prelude to an angry delusion of jealousy.

Mercury Poisoning

We know that colonial physicians during Dorothy's lifetime treated the bloody flux with mercury. We naturally wonder then if her paranoia could have been due to mercury toxicity. Could mercury poisoning have been at the root of Dorothy's distress?

Medical researchers have studied mercury poisoning extensively during the last few decades. Workers in various industrial settings such as thermometer manufacturing plants are subjects for these studies. Research in this area took on special urgency when scientists located a massive number of mercury poisoning cases around Minamata Bay in Japan. Now the syndrome caused by mercury poisoning is called Minamata disease.

Various psychiatric symptoms can occur along with other physical problems when someone is suffering from mercury toxicity. Among these problems are erethism (irritability, excitability, temper outbursts, quarreling), extreme shyness, anxiety, tension, depression, and forgetfulness. Other more severe symptoms can appear in advanced cases: hallucinations, suicidal tendencies, melancholia, or a manic-depressive psychosis.[48] These severe symptoms appeared among felt hat makers in nineteenth-century England, thus leading to their well-known moniker: Mad Hatters.

None of these symptom clusters precisely fit what we know of Dorothy's major problem: a jealous paranoia.[49] An even greater problem in relying on this organic explanation for Dorothy's psychosis is that we have no indication that anyone used mercury to treat Dorothy's dysentery.[50]

Cultural Maladjustment

Could the monumental task of adjusting to such a different culture have overwhelmed Dorothy? Did she discover that life in India was so different that she could not make the necessary adaptive steps?[51] We know that the family encountered numerous challenges that must have stretched them to the limits. Our handicap here is that we do not have the words, thoughts, and feelings of Dorothy recorded for our examination. We simply do not know how much these cultural factors bothered her.

If the religious and social milieu of India was a challenge to new Europeans, so was the weather. Physicians in the tropics have long noted what is sometimes called "tropical neurasthenia," or a neurosis triggered by life in the tropics. Observers usually list several symptoms of this condition: a sense of persecution, social withdrawal, and/or extravagant behavior requiring excessive stimulation.[52]

Actual disease undoubtedly influences the tendency to neurasthenia, especially perhaps intestinal infections. The fear of amoebiasis can be very real, leaving the patient riveting his attention on his digestive system and never being happy unless reassured by repeated examination.[53]

Life in the tropics with its climate and diseases can breed this type of neurasthenia. However, the description of tropical neurasthenia does not fit closely enough with what we know of Dorothy's symptoms.[54]

Heredity

The psychological literature does not suggest a genetic involvement in paranoid conditions,[55] but we do know that Dorothy and William's oldest son Felix had a period of considerable mental instability during his adult years. Could Dorothy's and Felix's emotional struggles be related? Could Dorothy's mental illness have connections with genetic conditions? To explore this issue we need to make a quick survey of the life of Felix Carey.

Felix may have suffered from a lack of attention from his very busy father and from his mother whose emotional struggles consumed her. He seemed to grow up too quickly. At fourteen years of age he wrote an enthusiastic letter to England telling of his conversion and of his zeal for missionary work. The Baptist Missionary Society replied immediately with the news that a package of gift books was on its way to him and that he was now officially regarded as a missionary of the society.[56] Felix was a gifted linguist who was very skilled in the vernacular, as is "usually experienced by children brought up mainly by servants."[57]

In 1804 at eighteen years of age he married fifteen-year-old Margaret Kinsey. The Serampore missionaries sent young Felix and his wife off to Burma where they hoped to establish a new mission. Felix had obtained some medical training in Calcutta and was eventually able to offer small pox inoculations to the family of the king of Burma.[58] Felix and Margaret had some struggles in Burma. "Mrs. Felix Carey had no missionary feelings and she did not like to be deprived of bread, butter, meat, etc."[59]

In 1807 Felix received news of his mother's death. The news hit him hard. During the next year he visited Serampore with his family. He returned to Burma alone since his wife was about to give birth to their third child. Margaret died soon after childbirth at nineteen years of age. William Carey took the three children (Lucy, Dorothy, and

William) and urged his son Felix to remain a missionary in Burma. In 1811 Felix married again and had two children by his second wife. A tragic river accident took the lives of his second wife and two young children. Death stalked his footsteps. His father William wrote, "I mourn for Felix in silence, and still tremble to think what may be the next stroke. I am dumb with silence because God has done it."[60]

Felix later came to Calcutta on a mission for the royal court of Burma. His father was upset. "He is shrivelled up from a missionary to an ambassador from the Burman Court to the supreme government of Calcutta."[61] When Felix presented his credentials to the government in Calcutta, officials found irregularities. Felix insisted that he was now an ambassador. He demanded preferential treatment and began to live very ostentatiously. He wore elaborate Burmese regalia and had a large retinue of attendants. The Calcutta officials were polite but refused to accept his "credentials" as an ambassador. His father wrote, "I am glad he was not received. I hope it is felt by him."[62]

Felix left behind a trail of debts that his father had to cover. "I never told you that Felix's extravagances had stripped me of all I had. Only my brethren have agreed that I shall pay it off by installments."[63] "It is possible that his conduct was merely the outcome of ambition unrestrained by much common sense."[64]

The best explanation we have for this strange episode in Calcutta is that Felix was temporarily suffering from a Delusional Disorder of the Grandiose type. Unlike his mother, the incident appeared to fade away and he had several productive years after these Calcutta struttings. "Megalomania seems to be the only explanation of Felix's extraordinary confidence in his own importance."[65]

Felix worked to some extent with Adoniram and Ann Judson in Rangoon. He disappeared from the scene of missionary work for a while to wander through the interior collecting botanical samples and making anthropological observations about the peoples he encountered.[66] At the urging of William Ward, he later returned to Serampore where he enjoyed several productive years translating.[67] He married two more times; his fourth wife outlived him. Felix died on November 10, 1822, at thirty-six years of age after a bout with high fevers.

Felix's grandiose episode is the strongest evidence we have of familial factors in his mother's mental illness. Yet the story of Felix may not point to heredity factors. His delusional bout may simply illustrate that both he and his mother shared heightened sensitivities to grief. Both of them became delusional after severe losses. Perhaps the story of Felix points more to the next explanation for Dorothy's mental illness: an intense grief reaction.

Grief Reaction

Loss is a painful human experience. Some people experience more loss than others, and among those who suffer massive losses are some who handle it well and some who struggle intensely with the grief. Felix lost two wives and several children before his grandiose episode. Dorothy buried two of her daughters in England, lost contact with her extensive family in Northampton, watched her sister Kitty marry and leave her, and then buried one of her sons in Mudnabatti. Her losses were numerous and severe. Other Baptist missionaries in Serampore also suffered severe loss.

> John Chamberlain was to lose all three of his children within nine months between midsummer 1811 and March 1812; and the first two months of 1812 would carry off Mrs. Mardon and her youngest child, Joshua Marshman's baby son, one of William Ward's daughters (he had married Fountain's widow), a servant of Hannah Marshman and a young boy boarder at the Marshman school.[68]

But people deal with grief differently. What one mother can handle and recover from, the next may not be able to withstand. Loss may have pushed Dorothy and Felix beyond their tolerance for loss. We know that paranoia and depression are related.[69] When reality becomes too painful to bear, the human personality has the capacity to retreat from reality, and to live in a less painful but unreal world. Felix's grandiose behavior may have temporarily covered over his painful grief. Dorothy's retreat from reality may have helped her move away from the pain of her own losses as she focused on the imagined sins of her husband. A psychotic state, such as Dorothy experienced, can thus be adaptive. As unreal as her imagination was, she could survive by focusing on the imaginary problems rather than actual events. She may have feared that if she faced her own grief, the pain would have been overwhelming.

Fears

The final explanation for Dorothy's mental illness deals with fear. We have seen fear before in Dorothy's story. She was fearful on the day Thomas talked her into going to India. She was fearful on the voyage. She must have been fearful of the tigers, crocodiles, and snakes so nonchalantly described by her husband. The profound religious and cultural differences all around her in the remote area of Mudnabatti must have frightened her. The jungle noise, the problem of educating her sons in this remote setting, the disease that killed her son, and the uncertainty of their future could all have triggered massive fears in Dorothy.[70] Carey himself admitted later that the education of the boys in Mudnabatti was not satisfactory. "I was in great distress at Mudnabatty because the education of these lads could not possibly be attended to in such a manner as it ought to have been."[71]

When Peter died, could Dorothy have feared that she would lose all her children? Carey tells us in his journal that Dorothy was disturbed that William always wanted to put himself on the level of those living around them. Could these and other fears have simply overwhelmed Dorothy?

Perhaps each of these factors played a role in the development of Dorothy's mental disorder. Psychologically discouraged by her long battle with dysentery, Dorothy must have been emotionally overwhelmed by life in the tropics with its many fear-provoking features. She had a ceiling of tolerance for loss, and when life pushed her beyond that capacity, she retreated from her painful world of reality into an unreal world that, though miserable, was at least tolerable.

Paranoia

Paranoia is not a new, twentieth-century phenomenon. Arnold wrote that suspicion and jealousy were the scourges of weak and gloomy minds.[72] In the late nineteenth century, the prevailing view about paranoia was that its roots were in sexuality.[73] In India, paranoia was a rare condition. Monomania was a common name for the condition. Early in the nineteenth century the disorder was described as having a slow onset, as being more common among males than females, and as a very dangerous condition for which no cure existed.[74] Many authors have connected the delusions of paranoia with dangerousness and violence.[75]

Current evidence confirms much of the above information. The best current data are that delusional disorders such as Dorothy had begin in middle or late adult life and are relatively uncommon. "Delusional Disorder is apparently slightly more common in females than males." "Immigration, emigration . . . and other severe stresses may predispose to the development of Delusional Disorder."[76] Psychodynamic theorists argue that the jealous person fears loss and attempts to compensate for this loss by possessing and being jealous of that person.[77] A violation of trust is another common predisposing cause. Perhaps William or John Thomas had promised Dorothy that once she arrived in India she would like the place. When India proved to be an extremely stressful country, she may have felt that her trust had been violated. What better way to express this violation of trust than by not trusting her husband?

Dorothy's retreat from reality in the first few months of 1795 added great misery and perplexity to William's life. We can also be certain that Dorothy was just as miserable and perplexed, even in her psychotic state. In attempting great things for God, Carey had never expected such great suffering in return.

7

A Bewildered Husband

From 1795 to 1807 William Carey had acquired some major new responsibilities. He now had to care for his wife who, at times, could not seek her own best good. He had to worry about his sons who were growing up in a highly stressful domestic environment. He had to monitor the safety of Dorothy, his own safety, and the safety of others around the family. During these twelve years Carey would see countless other projects buzzing around him at Mudnabatti and Serampore, but he would never escape the ongoing awareness of the responsibilities he carried for his wife and sons. These tasks would be like a drone string on a banjo—always contributing to the total effect but rarely changing.

Personal Resources

What resources did Carey have as he moved into this stage of his life? We can best answer this question by looking at two types of information we can glean from the Carey documents. First, we can examine how much he may have known about mental illness when his wife slipped into her psychotic state. Second, we can survey various features in his personality makeup that might help us understand his response to Dorothy's mental illness.

Mental Illness in Carey's World

Before Dorothy entered her state of paranoia, William personally knew about several others who struggled with mental illness. We have already referred to the mental illness of Mrs. Andrew Fuller in 1792. The Fullers had lost a six-year-old daughter after a long illness. Andrew Fuller was himself ill during his daughter's last days and could not be with her. He got off his sick bed to attend her funeral, which was preached by John Ryland. During this child's sickness, another child was born into the family.

> The circumstances attending this birth, amidst all the anguish of their watching over the little one whom God took from them, were too much to bear, and his beloved wife was seized with illness which led to distressing insanity, and ended in death.[1]

Two fellow pastors back in England had likewise struggled with mental illness. The pastor at the Hackleton Meeting House immediately before Carey moved to the area, Mr. Rands, "lost his reason" in 1774.[2] Andrew Fuller sent the following news of another pastor in one of his 1794 letters to Carey:

> Poor Faukner! His conduct has been such for a while before his derangement that we have been obliged to tell the church to cut him off! High misdemeanours tho' not amounting to the act of adultery! The Lord keep us![3]

Carey, like all other subjects of the English Crown, also knew about King George III. America's last king had at least four major episodes of mental illness: 1788–89 (the regency crisis with the Prince of Wales in charge), 1801, 1804, and 1810–12. Some experts have argued that the king's illness was based on a hereditary predisposition for mental illness and that he suffered from a manic depressive disorder.[4] Others claim that he suffered from porphyria, a rare and inherited metabolic disorder that allows toxins to build up in a system, thus producing temporary mental illness.[5] Whatever the true nature of his struggles, all of his subjects knew about his illness. Dorothy struggled at a time when the powerful and famous George III had his emotional battles also. All of the above examples prove that Carey knew about mental illness and that it had touched lives close to his.

After Dorothy's psychotic onset other cases of mental illness crossed Carey's path. Robert Hall, Jr., son of the author of *Help to Zion's Travellers,* had bouts of severe depression. While pastor of the St. Andrew Street Baptist Church in Cambridge, Hall became very depressed. He

Illustrations and Maps

Illustrations

1. Register of Dorothy Carey's baptism.
2. Dorothy and William's marriage license.
3. Dorothy's husband, William Carey.
4. Meeting House in Hackleton.
5. Drawing of the interior of the Careys' cottage in Moulton.
6. Drawing of the exterior of the Careys' cottage in Moulton.
7. Photograph of the Moulton cottage.
8. Leather-soaking trough in the Moulton cottage.
9. Moulton (Carey) Chapel in 1892.
10. Utensils and a cup from Dorothy's kitchen.
11. Dorothy's kitchen and living room in Leicester.
12. The Careys' cottage in Leicester.
13. Harvey Lane Chapel in Leicester.
14. Thomas Arnold, M.D., of Leicester.
15. John Thomas, friend of the Careys.
16. Note to Dorothy Carey's father.
17. Dorothy Carey's gravestone.

Maps

1. England
2. Northamptonshire
3. Bengal, India

1. In this official list of "Christenings for the year 1755," the ninth line records Dorothy's baptism: "Jan. 25. Dority (*sic*) daughter of Dan'l & Lusi (*sic*) Plackett was bapt. 1755." Photo by County Record Office, Northampton, England.

2. Dorothy's and William's marriage license shows the mark (x) Dorothy had to make because she was unable to sign her name. Her sister Lucy, one of the witnesses, did the same. The document reads: " Banns of marriage between William Carey and Dorothy Plackett, both of this parish, were published in this church on 2 formal Sundays ____ and May 6, 1781 ____. William Carey of this parish and Dorothy Plackett of this parish were married in this church by banns this tenth day of June in the year One Thousand Seven Hundred and Eighty-one by me, ____. This marriage was solemnized between us, [signed] Wm Carey [and] Dorothy Plackett (x), in the presence of [signed] Tho. Old [and] Lucy Plackett (x)." Photo by County Record Office, Northampton, England.

3. Dorothy Carey's husband, William, as painted by Robert Home (1752–1834).

4. The Meeting House in Hackleton. Drawing by Henry Stanhope (1923).

5. The interior of Dorothy and William Carey's cottage in Moulton. Drawing by C.E.M. (1892).

Plan of the Cottage

Sink where Carey soaked his leather

6. A drawing of the exterior of the Careys' Moulton home. By C. E. M. (1892).

7. A photograph of the Carey home in Moulton. By Andrew Fuller Carey.

8. The trough in which William soaked leather. For its location in the Careys' cottage in Moulton, see the inset in figure 5. Photograph by Andrew Fuller Carey.

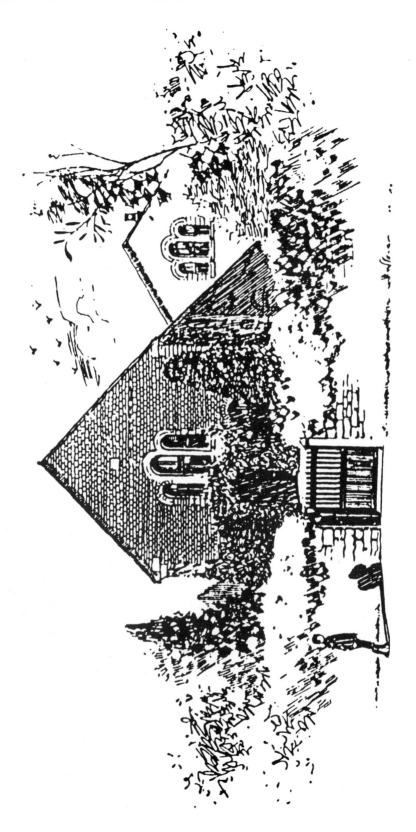

9. The Moulton (Carey) Chapel. Drawing by C. E. M. (1892).

10. A fork, knife, and cup from Dorothy's kitchen. Photograph by Andrew Fuller Carey.

11. Dorothy's kitchen in the Careys' Leicester home was also the livingroom, workshop, and classroom. The vantage point is that of one who has entered the front door, taken a couple of steps straight ahead, and then turned to the right. Drawing by G. Leader.

12. The front of the Carey cottage in Leicester. Drawing by G. Leader.

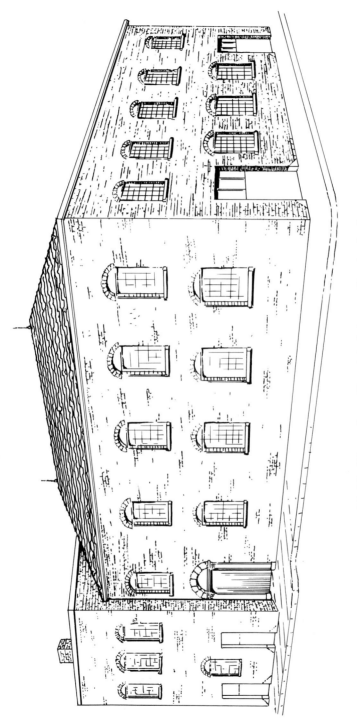

13. The Harvey Lane Chapel in Leicester. Drawing by Stevenson.

14. Thomas Arnold, M.D., of Leicester. Drawing by G. Ralph.

15. John Thomas, friend of William and Dorothy Carey and a fellow missionary. Painting by Medley.

16. We do not know who wrote this note to Dorothy's father, "Mr Daniel Plackett, Hackleton." It reads: "Dear Father, We are just going. The boat is just going out, and we are going on board—Thursday morning at five o'clock—June 14th, 1793. We are all well & in good spirits." Photocopy by Angus Library, Regent's Park College, Oxford.

17. Dorothy's gravestone. The inscription reads: "To the memory of Mrs. D. Carey, wife of the Rev'd W. Carey, D.D., who departed this life on the eighth day of 1807, aged 51 years, this small token of conjugal affection and filial regard erected by her affectionate husband and bereaved children." Photo by Raymond P. Prigodich.

England

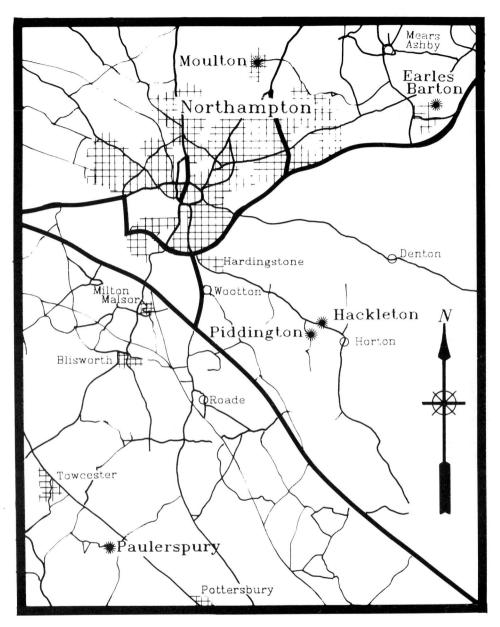

Moulton

Northampton

Mears
Ashby

Earles
Barton

Denton

Hardingstone

Wootton

Milton
Malsor

Hackleton

Piddington

Horton

Blisworth

Roade

N

Towcester

Paulerspury

Pottersbury

Northamptonshire

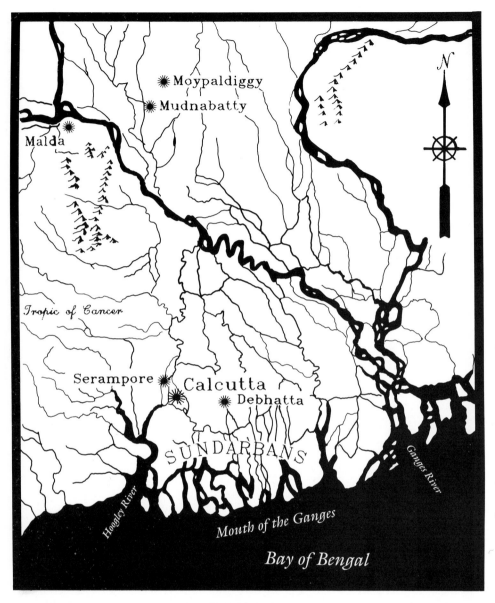

Bengal, India

confined himself to his room and spent long periods of time reading. Eventually he took a room in a neighboring village in an attempt to reduce his stress. In November 1804, a church member went to visit him. "He was engaged in one continual stream of incoherent talk."[6] Eventually Hall was institutionalized in Dr. Arnold's Leicester asylum. Hall's experience there was not good.[7] He returned to his pulpit, but in 1805 he began to decompensate. He became intermittently incoherent in a service commemorating the Lord's Supper, muttering about the millennium. This time friends hospitalized him under the care of a Dr. Cox in Fish Ponds, Bristol.[8] Carey probably heard about Hall's struggles through letters from England.

Closer to home, William knew of mental illness among missionaries to South Asia. In 1819 he wrote:

> Poor Mr. Wheelock the American missionary coming from Rangoon in a delirium which was attended with great despondency threw himself overboard last Friday and was drowned.[9]

Carey's colleague Joshua Marshman suffered from severe depression. After returning from a visit to England, Marshman had three major bouts. William Carey described Marshman's condition as a "morbid depression" in which "the merest trifle lies on his mind with unsupportable weight."[10] Marshman described his state as a combination of terror and anguish.

Thus when Dorothy began her emotional struggles, while she was in the midst of them, and even after her death, Carey was not ignorant of the existence of mental illness among Christians. He could not have concluded that Dorothy's problems were unique; others among his good friends likewise suffered from the ravages of psychopathology.

Carey's Personality

Some of Carey's personality patterns served him well during the twelve years of Dorothy's psychosis. Other traits added to the difficulty he had in dealing with his emotionally disabled wife. The sum of Carey's personality is very much like most Christian leaders: many strong, positive features with a few foibles sprinkled in among the positives. Yet Carey was also a unique combination of characteristics. He, like Dorothy, is worth understanding.

Attitudes Toward the Future

Carey was very much a visionary. He had a bright and nearly limitless view of the future and its possibilities. On the sea voyage to Calcutta when he had barely begun his own missionary career he was busy making notations of where the society could undertake additional mission outreaches.[11] As each country passed over the horizon Carey would dream of its spiritual future.

His visionary stance toward the future equipped him well for reverses. As soon as some plan proved unfeasible, he was ready within a few days with another ambitious alternative. If his attitudes toward the future contained any flaws, they were that sometimes his dreams were too big and too premature. For example, Carey wrote that all Christians interested in evangelism and missions should gather together for an international congress to conduct long-range planning. The proposal was a sound one but did not come true during his lifetime. The congress eventually did convene in Edinburgh, but over 100 years after Carey had first suggested the idea. Carey's wish to decline further support from England as soon as he had obtained his first salaried job in Mudnabatti is an example of a hasty, premature decision that would have been unwise.

Carey's basic vision and optimism for the future served him well as he and Dorothy began to journey through the long twelve years of her psychosis. Without a reservoir of optimism, Carey's depression and despondency might have been much worse.

Response to Stress

Carey responded to stress in one of three ways. The first—by far his most common response—was an even-tempered, take-it-in-stride attitude. Carey was a man of deeply held values. During his young adult years these moral and spiritual convictions solidified and became the driving force behind his entire life. These values determined both his short-range and long-range planning. Stress, obstacles, and difficulties simply drove him back to his core. Battered by failure, disappointment, or opposition, he would renew his effort to meet the challenge and develop some creative strategy around the obstacle. This tenacious grip on his core values gave him an equanimity of temper that served him well as a pioneer missionary with a mentally ill wife.

The second response to stress was by far less frequent: losing his temper and patience. We only have a few examples of this rare outbreak of frustration. Soon after he had obtained the salaried position at the indigo plant, he wrote a letter relaying the news and the promise of Mr. Udney to share part of the profits with Carey at the end of a good year. When that letter arrived in England people began to believe that Carey was not just taking a job with a salary to feed his family, but that he was entering into business and losing his focus on missionary endeavors. This misunderstanding by a misreading of correspondence is but the first of countless problems that have occurred in the history of modern missions through the mails.

The emerging public relations fallout in England forced Fuller and other society administrators to jump into action. Fuller called an emergency meeting of the committee because "Booth and the London friends are much afraid of this mercantile scheme."[12] Eventually truth prevailed over the rumors. Carey was the last man on earth to be detracted from his deeply held goals. Fuller wrote to Carey:

> When we considered you as *involved in affairs of trade,* we rejoiced with trembling. . . . We know that many worthy men who have stood firm in the day of adversity, have been melted into indifference by the smiles of prosperity.[13]

This misunderstanding pushed Carey's patience to the limit. He had just emerged from a year of near disaster, and the society at home implied he was awash in wealth and prosperity!

> I account this my own country now, and have not the least inclination to leave it tho repeated experience proves to me that I have nothing to expect in it but a bare living. . . . I am well satisfied and only mention this to rectify a mistaken opinion of our having grown rich in India, perhaps from my mentioning what might possibly be our income. We are neither rich or in situations equal to what mine was at Leicester considering the great losses we have met with from large floods, and the amazing expense of servants necessary here.[14]

On at least one other occasion Carey lost his patience. A serious misunderstanding developed between the Serampore missionaries and the society in England. The situation was serious and frustrating to both parties. In 1819 Carey wrote an eleven-page response to charges in an uncharacteristic, stinging style.[15]

The third response Carey exhibited to stress was a passive one. At times he would defer to others and not actively participate in problem solving such as he did in the early years with John Thomas. Carey later regretted his passivity because things would often get worse when he did not actively participate.

> I blame Mr. T. for leading me into such experience at first, and I blame myself for being led; tho I acceded to what I much disapproved of, because I thought he knew the country best.[16]

> You see that I have not been following my own plan, but I suppose I have complied with Mr. T's wishes contrary to my own private judgment.[17]

Carey's response to stress was normally one of resilience, although he could be passive and on rare occasions he could lose his patience. All three responses likely occurred as Carey attempted to live with Dorothy in her psychotic state. God was merciful in that Carey was primarily equipped psychologically as a patient responder to stress. Hence he possessed a major qualification for dealing with an insanely jealous spouse.

Attitudes Toward Work

Carey's capacity for work and productivity was phenomenal. The pattern of intense attention to work he established in his early years as a shoemaker and pastor continued into his career as a missionary. Carey had

> always entertained a dread of "becoming useless," as he expressed himself before his death, and he hoped that his life might terminate with his capacity for work.[18]

> He was a strict economist of time, and the maxim on which he acted was to take care of minutes, and leave the hours to take care of themselves. He never lost a minute when he could help it.[19]

Carey described himself as a plodder. One time when asked how he could accomplish so much translation work, he replied, "Few people know what may be done till they try, and persevere in what they undertake."[20] Carey used this plodding attitude to attack obstacles. The very fact that he got to India when, according to the East India Company, he was not supposed to be there as a missionary, is a testimony to this dogged attitude.[21]

An ingredient in this disciplined attitude toward work was his sense of responsibility. During the early months when he did not have a certain future in India, he wrote, "I am dejected, not for my own sake but my family's."[22] He attempted to be a worthy steward of funds donated by English and Scottish supporters, and he was committed to doing his share in making the mission succeed.

Although Carey was committed to work, he also knew the value of diversion. He always made time for his botanical interests. Carey was an inveterate collector of plants, birds, rocks, and shells from all over Asia. In every place where he lived a garden inevitably appeared. In his long correspondence with his son Jabez, who was living in India at some distance from Carey, he was always giving instructions regarding the botanical samples he wanted Jabez to send him. He asked Jabez to send seeds, bulbs, tubers, and plants.[23] He told friends in England how to ship live plants so they would survive the long sea voyage. He attacked his hobby as he did his work—vigorously!

How did this personality feature equip him to care for Dorothy? On the positive side, his commitment to work gave him reason to go on with his vision for evangelizing the heathen. On the negative side, his tendencies to workaholism provided him with an escape. Dorothy was craving attention from her husband. The more he avoided giving it, the more she likely became convinced that he probably was having affairs with other women.

Interpersonal Skills

People who knew Carey well described him as quiet and shy. "His conversation was grave and instructive; but he had no conversational talent."[24] Carey decried his hesitancy to initiate conversation especially as related to evangelism:

> A want of character and firmness has always predominated in me. I have not resolution enough to reprove sin, to introduce serious and evangelical conversation in carnal company, especially among the great, to whom I have sometimes access. I sometimes labour with myself long and at last cannot prevail sufficiently to break silence; or, if I introduce a subject, want resolution to keep it up, if the company do not show a readiness thereto.[25]

Carey was hard on himself, but he did seem to struggle with interpersonal communication. Yet Carey could be very direct, even if only in his journal:

Yesterday my mind was much hurt to see what I thought was a degree of selfishness in my friend (John Thomas) which amounted to an almost total neglect of me, my family, and the mission, tho' I don't think he seriously intends to neglect either.[26]

Even though Carey may have felt awkward in some social settings, he repeatedly demonstrated the capacity to make and sustain long-lasting friendships. We have seen the friends he made in Leicester among a wide circle of influence. His correspondence was wide-ranging: with botanists in England, with clergy of all denominations, and with persons of political importance.

When loss occurred in his life he grieved deeply. Of Felix he wrote, "His departure from God has nearly broken my heart. May God restore him."[27] After his second wife died he wrote:

My life is solitary and melancholy. I shall I think, endeavour to marry again, after some time but at present I know not where to look for a woman who will be a suitable partner for me. I hope the Lord will direct me in that matter as he has done in everything from my youth till now.[28]

His loss of Charlotte, the second Mrs. William Carey, was "the greatest loss I ever suffered."[29]

My loss is irreparable. . . . We had frequently conversed upon the separation which death would make, and both desired that, if it were the will of God, she might be first removed; and so it was.[30]

In spite of his shyness, Carey could form deep attachments to people, both family and friends. His grief at times of loss was great. His dislike for amiable, social chit-chat, however, may have ill suited him to spend time with his wife in daily conversation. His seriousness of purpose may have obscured the value he could obtain by spending more time with Dorothy. Before her psychotic breakdown, such attention might have borne fruit. After her retreat from reality, attention from Carey was probably too late.

Flexibility and Openness
Carey viewed the world as a wide place in which he had an obligation to represent God's mercy and justice. He did not have a small, rigid world in which his only concern was for the salvation of sinners and nothing more. His openness and flexibility regarding the issues around

him continue to be inspiring examples to all who have followed in his footsteps. He did not shy away from needed progressive reform:

> I consider that the burning of women, the burying of them alive with their husbands, the exposure of infants, and the sacrifice of children at Saugor, ought not to be permitted, whatever religious motives are pretended, because they are crimes against the state.[31]

Carey was open enough to see that "All things have not the same value"; thus his scale of values made him the friend of the disadvantaged and oppressed.[32] Carey maintained an impressive mix of social awareness and interest in evangelism, always giving respectful attention to the religion and culture of others.[33] Such openness and appreciation for a wide world of responsibilities characterize a person who is not rigid.

Carey's flexibility, perhaps in contrast to others of his day, is also present in his attitudes toward the Sabbath. He observed strict practices regarding Sunday, but he was not rigid about those standards. We have already seen how the Carey family took off from Hackleton in 1793, leaving behind a cloud of dust on a Sabbath! In 1829 when Governor General William Bentinck sent him the newly enacted ban on *sati* with a request to translate the law into Bengali, Carey excused himself from Sunday preaching in order to have this privilege.

These events point to a healthy amount of flexibility in Carey's personality structure. How did this quality help him with Dorothy's illness? He had to make many adjustments in the years following 1795. These accommodations must have frustrated him, but at least he seemed to have the capacity and flexibility to make them on behalf of Dorothy.

Spiritual and Moral Core

Carey was a social liberal. He abhorred slavery on the basis of scriptural principles. He abandoned the use of sugar while still living in England:[34]

> A noble effort has been made to abolish the inhuman slave trade, and though at present it has not been so successful as might be wished, yet it is to be hoped it will be persevered in, till it is accomplished.[35]

In 1803 Carey wrote a New York City Baptist pastor and asked about revival in America:

Has this glorious work spread into any more of the States? Has it contributed at all to the destruction of that disgrace of America, and every civilized nation, the Slave Trade?[36]

Carey's deep social and spiritual revulsion toward slavery evolved in India into an equal abhorrence of caste. Early in their ministry the missionaries made some accommodation for polygamy among converts, but they absolutely forbad any caste differentiations in the church.[37] The missionaries insisted that converts break class upon conversion.[38] God rewarded Carey's deep moral and spiritual courage in this matter:

His policy met with marked success. The scornful accusation that only the lowest castes or outcasts could be induced to accept a Christianity which abjured caste distinctions was completely refuted in the Serampore community.[39]

Deep at his spiritual core was a holy zeal and a sense of calling that propelled this Calvinist to become a missionary.[40] His sense of calling kept him on his evangelistic pursuit. He earnestly prayed for the conversion of his own sons.[41] At times, however, he put intense spiritual pressure on his sons. By today's standards such intensity seems risky. Carey wrote the following to his son Jabez, who was twenty-three years of age at the time:

All my hopes as it respects the usefulness of my children now centres in William and you, for Felix is become an awful profligate and Jonathan's religion, to say the least of it, is doubtful. One year of heartbreaking circumstances like what I have experienced in the present one will doubtless overset me. Indeed I shall never recover the wound I have received but expect it will bring my gray hairs with sorrow to the grave.[42]

Quite a heavy load to place on a son!

Carey's deep spiritual and moral core suited him well as Dorothy's husband. He trusted deeply in the God of providence, and he knew that God's sovereign hand was at work in Mudnabatti even though he at times must have felt that his world was caving in on him.

Family Relationships

How did Carey function as a father and as a husband? We often do not know the answers to such questions among our contemporaries, let alone about someone who lived 200 years ago. Hints occur in the

Carey literature that give us some clues. He loved Dorothy and his sons. He expressed this love in his sense of responsibility toward them and in his desire for their best. At times, however, he seemed to display poor domestic judgment:

> I wrote to you to interest yourself in sending out a young person as wife for my son Felix. I shall feel myself greatly obliged by your doing so; and with as little delay as possible. It will give me great pleasure to see him comfortably settled in the married state.[43]

He seems here to have little awareness of factors that might contribute to marital happiness or misery. Simply being married was the criterion.[44]

In some ways Carey had high ideals for marriage. In 1814 he wrote a "father-son" letter to newly married Jabez:

> You are now married. Be not content to bear yourself toward your wife with propriety, but let love be the spring of all your conduct. Esteem her highly that she may highly esteem you. The first impressions of love arising from form or beauty will soon wear off, but the trust arising from character will endure and increase.[45]

Knowing what to do in a marriage is sometimes different from actually doing it. We have some reason to believe Carey was able to get closer to this ideal in his second marriage than he was in his first marriage.

When compared to others of his day, Carey was not chauvinistic toward women. As a boy he had observed his father showing concern for the education of the girls of Paulerspury. Edmund Carey was a good role model for William. "Twice a week he (William's father) might be seen walking to the neighboring town of Towcester, there to teach a ladies' school writing and arithmetic."[46] Carey was an avid supporter of Serampore efforts to educate women and girls.[47] Earlier in his Harvey Lane pastorate, Carey made sure in the renewed church covenant that democratic votes would govern church meetings, including the vote for women. Perhaps as a caveat to males who feared such radicalism, the covenant also inserted: "Yet they shall not be permitted to dictate."[48] Carey is also well known for his relentless opposition to *sati*, the Hindu custom whereby a widow threw herself on the funeral pyre of her deceased husband. From the time he saw his first *sati* in 1799 until the practice became illegal in 1829, Carey worked tirelessly for its abolition.[49]

Carey was also a person of some sentiment. He could cherish memories and relish the role family had played in his own life and development: "My heart often flies into England, and I frequently visit the house, the orchard, and garden where I passed my juvenile years."[50] But sentiment was not the same quality as rigorous attention to the needs of his sons. The Marshmans, admirers of Carey though they may have been, were critical of his skills as a father:

> Though assiduous in the cultivation of his own mind to the highest standard of excellence, he was not sufficiently alive to the importance of improving the minds of his children. . . . His children came from Mudnabatty to Serampore without any culture; and for all the advantages of education they enjoyed they were indebted to the affectionate exertions of Dr. Marshman.[51]

The Marshmans attempted to bring some culture to Felix soon after his arrival in Serampore:[52]

> Owing to Brother Carey's domestic affliction, his perpetual avocations, or perhaps an easiness of the temperament not wholly free from blame, his two eldest sons were left in great measure without control; hence obstinacy and self-will took a very deep root in their minds while, he, like David, never displeased them.[53]

Carey's major flaw may have resided in his limited capacities for domestic relationships. He did not think that giving attention to his wife and children was wrong or unimportant. Nor did he regard members of his family as second-class citizens. He simply did not have this particular responsibility of life very high on his list of priorities. Other tasks and challenges interested him far more than spending time with his family.[54] We must be careful not to impose twentieth-century standards on William. We live in an age of leisure unparalleled in history. The time we now have to spend nurturing family relationships does not necessarily correlate well with other times and places. Nonetheless, Carey did not seem to give a lot of attention to his wife or sons.

When Carey thus came upon the heavy responsibilities of caring for his insane wife, he had some factors in his favor, some working against him. Like the rest of us, he was not perfectly equipped for what God was calling him to do. He did his best. One of the most pressing tasks in 1795 for this bewildered husband was to think about a long-term solution.

Long-Term Solutions

At some point Carey must have realized that Dorothy's problems were not short-term. People who loved her and cared for her must have kept alive some hope that her delusion would remit. But improvements were temporary and apparently infrequent. Dorothy no doubt also wanted some resolution to her distress.

The number of options available to Carey regarding the care of his wife during her psychosis were quite limited. Some of them he implemented, some he did not.

Consult a Physician

John Thomas, friend and colleague of Carey, was a physician. In a sense, Carey did consult with Thomas and thus may have thought further medical investigation of Dorothy's problems was unnecessary. Perhaps Thomas told Carey that nothing more could be done for Dorothy and so no more enquiries would prove helpful. Nonetheless, we have no evidence that Carey ever sought medical help for his wife, even after Thomas's death in 1801.

When the family lived in Mudnabatti during Dorothy's psychotic state (1795–99), the issue may have been moot: No physicians were around. Yet Carey did make trips to Calcutta during this time. In 1800 the family moved to Serampore, just thirty miles from Calcutta. During these last seven years of Dorothy's life, medical evaluation and care were much more feasible since British physicians practiced in the nearby city of Calcutta. But we do not know that Carey ever took Dorothy to Calcutta for medical attention.

We also know that Danish physicians were resident in Serampore in 1800.[55] In 1809 when Carey was ill with a delirious fever, colleagues called in physicians as they later did when Carey had a bad fall.[56] In 1812 William Johns arrived in Serampore as a missionary doctor to care for the missionary family there.[57] So Carey had access in Serampore to medical care even though he primarily seemed to consult physicians for illnesses of a physical kind. Carey did not appear to have any prejudice against medical treatment even though he sometimes complained about their cures.[58]

The best explanation for Carey's apparent reluctance to take Dorothy to a physician for medical evaluation is related to the strained relationship between the missionaries and the government. The East India Company knew about Carey and his missionary work all along, both

while he lived at Mudnabatti and later when the family lived in the
Danish colony of Serampore. Until 1813 official company policy
banned direct missionary work in company territory. The missionaries survived in this somewhat hostile environment by keeping a low
profile and by living as upstanding lives as possible.

Now we can imagine the awkwardness of taking Dorothy to a company physician. She would explain in the most convincing terms that
her husband was living a grossly immoral life. Whereas the doctors
would undoubtedly recognize her accusations as part of her paranoia,
the mere reporting of Carey's alleged behavior would have launched
awkward, official investigations. Carey was in a difficult position, and he
may have chosen not to risk ruining the reputation all the missionaries
had worked so hard to earn.

Return to England

Another long-term solution would be to return to England. We do
not know if Dorothy had asked him to take her home. If Carey had
consulted with physicians, they might have advised him that she could
possibly improve if she were back in familiar surroundings. Of course,
we have no idea if anyone made such a recommendation to Carey.

In Carey's replies to letters from England one can detect an occa-
sional clue that his correspondents may have suggested that he bring
Dorothy back to England. One example comes in a letter from Carey
to his father in 1804:

> I and my family am, through the good care of God as well as I ever
> remember, except my poor wife who continues in the melancholy situ-
> ation which she has long been in. You seem to think that the climate
> of this country has contributed to her derangement. I have no such
> idea.[59]

Perhaps his father had suggested that William bring Dorothy back to
England. In an important passage Carey goes on in this same letter to
relate why he feels the weather has not driven his wife insane.

> On the contrary I have every reason to suppose that it was gradually
> coming on before she left England tho then unsuspected by me. But I
> now recollect numerous instances of conduct which are best explained
> by referring them to this source. The enjoyment which I have in our
> family, which is one of the happiest in the world, and in my children,

two of whom I have had the pleasure of baptizing with my own hands, more than compensates for the distress which I have from any other quarter.[60]

Carey's reasoning here is that India has not necessarily caused her problems. She had problems before she left England. We wish we knew more about these behaviors which, by hindsight, seemed related to her insane jealousy. Had Dorothy been a possessive wife in England? Had she continually asked for more of his time and attention? Was she violent in England? We simply do not know, but the available evidence from her years in England, as we have previously reviewed, seems to indicate that she did not manifest overt symptoms of mental illness in those early years. Perhaps she did complain, however, about Carey's priorities and a lack of attention.

Families of a suicide victim will often reflect on and reinterpret clues that they missed. Or friends of someone in acute emotional crisis will experience the same phenomenon: Hindsight often teaches us something we previously missed. If Carey had been more specific in this letter to his father, we could have more confidence in its actual meaning. The bulk of the evidence that we do have, however, points to factors in India as being much more related to Dorothy's psychotic break than her experiences in England.

If Carey had returned with Dorothy to England for a prolonged time or permanently, he would have consulted with Thomas Arnold about her treatment. Arnold probably would have recommended a stay in his Leicester asylum that may or may not have helped Dorothy. Arnold was in favor of restraining violent patients, so Dorothy may have had an experience similar to that of Robert Hall, Jr., in the asylum.[61]

Commitment

At the end of the eighteenth century a psychiatric revolution occurred. The mentally ill were no longer seen as animals needing confinement in "madhouses," prisons, or workhouses, but as distressed human beings needing care in asylums.[62] Just such an asylum for Europeans existed in Calcutta. The asylum was operated as a private institution for those who were certified to be insane by the authorities.[63] The missionaries were later to take John Thomas there for treatment. Did Carey ever consider the Calcutta asylum for Dorothy?

Commitment to the asylum was probably a genuine option for Carey. Yet commitment, like confinement that was already in use with

Dorothy, would have exacerbated her condition. They did need to provide protection for her and others around her when she was violent, but any such restraint only fueled the delusion. In her twisted reasoning she would view the restraint as proof that Carey and all his friends had something to hide. Their zeal to lock her up was only proof to her that her accusations were correct. Besides, her confinement just freed Carey up to commit more adultery against her. The necessary strategy, confining her at times of violent outbursts, probably had the sad effect of adding confirmation to her delusion.

Pay More Attention

We do not know if anyone suggested to Carey that he might see some improvement in his wife's condition if he could give her some time and attention. The pathos of her delusion spoke volumes: She felt unwanted, abandoned, and alone. Perhaps the idea had occurred to Carey without anyone else suggesting it to him. We do not know if he tried such attention. The letters and documents suggest that others tried to reason with her, but her rage was so intense against her husband that communication may have been nearly impossible.

Attention may have been very therapeutic much earlier in their relationship. By the time she developed her full-blown delusion of jealousy, her condition may have been nearly irreversible.

Community Care

The one long-term strategy that Carey did implement was to arrange for a community of Christian care around Dorothy. Carey seemed to feel that community had ruined Dorothy. He not only decried the influence of Calcutta upon her, but he constantly berated the "carnal company" on the sea voyage. Calcutta was "highly injurious to the life of a missionary."[64] Their sea voyage was agreeable "tho the company on board a ship is the most injurious to the soul that can be occasioned, all in carnal gentility."[65] Carey was no doubt surprised to hear that his wife could swear and curse "like a sailor" when enraged, and he must have seen those foul-mouthed seamen as partly responsible for his wife's deterioration. So if community had contributed to her disorder, perhaps a Christian community might contribute to her healing.

Carey proposed that he and his English Baptist colleagues establish a Moravian-like mission community.[66] We have no evidence that Carey consciously developed this idea as a way of caring for Dorothy. If anything, he may have had some subconscious awareness that a community might be good for Dorothy, but she was not his primary reason for proposing such a novel idea.

Missionaries would keep a common table, would pool all of their resources and funds, and would operate in concert as a group. The society in England approved the plan. Carey proposed his idea in 1796, but the community did not begin to operate until additional missionaries came and they all settled at Serampore. There the women of the mission community must have shared in Dorothy's care. This long-term strategy was Carey's most successful one in terms of caring for Dorothy.

Prayer

Carey prayed earnestly for the recovery of his wife. His friends and colleagues in India prayed. His family and supporters in England prayed. God did grant Dorothy good physical health for the twelve years of her insanity, but he did not remove her delusion. She died unimproved. Carey's sister Polly once reminisced:

> It has greatly encouraged me of late, in reading over some of the first letters he sent, to see how he was enabled to act faith on a faithful God; and in how many instances God has answered his prayers for his own children, and the children of his brother and sister, as well as other relatives.[67]

We do not know why his prayers for the mental health of Dorothy went unanswered.

8

Dorothy's Dark Years

From 1795 until 1807 Dorothy was concerned with one thing: trying to convince others of her husband's unfaithfulness to her. People would listen; they would try to understand. But eventually they realized that her passion was a delusion, rooted deeply in hurts, disappointments, and betrayal of trust, but not anchored to reality. Carey's protestations meant nothing to her. His denials would only intensify her rage and confirm her conviction that he was cruelly unfaithful to her.

Confinement to her room fueled her delusion. At first, John Thomas reported that Dorothy was lucid and reasonable about other areas of life except her husband's loyalty to her. We do not know how long she retained these reasonable qualities in other areas. We have some indication that she deteriorated and that other delusions began to form. Thus we cannot easily tell how aware Dorothy was of events around her.

In these twelve years of her psychotic combativeness alternating with periods of relative quiet, activity was aswirl around her. She was consumed with her single-item agenda, but her husband was pursuing a vast number of projects. Changes, new faces, a 300-mile move, a new house, a different room in which t be confined, boys growing up, and a new professorship for her husband were just some of the changes she obviously knew about. Was she aware of the many other developments around her during these twelve years: the progress of the mission, the first convert, the baptisms of her sons, the titles coming off the new printing press, the new missionaries from England?

These twelve years were Dorothy's dark years. We will follow her story through this long tunnel of misery by looking at her condition and the events around her in three different time periods. Readers will have to use their imaginations to decide how much Dorothy knew of the developments taking place around her.

Mudnabatti, 1795–99

The Careys continued to live in their brick house near the indigo works in Mudnabatti. The Udneys and the Thomas family lived in towns not too far distant. News about Dorothy during the first few years of her mental retreat was sparse. Very little information about her condition, other than the letters informing supporters and family in England, survives from the years 1795, 1796, and 1797. This partial news blackout may have been related to fears of censorship.[1] England was still at war with France. British authorities in India were nervous about possible French spies in their territory. In this climate of war paranoia, the missionaries were not sure that officials opened their mail, but they strongly suspected that censorship was occurring. Perhaps they felt that too many descriptions of Dorothy's allegations in letters to England would arouse a bothersome curiosity on the part of the authorities.

The following four passages describe Dorothy during the Mudnabatti years of her insanity:

16 Nov 1796. Poor Mrs. Carey cannot, I think, be a greater burden than she is. She has even attempted my life. Mr. T. has been a too unhappy witness of her conduct, and I doubt she is absolutely inexclaimable.[2]

23 Mar 1797. My family trials which you intimate you have heard continue and increase. Some attempts on my life have been made but I hope nothing of that kind is to be found now. God has graciously preserved me, and given me that support that I have not been remarkably retarded in my public work thereby. I am sorely distressed to see my dear children before whom the greatest indecencies and most shocking expressions of rage are constantly uttered and who are constantly taught to hate their father; tis true they don't regard what is said, yet it invariably imbues their minds with a kind of brutish ferocity, and lownishness which is to me very distressing . . . but Mr. F., Mr. T. or any one else can give a much more impartial account of these things than I can.[3]

16 Jan 1798. We are all well. Mrs. C. as usual.[4]

18 Jan 1798. Poor Mrs. C. is as wretched as insanity can make her almost and often makes all the family so too. But we are supported by a gracious God.[5]

Dorothy's violence was obviously the most pressing problem. She made at least two attempts on her husband's life. These frightening incidents led to her confinement. William must have wondered whether his sons were safe with Dorothy. We have no evidence, however, that she ever struck out at anyone but him. The violence appears to have occurred early in her illness. During most of 1795 she was pregnant. Jonathan was born early in 1796 and presumably she fed and cared for her newborn. These episodes of violence and uncontrolled rage form an odd mix of behaviors when compared to her mothering and childcare tasks.

Dorothy was thirty-eight years of age when her psychosis began. Her three older sons were ten, seven, and six. William worried greatly about them. They were pawns caught in the middle of Dorothy's wild accusations and William's futile denials. Dorothy was frustrated by the refusal of other adults to believe her allegations. The children became potential allies in her cause. Surely they would believe her. She began to recruit them to join her side of this ongoing dispute.

Children caught in such a bind face a dizzying array of developmental tasks. Such children often learn to survive by being flexible—listening to each parent while trying not to get caught in the cross-fire. The older ones may have tried the impossible, to serve as negotiators or reconcilers. Such efforts would have failed, and the children would have resorted to more passive strategies. Listen to mom, agree with her as much as we can, mind her, and love her. Listen to dad, agree with him as much as we can, mind him, and love him. Children are adaptable. Felix, William, and Jabez must have learned the art of flexibility. Baby Jonathan would become aware of all these tensions soon enough, but in 1796 he was innocently unaware of all the misery around him.[6]

Life for the Carey family in Mudnabatti was not easy. The heat was unbearable at times. Carey tried to grow watercress in the infamous crocodile pond, but the water got so hot that the plants died. Summer was the worst.

> When we bathe in those months it is often necessary to dive to the bottom because the water is so hot in the surface as not to be borne, till it has been stirred up and mixed together.[7]

Floods periodically ravaged the area. When the waters were high, Carey would make his ten- to twelve-mile-long inspection trips by boat over trails submerged under water.

Jonathan grew quickly. By January 1798 he was running about jabbering fluently. William was proud that Jabez, William, and Felix were speaking Bengali, Hindustani, and English with great facility.[8] William, a "fine tempered" lad, seemed to have some difficulty learning, however.[9]

The family soon acquired a considerable number of servants. The family workforce was large because of the difficulty of tropical living and food preparation. Arranging for the complement of servants was also cumbersome because of strict prohibitions among the nationals against mixing kinds of work. "One man will not do all these things, nor any two of them." Carey complained of the expense of maintaining the following: two female millers to turn the hand mill, a baker, a man to fetch toddy (the sap of a date tree used in place of yeast), a cook, a butler, a cleaner, two bearers, a man to shop for provisions, one man each to care for the horses, cows, hogs, and poultry, a washerman, a tutor for his boys, a teacher of the nationals, a nurse for the children, and several gardeners.[10] And Carey added that he kept fewer servants than most Europeans in the area.

School for the children continued to be a problem. Carey wrote, "Mine are very badly off for want of a school. My many avocations prevent me from paying all the attention to them that they require. Yet they are not very bad boys."[11] Carey may have indulged the boys in a misguided effort to compensate for the invective hurled at him in the presence of his sons by his deluded wife. Still we are somewhat puzzled by Carey's neglect of the boys' education. He had grown up in a home where education was primary. He himself was committed to the learning process. He had great dreams for his boys that could only be accomplished with a solid educational background. In 1796 he had outlined for the mission society in England his suggestions for the schooling of missionary children:

> The importance of a proper and practicable plan of education for not only the children of natives but also of missionaries some of whom, it is

to be hoped, might in time be converted by the Grace of God, and become missionaries themselves or be otherwise serviceable in the mission is obvious.[12]

Carey clearly knew the importance of education for his children, but he seemed unable to arrange for schooling for his own sons that would satisfy his own standards. During these years he was supervising hundreds of men in the indigo plant, keeping a watchful eye on the custodial needs of his wife, and trying to pursue his ministry. The schooling of his children apparently did not get a high priority.

We know that Carey attempted to maintain a crushing schedule during these years. Translating and correcting his prior work took up all his evenings and many afternoons; he was also trying to learn Sanskrit as well as continue his work in Bengali.[13] He aimed at translating twenty verses of the Bible per day. As early as October 1796 he had finished with Genesis, Exodus, Leviticus, Matthew, Mark, Luke, John, Romans, 1 and 2 Corinthians, Galatians, and James.[14] No wonder he did not have time to attend to the needs of his boys.

His work of supervising the manufacture of indigo required that he travel a circuit to inspect various farms where workers were growing the plants. His territory encompassed twenty square miles and contained 200 villages or small settlements.[15] Apparently Dorothy's condition allowed him to leave her at times in the care of servants. Travel was not easy. He had to take corn to feed the horses and a groom to care for them. If their travel was by boat, six watermen would have to accompany them. They had to carry their beds, clothes, and every convenience.[16]

Other major events included the arrival in 1796 of John Fountain at Mudnabatti. A single man, he was the third missionary sent to India by the Baptist Missionary Society, after Carey and Thomas. For a brief time Carey hoped that his good friend, Samuel Pearce of Bristol, would join him as a missionary. Pearce had volunteered to the society after his wife prayerfully gave her consent. The leadership, however, decided he was more important to them in his influential Bristol pulpit so they did not appoint him. Carey reluctantly agreed that the decision was sound.[17]

John Thomas was around in 1796 to lance an abscess in Carey's throat, but in 1797 he resigned from the superintendency of the Moypaldiggy indigo factory. When he attempted to get his job back in January 1798, he discovered that Mr. Udney had hired Thomas's cousin,

Samuel Powell, as the new superintendent.[18] For two years Thomas faded into the background.

Carey's longed-for dream came true when they organized a small church at the end of 1795:

> I can with pleasure inform you . . . that a Baptist church is formed in this distant quarter of the globe. Our members however are but four in number, viz. Mr. Thomas, myself, a Mr. Long, and a Mr. Powell, the last of whom accompanied Mrs. Thomas from England. Mr. Long had been baptized by Mr. Thomas when he was in India before; and on the first of November this year I baptized Mr. Powell. At this place we were solemnly united that day as a Church of Christ; and the Lord's Supper has been twice administered among us. Mr. Powell is a very hopeful young man; burns with zeal for the conversion of the heathen; and I hope will prove a valuable acquisition to the Mission.[19]

The church in Leicester responded on March 18, 1798, by sending Carey's church membership letter to the new church in Bengal along with assurance of prayer that the small church in Mudnabatti would "fill all Asia" with the fruit of the gospel.[20]

A second dream of Carey became reality when he saw a newspaper advertisement for a printing press. An Englishman nearby gave him the 400 rupees to buy it.[21] Carey pointed all his translation labor toward the ultimate goal of putting Scripture into the vernaculars of Asia. Now he could start on that enormous goal. Fountain and Carey showed so much fascination with their new press that nationals in the area wondered if these white men had just acquired a new idol!

The manufacture of indigo was not a stable industry. Mr. Udney was first attracted to this cash crop because of a decline in supply of the dye from western India, North America, and the West Indies. Bengal indigo was of a higher grade than that found in most parts of the world. The textile industry in England needed large quantities of this blue dye for the manufacture of military uniforms. England was on a wartime economy because of the war with France, but the world market was nonetheless fickle. Thomas had at one time encouraged Carey to get out of the indigo business and into sugar and rum.[22] Carey showed some interest but decided to stay with indigo.

In 1796 prices began to falter. Between 1797–98 and 1798–99 production in Bengal fell 56 percent.[23] Mr. Udney again gave signals that he could not keep the plant open much longer. A flood in the fall of

1799 sealed the fate of the factory. Carey asked his friends in England to understand why he was not writing them more often in light of "such a time of wandering up and down and perplexity as we have had."[24] Carey was discouraged. "My second son (William) is now dangerously ill with a fever, it appears uncertain whether he will recover."[25] By November 9, 1799, Udney had made the decision to abandon the factory. "This, with my large family will reduce me to serious difficulties."[26] Udney gave Carey his salary until the end of the year.

Carey then made a quick move to purchase a small indigo plant at Kidderpore seventeen miles away. He hoped to found his missionary colony there. Meanwhile several new missionaries from England had arrived in India on an American vessel. The captain of that ship, a man friendly to the cause of missions, advised the new missionaries from England to proceed immediately to Serampore rather than to enter Calcutta. When the immigration officials boarded the ship as it entered the bay, the missionaries reported that they were on their way to Serampore. The official allowed them to transfer to another boat for their journey up the river to the Danish colony.

Meanwhile the American ship captain received orders, when he docked his ship in Calcutta, that he could not unload his cargo until he handed over to the authorities the missionaries who had just gone to Serampore. The East India Company was becoming more resolute in its attempt to prevent missionary work in India. This little band of British Baptist missionaries had stepped into some international intrigue. The Danish governor of Serampore accepted the missionary party and offered them his protection. Although Serampore had no more military protection than a small gun used to fire off salutes, international law prevented the British from interfering in matters on foreign soil. The crisis passed.

The governor of Serampore, Colonel Ole Bie, offered the missionaries a deal they could not resist if they would settle at Serampore. He would give them the use of a church he was currently building, allow them to install a printing press for the publication of Scripture, and issue them Danish passports so they could travel in and out of surrounding British territory without hassle.[27] Ward, accompanied by Fountain, went immediately on his new Danish passport to meet Carey who was living deep in British territory at Mudnabatti. They urged Carey to abandon the newly purchased site at Kidderpore and to join them at the Danish colony of Serampore. Ultimately Carey agreed to move to Serampore even though he would lose money. Dorothy would have to move one more time. It would be her last move in India.

Serampore, 1800–1801

The Carey family arrived at Serampore on January 10, 1800. The journey from Mudnabatti was a long one, over 300 miles, but because they had sailed downstream the trip was quicker than when they had originally moved to Mudnabatti in 1794. We know little about how the family fared on the trip.[28] Dorothy must have been stable and able to travel. Carey must have explained to her that Serampore would be a better place for the family and especially the boys. Carey was correct. Serampore was a safer and more stable place to live. Dorothy may not have had the capacity to believe him, yet somehow she made the trip and arrived safely at the Danish colony.

Serampore was thirty miles upstream from Calcutta on the Hooghly River. The Danes ruled two small trading colonies on the Indian subcontinent: Tanquebar in the south and Serampore in Bengal. The king of Denmark, Frederick IV, established a missionary presence in the southern colony in 1705. A later missionary there greatly influenced a young Danish officer in Tanquebar, Colonel Ole Bie, the very official who offered the bedraggled group of missionaries their first secure and safe foothold in India.[29] The colonies, including Serampore, were sold in 1845 to the British.

The British operated a large military facility at Barrackpore immediately across the river from Serampore. On April 12, 1801, British troops crossed the river and occupied Serampore for the next fourteen months. The governor was technically a prisoner of war since Britain was at war with Denmark. But even in these times of official occupation by the British, the missionaries enjoyed relative safety because of their ongoing, good reputation with British officials.[30]

Though Dorothy may have handled the move to Serampore quite well, she soon suffered a relapse. The following comments about her help us trace her condition during these first two years at Serampore.

22 June 1800. Mrs. Carey is stark mad.[31]

29 December 1800. My love to Mrs. Carey's relations. I will try to get time to write them. Mrs. Carey is worse than ever with respect to her mental derangement.[32]

8 April 1801. Love to Mrs. Carey's friends. She is much worse.[33]

15 June 1801. Poor Mrs. Carey is a miserable creature. I dare not let her have liberty in the night for fear of murder. She has been cursing tonight in the most awful manner, till weary with exertion she is gone to sleep.[34]

23 November 1801. Mrs. Carey is obliged to be constantly confined. She has long got worse and worse, but fear both of my own life and hers, and the desire of the police of the place obliged me to agree to her confinement.[35]

23 November 1801. Indeed I have the greatest reason to bless the Lord for the great work he has wrought in my children. It is a consolation which supports me greatly in the midst of very heavy family trials of another kind. I mean my poor wife, who has been obliged to be constantly confined in her room for more than half a year past, being totally insane.[36]

These brief references to Dorothy's misery represent intense pathos. Her suffering and the suffering of those around her seem to have considerably worsened in Serampore. By the time of their move to Serampore, Dorothy had been delusional for six long years. The end was hardly in sight. Moves are always difficult, but Dorothy's decompensation may be due more to her declining influence with her sons than to the move itself. In Mudnabatti the family was isolated and in contact with only a few other Europeans. In Serampore a growing community of missionaries and their families gave the boys many more role models.[37] Perhaps she felt that her one remaining area of influence was declining and disappearing.

Her ravings, especially when Carey was with her, were nearly constant. She exhausted herself spewing out accusatory rage until weariness and sleep silenced, temporarily, her verbal assaults.[38]

John Clark Marshman later wrote:

It will serve to give some idea of the strength and energy of Dr. Carey's character that the arduous biblical and literary labours in which he had been engaged since his arrival at Serampore, were prosecuted while an insane wife, frequently wrought up to a state of the most distressing excitement, was in the next room but one to his study.[39]

Carey also made reference to the Serampore police. We do not know the background of this comment. Perhaps officials had encountered Dorothy during the course of a routine census of the colony and volunteered the confinement advice to her husband. A more likely explanation is that Dorothy wandered out into the community and created some type of incident that triggered the police evaluation of her condition.[40]

Among the new missionaries at Serampore were William Ward, a printer Carey had met in England several years before, and Joshua and Hannah Marshman. Carey, Marshman, and Ward became the famous Serampore Trio.[41] The group worked together with uncommon unity for many years.

Part of the success of the Serampore missionary community stemmed from the Moravian-like community that they immediately established. Carey had proposed that all the missionary families share a common meal table, pool all funds, and convene a weekly meeting on Saturday evenings to iron out the inevitable tensions and disputes that would arise from this ambitious plan. Although the community formed earlier, the missionaries put the actual principles and practices of the community on paper in 1805; they renewed the pact on an annual basis.[42] When Carey had first proposed the community to the society in England, Andrew Fuller sent back his blessing:

> We have nothing to object. The experience of the Moravians seems to sanction it. But I suppose you could not carry it into execution without some active, amiable women amongst them. Do whatever your own judgment dictates, all circumstances considered.[43]

Hannah Marshman was just the kind of woman Fuller wrote about.[44] Hannah earned the title of the first woman missionary to India.[45] She was a gifted woman who adapted well to India even though she struggled with health problems.[46] She and her husband were active in the establishment of schools at Serampore for national and European children. In this capacity they both became active in the nurture and education of the Carey boys. We can assume that Hannah also took an active role in arranging for the ongoing care of Dorothy.

William Ward took an immediate liking to Felix, the oldest Carey boy. Ward took Felix on as an assistant at the printing press and began to meet with him and his brother for prayer and Bible study. Ward was an effective mentor who made a deep and lasting impact on Felix. Yet

Ward's interest in Felix was a threat to Dorothy, who soon became delusional about the relationship. Ward wrote about Dorothy in his journal: "We keep her from table. She has got an unfounded idea that I beat the boys; and she calls me all the vile names she can think of."[47]

The community may have initially tried to include Dorothy in their communal meals, but experience soon made this impossible. As Dorothy began to sense that Felix was developing a closer and closer relationship with William Ward, she reacted in her psychotic way, spinning a delusion to cover her personal sense of threat and jealousy. Ward's comment about her delusion about the boys and her verbal attacks on him is our only evidence that Dorothy's delusions spread beyond her original jealous paranoia regarding William. Dorothy probably expressed any number of such delusions, although records of her spreading delusions do not survive. Dorothy clearly regressed during these initial years in Serampore. They were dark years for her, but bright years for the mission.

The missionaries soon organized a church with William Carey as the pastor.[48] They continued to pray for their first convert. One promising inquirer named Fukeer, a Mohammedan, expressed faith but disappeared before his baptism. One day a Hindu named Krishna Pal came into the Serampore compound with a dislocated shoulder. The missionaries immediately summoned John Thomas to help with this medical emergency. Carey and others assisted by bracing and holding the injured man against a tree while Thomas reset the shoulder—without any anesthesia, of course. The grateful Krishna then listened to a gospel presentation. Eventually he became the long-prayed-for first convert to Christianity. Several years had elapsed since the arrival of Thomas and the Careys in November 1793. But they rejoiced that God had finally answered their fervent prayers. Carey wrote, "Yesterday was a day of great joy. I had the happiness to desecrate the Ganges by baptizing the first Hindu, viz. Krishnu and my son Felix."[49]

The baptism scene was a victorious celebration for the missionaries. It was accented, however, by a cacophony of insane ravings from Dorothy and John Thomas who had just recently lost his sanity. George Smith described the incongruities well:

When Carey led Krishna and his own son Felix down into the water of baptism the ravings of Thomas in the schoolhouse on the one side, and of Mrs. Carey on the other, mingled with the strains of the Bengali hymn of praise.[50]

The momentous symbolism of this baptismal service in the most sacred of all Indian river systems coupled with the madness of Dorothy and Thomas reminded everyone present on the river's bank of the tremendous cost paid by this band of missionary families for their first convert. The victory was salutary, but the price they paid was high. Seven years of hard labor had passed before they saw even the smallest hint of future harvest.

John Thomas had started to decompensate during the week before the baptism of Krishnu. Thomas had come to India fifteen years before. He too had waited a long time to see evangelistic fruit for his labor. Contemporaries always attributed to Thomas a keen interest in the evangelism of India whatever else they may have said about him. His colleagues felt that the impending excitement of actually seeing a Hindu baptized nudged Thomas over the brink. On Tuesday of that week his missionary colleagues placed Thomas into a straitjacket.[51] He failed to improve, and they made a decision to arrange for hospitalization in the Calcutta Asylum for Lunatics. On Monday some of them went to Calcutta but were unable to make all the arrangements.

Mr. Udney helped them contact Claudius Buchanan, one of two East India Company chaplains in the city. He wrote the following letter to the governor general, the Marquis Wellesley:

> I beg leave to represent to your lordship in behalf of Mrs. Thomas that her husband John Thomas formerly Surgeon of the Oxford Indiaman and lately a manufacturer of sugar . . . is at present in a state of lunacy, and that she earnestly requests that he may be admitted into the Hospital for Lunatics at Fort William. She is in destitute circumstances and altogether unable to make the usual allowance for his support in the hospital; and therefore humbly craves that this allowance may be afforded by the Government.[52]

On the basis of his past government service as a surgeon, Thomas was admitted at the expense of the government. On January 1, 1801, Carey and Marshman took him to Calcutta to admit him under the care of Dr. William Dick. We do not know if Carey took a tour of the asylum, but he did have the opportunity to see the facility. Did he consider placing Dorothy there? If he did consider such a move, he apparently decided against the idea because he never took Dorothy there.

Thomas was a patient in the asylum from January 1 to 24. The missionaries agreed that Thomas should go to Dingapore upon his release.

Perhaps the pressure would be less intense. Two days after his release Thomas received a letter from the society in England giving him a mild rebuke. Thomas did not receive these restrictions well in his weakened emotional state and soon relapsed:

> Poor Mr. Thomas has been deranged. . . . He is better and the doctor has sent him out again. But I think he is far from well. Poor man he has increased his debts by borrowing more money of a native man. I can make no apology for him except that he be considered as constantly insane in a degree tho not always maniacal. I am of this opinion.[53]

John Thomas died at Dingapore on October 13, 1801, after suffering from a high fever. His career, though checkered, included many commendable accomplishments. He was the person most responsible for Dorothy's going to India. He and his wife were best friends of the Carey family when they were in the indigo business near Malda. He tried valiantly to talk Dorothy out of her delusion and was the only person with whom she could be calm. But the stress of life left him in emotional shambles at the end of his life, and he died a broken man. We do not know if Dorothy grieved for him or if the Serampore community even informed her of his death.

Carey followed his usual pattern in Serampore of working long hours on his translation projects. His work tasks "and attending to my share of domestic concerns occupy my time so much that I am sometimes forced a little to transgress the just bounds of propriety and infringe upon the hours of sleep."[54]

Carey mentioned an interesting newcomer to his good friend John Sutcliffe:

> I was last evening employed in teaching the English language to a German lady who I hope professes the grace of God. She is a person of large fortune. I believe her father was a Count but she informs me that he would never accept any but his hereditary title. She is from Schleswik and has been instructed in the school of affliction. Came last year into this country for her health not having been able to speak or stand for some years. Her speech is restored, and she can walk a little. Her name is Rumohr. I trust she has met with some good to her soul in this place.[55]

In a letter to Ryland, Carey said the governor of Serampore had asked him to teach her English. "I . . . have reason to believe that my visits have been blessed."[56] Charlotte Rumohr was later to become the second Mrs. William Carey.

In 1800 the governor general in Calcutta established Fort William College for the training of company management. Young recruits came from England in need of language training for their new responsibilities in India. The East India Company evangelical chaplain, Rev. David Brown, became provost of the new school and Rev. Claudius Buchanan assumed the post of vice-provost and professor of Latin, Greek, and English.[57] The school became an "Oxford of the East" for these civil servants.[58] The missionaries in Serampore had concentrated on learning the vernacular languages. British officials had focused more on the official languages of Sanskrit and Persian. Buchanan thus suggested William Carey for a teaching post at the new college based on Carey's impressive knowledge of Bengali.[59] On April 8, 1801, British officials summoned Carey to cross the river to Barrackpore where they made him a job offer he could not refuse.

After consulting with his Serampore colleagues, Carey accepted the job. He commuted to Calcutta each week to assume his teaching responsibilities. No one would have offered Carey such a position in England, since the law specified that all persons in government posts be members of the established Anglican Church.

> As a non-conformist missionary, despite his being acknowledged to be the most suitable person for the purpose . . . he was discriminated against in the matter of salary and status. Whereas the other European teachers received a monthly salary of R. 1000 each and were designated professors, Carey was given a salary of Rs. 500 a month only and called teacher of Bengali although he worked as much or even more than they.[60]

Carey did not quibble over details of prestige. The salary was quite generous from his standpoint, and the income became an important source of revenue for the Serampore mission community.[61] In his new post he taught many of India's future colonial administrators and was able to advance his fight against some of the social horrors of the society around him.

Carey outlined his weekly schedule in a letter to his father.[62] On Tuesday he left Serampore at 3 P.M. and arrived in Calcutta at 6 P.M. (He kept a horse and buggy on each side of the river and crossed the Hooghly by boat to get to Calcutta.) From 6 P.M. to 8 P.M. he worked on grammar before going on to an 8 P.M. prayer meeting. He lectured on Wednesday from 9 A.M. to 3 P.M. on Bengali and Sanskrit. Before 9 A.M. he devoted time to his private reading and at 3 P.M. he had dinner. He worked on various projects until the 8 P.M. church service after which he wrote letters. On Thursday he went out to breakfast with various religious friends before working with his language pundits from 10 A.M. to 3 P.M. After Thursday dinner he preached each week at a Portuguese man's home. Thursday evening he attended a philosophical and chemical lecture in the city of Calcutta. On Friday he lectured until 3 P.M. The buggy was waiting for him at the door after dinner and he could make the fourteen-mile trip home in time for evening tea. After evening tea in Serampore he held family worship and conducted a planning meeting with the Hindu believers. Saturday was no less busy. He spent a half-hour in the garden and held family prayers before breakfast. The bulk of Saturday was spent translating and proofing material ready for the presses. Saturday evening was the family meeting of the entire mission community. On Sunday he preached four times: on the streets of Serampore in Bengali, in the mission house in English, and two more services in the evening. He spent each Monday as he did Saturday except he lectured to the school children on the compound in geography, astronomy, and natural history. After a Tuesday morning prayer meeting his week started up again with his weekly trip to Calcutta.

Carey was absorbed in his work. He must have visited with Dorothy on the weekends, but the visits must not have been long ones. He tried to make use of the three-hour commute that he made every week. "He never lost a minute when he could help it; and he thus read through every volume of the 'Universal History' during his periodical journeys to Calcutta on his college duties."[63]

Serampore, 1802–7

Dorothy's final five years were likewise eventful for others, tedious for her. During 1802 Dorothy did not get better but in fact seemed to slowly worsen.

17 Mar 1802. Poor Mrs. Carey is quite insane, and often raving, and is obliged to be constantly confined.[64]

28 Mar 1802. Mrs. Carey is now almost constantly confined to her room.[65]

29 June 1802. Poor Mrs. C. is quite insane. I greatly need your prayers.[66]

1 Dec 1802. Poor Mrs. Carey has been long deranged in her mind. She is obliged to be confined or closely watched continually. There is I fear no reason to hope that she will ever recover.[67]

2 Dec 1802. Poor Mrs. Carey, no better but worse.[68]

Carey expressed despair that Dorothy's condition would ever improve. He faced another discouragement when Charles Short died. Charles' wife, Dorothy's sister Kitty, was in England at the time and Carey had the responsibility of writing to tell her the sad news. Carey was executor of the Short estate.[69] Kitty never returned to India. We do not know if Dorothy even knew that her sister had returned to England or if Dorothy could understand that her sister would not be coming back.

The year 1802 included the first convert from the writer caste and the first Brahmin convert.[70] God was blessing the work. The first marriage of a Hindu convert occurred in the mission house on March 29, 1802. Carey preached on the nature of marriage and exhorted the young groom and bride to enter their marriage with Christian joy.[71] We wonder if Carey thought of his own marriage as he conducted the ceremony.

News of Dorothy slowed to a trickle in 1803 and 1804.

24 Aug 1803. Poor Mrs. C. is much as she has been for some years, if anything she is worse.[72]

14 Dec 1803. Mrs. Carey is as she has been for some years past.[73]

27 Feb 1804. Poor Mrs. Carey is as bad as ever. I wish to feel aright under this dispensation but fear that at present I have profited little.[74]

9 Mar 1804. Poor Mrs. Carey is if anything worse. . . . Oh that I may be sanctified by the strokes I have had, and learn to commit all my ways to the Lord.[75]

23 Aug 1804. Poor Mrs. C. is rather worse than better, a very distressing object indeed. This affliction is heavy. O may I bear it like a Christian and may it be of benefit to me.[76]

These passages read like a litany of sorrow, both for William and for Dorothy.

A highlight of 1804 for William was a glittering event in the government House Throne Room in Calcutta. The governor general, Lord Wellesley, arranged for the annual Fort William College speech day. Wellesley's brother, the Duke of Wellington, as well as the Supreme Council of India, an envoy from Baghdad, and the upper levels of society were all present.[77] Some of Carey's students debated the following thesis before the assembled crowd: "The translation of the best works extant in the Sanscrit into the popular languages of India would promote the extension of science and civilization."[78] After his students had debated, William Carey stood to address the governor general and his guests in Sanskrit. He unapologetically described himself as a missionary, at a time when official policy still forbade missionaries in company territory. He paid glowing tribute to the governor for establishing the college and promoting its linguistic work. But Dorothy was not there to share this day of glory with her husband.

In 1805 Carey wrote about Dorothy's morbid preoccupations with the safety and health of her children.

7 Jul 1805. Poor Mrs. Carey is a very distressing object. Her whole life is a life of fear and rage arising from ideal troubles, indeed her insanity is of that distressing nature that she never has any of those pleasing illusions which many in that unhappy state have, but seems to be wholly under the influence of malevolent impressions. A solicitude for her children, an idea that they are ill or injured & etc. constantly occupies her mind, and fills her with almost boundless rage against the supposed enemies of her offspring.[79]

11 Jul 1805. My wife is still a very distressing object. Her insanity increases, and is of that unhappy cast which fills her with continual rage, or anxiety.[80]

31 Dec 1805. Poor Mrs. Carey is much worse. She is a most distressing object.[81]

Carey stayed busy but began to complain of failing eyesight. The year 1806 was a quiet year with very little news of Dorothy in the letters home. "Poor Mrs. Carey grows worse. She is a very distressing object."[82] "My wife is in the state she has been in for years."[83] Claudius Buchanan drew up a proposal to solicit funds for the Serampore group for translating the Scriptures into fifteen languages. He distributed the pamphlet to nearly all company officers.[84] Thirteen-year-old Jabez was busy studying Chinese under the tutelage of an Armenian from Macao.[85] Language and linguistic concerns occupied the attention of everyone. Dorothy's only verbal contributions were rageful ravings and curses.

In 1807 a hint of Dorothy's depression characterized Carey's comments about her.

> 7 Feb 1807. My poor wife remains as she has been for several years, a melancholy victim of mental derangement.[86]

> 25 Feb 1807. My poor wife remains a melancholy spectacle of mental imbecility.[87]

> 3 Mar 1807. My poor wife has been deranged in her mind for many years which is a heavy trial.[88]

> 1 Oct 1807. Poor Mrs. C. is no better.[89]

Two major honors came Carey's way during 1807. Brown University in Providence, Rhode Island, awarded an honorary Doctor of Divinity degree to Carey. Rev. Samuel Stillman of Boston recommended Carey for the degree to President Asa Messer. "His literary and religious character is excellent." The degree was awarded at Brown's commencement, September 3, 1807.[90] The very next month Carey was given a private audience with Lord Minto. As the world was giving more and more recognition to Carey, the prolific linguist and translator, Dorothy was slipping toward the end of her life, probably unaware of these honors.

Dorothy died on the evening of December 8, 1807. William Ward's diary provides us with the most detailed account of her last days:

> 27 November 1807. Mrs. Carey is ill of a fever.

> 2 December 1807. Mrs. Carey was better but has been taken worse again.

> 8 December 1807. This evening Mrs. Carey died of the fever under which she has languished some time. Her death was a very easy one; but there was no appearance of the return of reason, nor anything that could cast a dawn of hope or life on her state.

9 December 1807. Mrs. Carey was buried this evening. Bro. Carey is just gone into his new house. Poor Mrs. Carey did not live to go in.[91]

Carey broke the news to Felix, who was to have the hardest time adjusting to Dorothy's death. Carey wrote that Dorothy slept for most of the two final weeks of her life and "was not awake more than twenty-four hours" during that time.[92] She was easing into her eternal rest, desperately weary from her twelve-year-long struggle with haunting delusions.

Supporters in England learned of Dorothy's death from the briefest of notices in the *Periodical Accounts:* "Mrs. Carey, after having been ill about a fortnight, died."[93] What a vast scope of events was summarized in that brief sentence! William and the children erected a fitting memorial on her grave. It reads: "This small token of conjugal affection and filial regard erected by her affectionate husband and bereaved children."

Her great-grandson Samuel Pearce Carey envisioned Dorothy as her Savior welcomed her:[94]

> The wildered brain,
> The pain—
> The phantom shapes that haunted,
> The half-born thoughts that daunted—
> All, all is plain.
>
> A fever fit that vanished with the night—
> Has God's great light
> Pierced through the veiled delusions,
> The errors and confusions;
> And pointed to the tablet, where
> His name was graven all the time?
> All the time!
>
> 'Tis God that takes to pieces
> The inveterate complication,
> And makes a restoration
> Most subtle in its sweetness,
> Most strong in its completeness,
> And so appoints your station
> Before the throne.

9

Carey's Life after Dorothy

William Carey's brilliant career continued for twenty-seven years beyond Dorothy's death. Dorothy knew about the hard, barren early years. She did not live to see most of Carey's greatest accomplishments.

Carey was an enigma. He repeatedly expressed great self-doubt, yet the sheer magnitude of his achievements continues to impress us.[1] He overcame obstacles that would deter most of us. He succeeded in entering India when missionaries were not supposed to be there; he became a professor in a government college as a nonconformist without a college education; he stimulated reform efforts in Indian society that still evoke admiration by Indian nationals.[2]

Carey's life was multifaceted. We can only mention in this brief chapter a few highlights of his career in missions, linguistics, social reform, and science in the years following Dorothy's death.

Family Developments

Dorothy died in December 1807. Carey immediately informed Felix, who just days before had left for Burma. In his letters to England Carey described Dorothy's last illness and her final release from insanity. Dorothy's sister Kitty responded: "I have received your letter respecting the death of my poor sister. I loved her much but can say the Lord gave and the Lord hath taken away."[3] Andrew Fuller responded, "Poor Mrs.Carey! Well, it is the Lord."[4]

When Carey informed his sisters, he paid a fitting tribute to his sons: "The affectionate attendance which my sons paid to her made a very deep impression upon my mind."[5] The Carey boys had successfully maintained their love for Dorothy under the most difficult of circumstances.

Carey's letter to his sisters informing them of Dorothy's death continued with a most interesting announcement:

> I am well aware that there is a degree of indelicacy in mentioning so early my design to marry again after a proper time. But as I shall not be able to write to you very often, and as some things connected therewith may contribute to your comfort I shall inform you that I do intend, after some months, to marry Miss Rumohr. I have proposed the matter to her and she has testified her agreement thereto. She is one of the most pious and conscientious persons with whom I am acquainted; and is two or three months older than myself. . . . She possesses some property which will enable me to do something for my relations, and it is in consequence of a wish she expressed, that I communicate my intention to you so early. She wishes to do something which may assist Bro. Hobson in giving his younger children a better education than they could otherwise enjoy.

Carey's early intention to remarry, within weeks of Dorothy's death, sent shock waves through the Serampore missionary community. Initial objections to his plans for remarriage, however, soon gave way to approval. Clearly, the emotional attachment between Dorothy and William had deteriorated under the relentless accusations of Dorothy and the futile denials of William. Carey was obviously pleased with his fiancee's willingness to help financially with his impoverished relatives in England.[6]

William Carey and Charlotte Rumohr were married on May 8, 1808. Carey had been her language tutor and the pastor who baptized her, and now he was her husband.[7] Charlotte and William built a loving relationship and were able to enjoy many common interests. "I have a very affectionate and pious wife, whose mind is highly cultivated by education and extensive reading."[8] Their thirteen years as a married couple were happy ones.

Charlotte Carey died on May 30, 1821. For the second time Carey followed the funeral cortege of a wife to the missionary burial ground. He wrote that her death was "the greatest domestic loss that a man can sustain."

> She had lived only for me. Her solicitude for my happiness was incessant and so certainly would she at all times interpret my looks, that any attempt to conceal anxiety or distress of mind would have been in vain.[9]

Carey later wrote to his sisters, "I am lonely and frequently very unhappy. My house becomes a wilderness and the gloom of having no one to whom I can communicate my feelings is very great."[10] Carey's second marriage was clearly much more fulfilling for him than his first one. Charlotte was a very different woman from Dorothy. Charlotte was in India by her own choice. At the same time, perhaps Carey changed somewhat in the care and attention he invested in order to make his second marriage such a happy one.

Carey married a third time to Grace Hughes. Grace provided William loving care during his years of declining health. She outlived her husband by one year.

Carey's sons continued to grow up. William Ward took a fatherly interest in Jonathan and Jabez as he had with William and Felix.[11] We have already traced some of the life of Felix. The sons all married, giving Carey at least sixteen grandchildren.[12] The first grandchild to die was in 1810, the last one to die was in 1937.

Evangelism

William Carey's great passion, from very early in his career to the very end, was to see the heathen respond to the gospel of Jesus Christ. His evangelistic motivation pervaded the *Enquiry*, guided all of his major decisions, and served as the reason for his translation work. The lack of India's receptivity to the gospel challenged Carey's evangelistic zeal. Carey's initial enthusiasm slowly gave way to a more realistic view regarding the responsiveness of the Indian subcontinent to Christianity. India did not become a Christian nation, but a small yet strong Christian church took root in Bengal where it continues to this day.

Carey carried on his missionary effort in Bengal without the benefit of a missiological education or a course in cultural anthropology. He seemed to possess a natural sensitivity to matters of culture, and thus was ideally suited to be a pioneer missionary since his attitudes set the tone for later work. The strategies of Carey, Marshman, and Ward adumbrated most all modern missions policy.[13] The fame of Carey's work spread even during his lifetime. Smith claimed that stories of the missionary work of Carey told by Charles Simeon in his rooms at King's College, Cambridge, led Henry Martyn to India.[14] By 1818 the Serampore missionaries had seen 600 baptisms.[15]

Not all developments in Carey's missionary efforts went smoothly. Financially, a great economic crash in Calcutta in 1830 created havoc in their ministry plans.[16] Evangelistically, the small number of those who gave little heed to the message of Christianity brought discouragement to Carey.

> When we look around upon the multitudes who care nothing about God, who are given up to every vice and to every lust, we are filled with distress, and sometimes yield for a season to discouragement; and indeed it is a melancholy reflection when we meet thousands of people on the road, to think there is not among them a single person concerning whom we can reasonably entertain the smallest hope that he is acquainted with the grace of God in truth.[17]

A major setback for the Serampore Trio began to take shape when additional missionaries came from England. These younger missionaries had struggles working with Joshua Marshman. Misunderstandings began to characterize the relationship between the society in England and the missionaries in Serampore. The situation worsened when Andrew Fuller died in 1815. For years Fuller had given steady leadership to the society in England. He realized the need to train a replacement and had tried several times unsuccessfully to recruit Rev. Christopher Anderson of Edinburgh as his replacement.[18]

The exact reasons for the Serampore controversy are complex and beyond the scope of this short review, but the dispute between missionaries and the sending society was long and bitter. Carey had been in India so long that few on the governing board personally knew him. Visits made to England by William Ward (1818–22), Hannah Marshman (1820–21), John Clark Marshman (1822–23), and Joshua Marshman (1826–29) did little to help resolve the controversy.

In 1818 a rival mission of younger missionaries began in nearby Calcutta. In 1827 a formal separation occurred between the missionaries in Serampore and the society in England. The breach was not healed until 1837, a year after the death of Joshua Marshman and three years after Carey's death.[19]

Linguistic Achievements

Carey's accomplishments with his printing press in Serampore were amazing. Carey knew that Sanskrit was a vital language to know because of its relationship to the official life of India, but he also knew the importance of the vernacular languages of India. Carey learned Bengali, a vernacular language for Calcutta and the Bengal, better than had any European to that time.[20] Bengali, in comparison with other Indian languages, had lagged behind in the development of prose expression. The work of Carey and the Serampore printing press served to stimulate such prose.[21] Carey's work also helped standardize Bengali.[22] Part of this Serampore influence on Bengali and other languages of India stemmed merely from the sheer volume of material that came off the presses. In one nine-year period, 99,000 volumes were printed in Serampore, including 31 million pages of the Old and New Testament Scriptures.[23] Or to calculate their printing productivity in a different way, a total of 212,000 items came off the presses in 30 years in 40 different languages.[24]

The main focus of the Serampore Trio was on Bible translation and printing. The actual accomplishments in Bible translation by Carey and his colleagues prompted critics in England to charge them with fraud.

> The Serampore missionaries were actually charged with having fraudulently invented the names of languages which did not really exist in order to claim to have learned them and to have translated them, and printed the Scriptures in them, thereby winning the applause and gather in the money of credulous admirers.[25]

The languages may have been unknown to some in England, but they were living languages nonetheless. The translation work of Carey was primitive by today's standards of Bible translation. By 1908 none of the versions produced by the Serampore Trio were still in use. The quality of the translation work may have been foundational, but the quantity was phenomenal. By the time of his death Carey had issued six complete translations, the New Testament in twenty-three more languages, and separate books of the Bible in ten more languages.[26]

> John Foster, the church historian, put the point vividly. During the first eighteen centuries of Christian history, he said, the Bible was rendered into some thirty languages, and then, in the first third of the 19th century, by the work of Carey and his co-workers in Calcutta and Serampore, that number was doubled.[27]

Carey focused on other linguistic work also. In 1823 he took on a government job of translating official documents and attacking an eighteen-month bureaucratic backlog of such documents. The Serampore

Trio founded the *Friend of India,* a magazine for Europeans and Anglo Indians.[28] Other journalistic efforts included a Hindi educational periodical, a newspaper, and a Persian newspaper.[29] Carey viewed these journalistic efforts as a valuable and effective way of promoting social justice.

The Serampore group, inspired by Carey's unrelenting energy and vision, eventually developed one of the most impressive type foundries in all of Asia. They imported a steam engine to power their own paper mill.

> All in all, the press was a supreme achievement by men without adequate resources or backgrounds, who were however inspired by a profound faith. In the field of printing, it has achieved everlasting fame; its type-foundry was a colossal achievement in the face of adverse circumstances; its papermill was an inspiring attempt which also left its mark on contemporary history.[30]

The entire printing enterprise once came to an immediate halt when a fire raced through the print shop. Carey was in Calcutta at the time, so Marshman went to the city on a Thursday morning to break the news to Carey. When they returned to view the ruins, "Tears filled Carey's eyes."[31] The fire destroyed a host of manuscripts and works in progress. When the ruins cooled, they found three-and-one-half tons of lead melted into lumps on the floor.[32] They soon moved the press to a nearby warehouse and began printing. Some books survive from this era, demonstrating how they used some paper scorched on the edges when the press began to produce books again.

Social Reform

A major component of Carey's fame stems from his distinguished commitment to social reform. Carey's evangelical contemporaries in England, of whom William Wilberforce is a prime example, made an impressive mark on English society with their relentless opposition to the slave trade. Carey took that same zeal into an Indian context and worked on several issues of concern to him. The most well-known target of his reform efforts was *sati,* the Hindu custom of widow burning.

Sati became illegal in other parts of India before officials banned the practice in Bengal.[33] Carey planned his assault on the practice carefully. He first examined sacred Sanskrit texts to determine the status of *sati* in Hinduism. He discovered that the custom was not part of

Hindu law but that the sacred texts merely countenanced the practice. Then he and his colleagues began to collect data regarding *sati* in the area around Calcutta. These statistics revealed that more deaths occurred as the result of *sati* than previously thought. Many of the widows who felt compelled by religious custom to throw themselves on their husbands' funeral pyres were only adolescents.

Meanwhile the famous Bengali Brahmin Rammohun Roy began to crusade against the practice after a female relative of his died in the practice. Roy published a treatise questioning *sati* in 1818, thereby upsetting some influential Brahmins. Roy traveled to England to testify in Parliament against the custom. He died on that trip and was buried in England.

The government had initially resisted banning *sati* out of fear of offending Hindu sensibilities and creating unrest, but in 1829 *sati* was declared a culpable homicide. The ban greatly enhanced the status of women in Indian society.[34] In recognition of Carey's indefatigable campaign against *sati,* Governor General Lord Cavendish Bentinck asked Carey to translate the new law into Bengali.

Carey and the other Serampore missionaries took center stage in England in 1813 when Parliament debated the renewal of the Ea+st India company charter. As early as 1807 Carey showed some political savvy by suggesting that the Christian public flood Parliament with petitions, perhaps as many as one million.[35] Wilberforce, who was appalled at aspects of Hinduism, led the fight in Parliament.[36] The essence of the appeal to Parliament was that England had a spiritual obligation "towards the populations committed by Providence into Britain's charge."[37] Parliament approved by a majority of twenty-four votes the Wilberforce resolution to allow missionaries to enter East India Company territory.[38] "Mr. Pendergast asserted some gross falsehoods of me in the house but the spirit of the country could not be withstood."[39]

Carey also worked against the mistreatment of lepers. In 1812 he witnessed the burning of a leper. Eventually the government joined in more humane treatment of lepers.[40] Carey highly valued education. He and his colleagues established Serampore College, which operated under a special charter from the government of Denmark. In 1845 when Denmark sold the small colony of Serampore to England, the international treaty ensured the ongoing life of Serampore College, Carey's greatest educational legacy.

Botanical Interests

Carey maintained a keen interest in gardens, plants, and flowers during his entire life. He did not merely indulge his botanical interests as a hobby; he pursued his love of plants with the same passion evident in most all areas of his life. He established a botanical garden at Serampore where he planted specimens that friends gathered for him from all of South Asia. He soon began correspondence with prominent botanists in England who were fascinated with all the exotic specimens Carey was discovering.

In 1820 Carey issued a prospectus for the "Formation of an Agricultural and Horticultural Society in India on 15 Apr 1820."[41] His effort was to establish a group that would unify efforts to improve agriculture in India. He proposed the introduction of new drainage procedures, better crop rotation, and fertilizing. He hoped to introduce new crops and the use of some European agricultural implements. "Once again the catholicity of the missionaries' interests supplied an example for future developments."[42]

In 1823 the prestigious Linnean Society of London elected Carey as a fellow.[43] Carey also became a member of the Geological Society in London and a corresponding member of the Horticultural Society of London.[44]

One of Carey's botanical correspondents was William Herbert, who named variation 7 of the Amaryllidaceous, Careyanum.[45] The plant is a native of Mauritius from whence Carey obtained it and forwarded it to England.[46] Carey also edited three volumes of William Roxburgh's *Flora Indica,* which was published in 1832 in Calcutta.[47]

Carey's Last Years

During Carey's forty years in India, he was seriously ill at several points. In 1809 he suffered with a high fever that triggered vivid hallucinations. He remembered details of his delirium after he recovered. We do not know if his brief experience with severe mental impairment gave him any deeper empathy for all that Dorothy had suffered. Carey's brush with death prompted his colleagues to arrange for a portrait by Robert Home.[48]

Carey injured his foot in a buggy accident from which he never fully recovered. He retired from teaching in 1830 at sixty-nine years of age when Fort William College cut back from a teaching school to an examining body. Out of respect for his long teaching career, officials awarded him a pension equivalent to one-half his salary.[49]

Toward the end of his life he suffered from a series of strokes and was confined to his couch for several months. He enjoyed being wheeled around his garden. When he could no longer leave the house, friends brought plants into his room for him to enjoy. Frequent visitors during his last illness included the wife of the governor general and the bishop of Calcutta.

> I have every comfort that kind friends can yield and feel generally a tranquil mind. I trust the great point is settled, and I am ready to depart. But the time when, I leave with God.[50]

> I am not worse.[51]

On June 9, 1834, Carey died. At his death the flag on the Danish Government House flew at half-mast. Crowds of Hindus, Mohammedans, and Europeans lined the road to the cemetery. Joshua Marshman preached the funeral sermon of his longstanding colleague. Only one memorial sermon has survived in print, preached by Rev. Christopher Anderson of Charlotte Chapel in Edinburgh.[52]

In his will Carey renounced all rights or titles to any property in Serampore, a final frustrated effort to quiet the simmering Serampore controversy. He willed his museum to Serampore and directed that his library be sold to pay for an inheritance for Jabez. He had previously given a portion of his estate to his other sons. He asked to be buried by the side of his second wife Charlotte.

Many memorials exist to the remarkable and unparalleled career of William Carey, but two are particularly poignant. The first is a Sanskrit verse still known among Bengali Hindus that remembers five Europeans, one of whom is Carey:

> By remembering daily the names of these five Europeans great sinners will get salvation. In this way Carey is still, after one hundred and fifty years of his death, occupying a revered place in the hearts of Indians, though it may sound incredible that the Indians should thus celebrate a Feringhee in the sacred tongue of their ancestors.[53]

Carey is obviously respected deeply by Indian Christians who recognize the great heritage they have received from him. The respect paid his memory by Hindus also speaks to the dramatic impact this humble shoemaker had on his beloved India.

The second impressive memorial is found in London's Westminster Abbey. The lectern, from which Scripture is read at all services (royal weddings, coronations, daily evensong), is dedicated to William Carey. In this vast abbey, where Britain pays tribute to her national heroes, stands a fitting memorial to the humble Baptist pastor who became a missionary and translator of the Bible. On the walnut lectern is inscribed the great message of his life:

> Attempt great things for God,
> Expect great things from God.

Conclusion

The life of Dorothy Plackett Carey comes to us from the pages of history as a sad chapter in the chronicle of modern missions. Her sacrifice of sanity, however, could lose all potential value to us if we fail to see her story as more than just a tragic biography. Her story is also very true, painfully true. We have an obligation to learn from lives such as Dorothy's and thereby to reap some of the benefits that can emerge from the costly sacrifice she made. She would not wish us merely to pity her. She would want instead that we benefit from the example of her life so as to help others who follow in her train.

This chapter explores in a reflective manner some of the value we can derive from our knowledge of Dorothy's life and sacrifice. Other reflections will no doubt occur to readers. These reflections will hopefully stimulate profitable discussions throughout the mission community so that we all may derive the benefits of Dorothy's sacrifice.

We will reflect upon Dorothy's life with three different strategies. First, we will ask some "What if . . . ?" questions. These hypothetical queries will help us understand better some of the underlying and powerful dynamics in Dorothy's experience. Second, we will explore some lessons of value that we might learn from her story. These tentative suggestions do not exhaust the meaning of Dorothy's insanity, but they may stimulate us all to look at ways in which her life could enrich ours. Third, we will examine the legacy that Dorothy has already left behind for Christ, his church, and us.

What if . . . ?

"What if . . . ?" questions are among the easiest to ask and the hardest to answer. Because these questions are so hypothetical, we can only

175

guess at their answers. But because these questions flood our minds as we interact with Dorothy's story, we can benefit by acknowledging the "What ifs?" and trying our hands at giving some answers to them.

What if Dorothy Had Not Gone?

The most basic "What if . . . ?" question goes back to May 24, 1793. Readers will recall that on that day John Thomas and William Carey made their hurried trip back to Northampton. Their purpose for that trip, in part, was to approach Dorothy again about going to India with them. Dorothy's response for the first hour or so of their quick visit was to hold to her longstanding preference not to go. Only after a rather intense session with John Thomas did she relent and switch to a new position: "I will go if Kitty will go with me."

What if the events of that morning in Hackleton had not occurred? What if Thomas and Carey had been able to sail on the *Oxford?* What if they had been unsuccessful in persuading Dorothy to change her mind? What if Thomas, Carey, and Felix had gone ahead with their bookings on the *Kron Princessa Maria?* We are aiming the thrust of this first "What if . . . ?" at May 24, 1793, because the events of that day gave sudden and new direction to Dorothy's future.

No one could change the personalities of any of the main actors in this drama: John Thomas, William, or Dorothy. No one could change the risks of the trip and the initial few months of their stay in Bengal. No one could have prevented Dorothy's twelve-month siege with illness. But the events of May 24, 1793, could have gone in a much different direction.

If Dorothy had remained in Hackleton with William, Peter, and Jabez, Carey would have been under great pressure from colleagues and the society to return home later for his family. After the initial forays of exploration regarding the possibility of missionary work in Bengal, Carey could return home much more informed about the realities of life and ministry in India than he was on that fateful Saturday morning he and Thomas returned to Hackleton. Carey would also have had the chance of building or acquiring suitable housing for his family. He would have been able to give Dorothy and the boys much more information about what they would face.

We can be fairly certain, given Carey's personality and determination, that he would have returned from such an initial visit to India with the conclusion "Let's go!" He was not the type of person who would say, "I think we should re-evaluate and open our first mission field in the South Seas." He was an optimist who did not shun challenges of monumental magnitude. Even if he would have returned home with enthusiasm for taking his family to India we still do not know if Dorothy would have consented at that point. Andrew Fuller, for one, was prepared for Dorothy to say no again. Whether Carey would be prepared for that answer, we do not know.

If Dorothy had not consented to go with her husband that hurried day, she would have continued to live in Hackleton with her sister and three boys. Her extended family, as well as the mission society itself, would have given her financial and emotional support during the separation. She would not face pregnancy for a while. Her body might have had a chance to recoup some strength. She might have profited from Carey's descriptive letters from India. And she just might have decided later that she would go with him.

If Dorothy had been able to abide by her original decision not to go, and if Thomas and Carey had not manipulated her into agreement, we can be certain of several resulting facts. First, Dorothy's integrity as a person would not have been trampled. With all her being and perhaps to the best of her capacities she had decided not to go. When those around her did not allow her the freedom to make such a decision, her value as a person was discounted. Granted, eighteenth-century wives did not have much opportunity to participate in contributing to basic family decisions such as this one. Yet Samuel Pearce said that he was willing to abandon his interest in the mission field if his wife expressed hesitancy. What if Thomas and Carey had given such respect to Dorothy?

Second, if Dorothy's integrity had not been trampled, could she have remained emotionally stronger? Would a later, more freely given consent to go to India have been easier for her? Could she have escaped the tragedy of losing her sanity if she had a more grounded sense that she was in India by her own choice?

Third, we have previously wondered in this book about the possibility that Dorothy's paranoia was related to a violation of trust she once had in her husband. Perhaps her disillusioning early weeks in India were the exact opposite of what she had been promised and thus she felt a massive betrayal of trust that manifested itself in her unfounded delusion. If Dorothy had not decided to go on May 24, 1793, her trust might not have been so badly shattered and her emotional health might have remained stronger. All of the above discussion, of course, is speculation. Such is the best we can do with "What if . . . ?" questions.

What if Peter Had Not Died? What if Kitty Had Not Left?

Of all the what if questions we can ask, these two are the most frivolous. Of course Peter died and of course Kitty decided to marry. We cannot change history, but by asking these questions we can perhaps sharpen our understanding of why events affected Dorothy and her mental health as they did. These questions force us to make a judgment about the role of loss in Dorothy's mental illness.

The deaths of infants, toddlers, and children formed a far more central role in eighteenth-century domestic life than today. The similarity between the experience of losing a child then and losing a child now is the massive pain and loss that occurs to the parents and siblings. But in earlier centuries families were aware of the very large possibilities of losing a child. Mortality rates for infants and children were much higher than they are today.

If everyone in the eighteenth century was aware of the probabilities of losing a child, why then did the death of Peter appear to have such a massive impact on Dorothy? She had survived the grief of losing two daughters. Why would a third death be so difficult? We can only speculate about why. Peter's death may have confirmed some haunting fears that Dorothy had. We know she later was very solicitous concerning the health and well-being of her children. Perhaps she had always been that way to a degree. She may even have resisted going to India out of concern for her children and their future welfare. We know that most government, military, and company officials did not take their wives with them to India, and they certainly did not take their children. Peter's death may thus have threatened to set off an overwhelming flood of fear that she would continue to lose her sons until she had nothing left. Dorothy may have retreated from reality so as not to live with her other "reality," the dreaded loss of more children.

We also know that Kitty played a strategic role in Dorothy's presence in India. Kitty was a godly sister who helped Dorothy survive those early months in Bengal. We know that Kitty agreed often with Dorothy about the unsuitable arrangements that Carey was making for his family. If they had not complained vigorously, their eventual settled home may have been far less adequate than their brick house in Mudnabatti turned out to be. Kitty must also have been strategic in the care of the four boys. In those early months the family could not afford servants, yet the tasks of feeding and caring for the large family were unrelenting.

We have already entertained the possibility that Kitty decided to marry because she thought that Dorothy was strong enough to carry on by herself. This explanation for her leaving Dorothy is insufficient because we know that Dorothy was still very ill with her dysentery at that time. The answer as to why Kitty decided to marry and leave Dorothy must be more complicated than that. The tug of love and the lure of a married future must have pulled against Kitty's care and concern for her sister Dorothy. We do not know how much Kitty struggled with this dilemma. We merely know that she did settle the issue by deciding to marry Mr. Short. If Kitty had stayed with the family, would Dorothy have been stronger? Would Dorothy have been less alone and less lonely? Could she have weathered Peter's death better? We wish we knew. We can be confident that Kitty's leaving did contribute to Dorothy's overall sense of loss that seemed to make her vulnerable and emotionally weak.

What if Dorothy Had Received Treatment in India?

When her psychotic state first began, Dorothy and William were living in a remote area where medical care was difficult to obtain. The situation changed considerably when the family moved to Serampore, where medical help was available both there and in nearby Calcutta. We have already discussed some of the pragmatic reasons why William apparently never had a doctor other than John Thomas examine Dorothy. The awkwardness of having her charges of infidelity investigated by officials who seriously questioned whether missionaries should even be in company territory is obvious.

Yet we still can wonder what would have happened if Carey had obtained help for her. The stark reality of the matter, however, is that even if he had consulted physicians in the area they probably could not have done much to help Dorothy. Today we would at least be able to use some tranquilizing agents to take the raw edge off the paranoiac rage and violence. No such medication was available in Dorothy's time. Would the doctors have suggested that William spend more time with Dorothy? If they had made such a suggestion, would Carey have done it and would such attention have been anything but a response that was too late? We do know that Dorothy did tell her story to the Thomases and other Europeans without any relief. So the mere experience of being able to share her delusions with a physician evaluating her would likely have been as futile.

What if Dorothy Had Returned to England?

We have already discussed this possibility that must have been a real option for William. Given Carey's dedication to the task, however, we concluded that he probably dismissed the idea as an option because it would take him away from the task to which God had called him. In some ways this question is much more related to our current practice of missions than to missions in Carey's day. William Ward and the Marshmans did make trips back to England later in their careers, but much of the motivation for these return trips related to the misunderstandings between the missionaries in India and the sending society back in England. Periodic returns to the homeland for rest and reporting to supporters came later in the development of the missionary enterprise.

Still, if Carey had taken Dorothy home for an extended period of time or if he had allowed her to return permanently to England, would her life have been any different? She certainly would have benefited from renewed contact with her extended family. The familiar English diet, climate, and manner of life may have been welcome, but we cannot say that such a change in environment would have rolled back her paranoid thinking and restored her to full mental health.

The prognosis, or estimated chance of recovery, in severe paranoid conditions such as Dorothy's continues to be very poor in spite of advances in the treatment of many mental disorders. Some jealous paranoias never subside until the relationship on which the delusion focuses is dissolved. If Carey had brought Dorothy home to England and returned later to India without her, the situation would not have been good. Dorothy would continue to be troubled by Carey's supposed infidelity, perhaps even to a larger degree, if she were even farther away from him. This "what if" question leads us naturally to the next query, however.

What if Dorothy Had Received Treatment in England?

Thomas Arnold would have been the natural person to work with Dorothy in such a case.[1] We know that people traveled from neighboring shires, as did Robert Hall, to Arnold's asylum in Leicester.

Given Dorothy's violence, Arnold would surely have recommended hospitalization in his Belle Grove facility. We know that Arnold's practice was thriving during these years. From 1801 to 1812 Arnold admitted 142 patients to his asylum, making Belle Grove one of the largest psychiatric facilities in all of England at that time.[2] Arnold was known for his charity; he advertised as early as 1785 that he admitted some patients at lower fees and took two patients at a time without any charge.[3] He advocated the use of chains with the poorer violent patients since the cost of providing attendants to watch them would be prohibitive.[4] But Arnold may not have regarded Dorothy as his typical low fee patient because of his friendship with Carey. She might have received fairly good care at his Leicester facility.

Would she have improved with treatment in England? We would like to know. We are left with uncertain answers to all of these "What if . . . ?" questions. We can not stop wondering, however.

Lessons We Can Learn

We move now to a brief review of areas where the story of Dorothy Carey can teach us valuable lessons. Some of the following areas represent issues with which many have already struggled. Some challenges that emerge from her story are new ones for us as we move shortly into the third century of the modern missionary movement. All of them represent potential value that we can derive from Dorothy's sacrifice of sanity.

New Perspectives on Carey

Proverbs 3:5 +6

Biographies of William Carey have all acknowledged the mental illness of his wife, but all too often Dorothy's role in his life and ministry receives only a cursory tip of the hat. Rarely do we find a vigorous examination of how her struggles helped shape the course of missions in Bengal during those early years. This serious oversight in part reflects scholarship trends. In the past we have often not focused significant attention on the role played by women and wives in the unfolding of events in the history of missions. Likewise, we have not always felt free to examine issues of mental health and illness such as are directly relevant to the Carey story. As a result we sometimes have only a partial understanding of events that we now need to re-examine.

Throughout the previous chapters we have referred to some of these gaps in the Carey story that we need to understand more fully. The part played by Dorothy's psychotic behavior in Mudnabatti is but one example. In those years, Carey and Thomas had no converts. They obviously would have preferred to present their Christian witness against a background of domestic tranquility, but they could not hide Dorothy's struggles. Did such a stark reminder of the harsh realities of life help or hinder their proclamation of the good news of Jesus Christ to their Hindu and Mohammedan neighbors? How did the Indian nationals react to these struggles within the Carey household? Did Dorothy's insanity tarnish their perception of Christianity? Or did Carey's ensuing treatment of her speak to them of Christian patience and forbearance?

In the Serampore community of missionaries, everyone knew of Dorothy's condition. How did her disabilities affect the development of the communal living arrangements? Did her struggles propel all of them to invest heavily in the success of their interpersonal functioning, thereby helping us understand the uncommon success of the Serampore community? Did Dorothy's plight help them all see the importance of mutual support when disease and death struck those within the missionary circle?

How was the ongoing relationship of the missionaries with the national believers affected by Dorothy's condition? Did the missionaries feel they had to hide Dorothy or were they able to somehow incorporate her as naturally as possible in their relationships with national believers?

William Carey's story is incomplete without Dorothy Carey's story. We have only begun to explore the potential ways in which her experience, when fully attended to, can help us understand more fully the remarkable William Carey saga.

The Value of Teams, the Danger of Isolation

Carey had no option in putting his missiological dream into action other than to start it. Beginnings are always small. The society did send out a team of workers, the Thomas and Carey families. Still, the fact remains that those early missionaries had to struggle alone far more than we would say is optimal. Once the Careys arrived in Mudnabatti they were alone. A few other Europeans lived in the area, but they were not committed to the same missionary tasks. For about half of the time the Careys lived in Mudnabatti, the Thomas family was nearby in Moypaldiggy. The Thomases were close yet far away at the same time considering the difficulties of travel.

How much did this relative isolation, albeit necessary at the time, contribute to Dorothy's emotional demise? Could she have fared better within a network of supportive co-workers? Could better friendships have stemmed her tide of loneliness and thus given her more resilience for upcoming tragedies? Everything we know about human functioning propels us to guess in the affirmative direction. People in highly stressful conditions tend to do better when in groups than when in isolation.

If indeed such is a valuable lesson we can learn from Dorothy's story, we also need to develop means of identifying the types of people who work best on teams and who can best profit from interpersonal networks. Perhaps we have glorified the highly independent pioneer missionary so long that we have ignored the need to recruit people who can function well in teams. The days of the Lone Ranger on the mission field may be over. Are we prepared to combat the known dangers of isolation in ministry? An even more complicated task may yet be ahead of us as we send more and more missionaries overseas to work directly under national church supervision and direction. Are we retooling our recruitment procedures to find people capable of such teamwork?

A Missiology of Suffering

Theologians struggle with theodicy, the attempt to understand God's goodness in the face of suffering and evil. Likewise we may need to struggle to understand the role of suffering in missions. The Carey story is a saga of accomplishment under the most adverse of circumstances and at the highest of costs. The Careys were not the first to encounter suffering in the course of obeying the Great Commission. Nor were they the last. Yet their story epitomizes the role of suffering in the mission of the church as few other stories do.

Carey himself attempted to hammer out a theology that would help him understand why his family was so ill and impaired. He used the very best understanding of piety and sanctification that his exposure to English Baptists had given him. His journal provides us with glimpses into his soul as he struggled with the spiritual monster of suffering.

Carey's sister Polly suffered greatly from a debilitating physical condition that left her virtually paralyzed except for her writing arm and hand. Polly's letters to her brother William do not survive, but we can surmise some of their contents from the responses Carey made to her. In a 1796 letter to his sisters (Polly lived with Carey's other sister Ann Hobson), he politely rebuked Polly for her complaining attitude.

Instead of always looking at the dark side of life he urged them to "take a peep on the other side of what God has wrought." The promises, the power, and the omniscience of God all should serve to help us understand the difficult things in life.[5] Carey no doubt started his own pilgrimage through suffering at this very point. We should try to find hints of God's goodness in even the bleakest of circumstances.

In a later letter to his father he refers to a second approach to suffering that he likewise personally used to understand why God would allow Dorothy to lose her sanity. We have already seen how Carey was cautious in what he wrote to his father due to Carey's concern for his father's salvation.

> These things my poor father are all under the directions of a wise and gracious providence which watches over all our concerns, and even attends to the minutest circumstances thereof.[6]

Carey never strayed far from his Calvinistic roots when reflecting on his God of providence. God was a God of order and control. Even the smallest of details did not escape God's attention or care. Even though we might not be able to understand the sometimes mysterious ways of this God of providence, we nonetheless can trust him to care for us well. Life's struggles and sufferings are but a small part of the larger picture, and God is God over both. At times Carey felt "tossed up and down on the Waves of Providence," but never did he fail to put his trust in the one who tossed the waves![7]

The final theme in Carey's ongoing struggles with his suffering has to do with the refining or purifying effects of suffering:

> Oh that I may be sanctified by the strokes I have had, and learn to commit all my ways to the Lord.[8]

> This affliction is heavy. O may I bear it like a Christian and may it be of benefit to me.[9]

Carey's attempts to understand these profound mysteries of life are also our tasks. Suffering continues to be a part of missions. And so do matters of mental illness. Carey spent much concentrated time mastering the arguments of Robert Hall, Sr., in his helpful book, *Help to Zion's Travellers*. We also know that Carey had this book with him in India. Visitors to Bristol College in England can view marginal notes in Carey's careful handwriting on the very pages where Hall wrote about the mentally disturbed. Hall argued that those without natural ability are not condemned by God for not having those abilities. God only asks for the right use of natural abilities that we do possess:

> It is not the sin of the blind that they don't read the Scriptures; nor are the deaf blameable for not hearing the sound of the gospel; nor the dumb culpable on account of their not pleading for God. Nor is it the duty of any to work or war with their hands who have got none. Nor are any blamed for being sick, though it should be unto death. The reason is, because they could not be or do otherwise if they would.[10]

Hall went on to write, "When rationality is absent, the words and actions of such people are never accounted criminal."[11] Hall's theology may have helped Carey accept that God could remove, or allow to be removed, some natural abilities in people such as his wife Dorothy, and that in some mysterious way all was well even in spite of the pain and suffering of the moment.

Have we made any more headway in understanding how and why suffering occurs in the course of obedience to the Great Commission? A missiology bereft of a capacity to integrate a view of suffering runs the risk of becoming something akin to a martial missiology: conquest, victory, and triumph, but never defeat, retreat, or loss.

The Role of Psychology in Missions

Psychology was not a separate discipline of scientific inquiry when the Careys labored under their mental health struggles. Even psychiatry was just in its infancy as a medical specialty. Nonetheless mission sending agencies have had to deal with issues of mental health and illness among the missionary force from the very beginning. Too often we are tempted to believe that psychological disturbance is a new phenomenon to the twentieth century and is just one more indication of the deterioration of our society. Yet problems of mental health have always been with us. We just have new categories of professionals in our day who try to work with these longstanding issues.

Increasingly, psychologists are involved in the selection of missionary candidates. Research data is now available pointing to certain factors that appear related to successful cross-cultural adaptation. New instruments are also available to help predict a person's capacity for the massive task of successfully becoming bicultural. Other trends among the mission societies of North America include offering re-entry seminars for adolescents who are returning to pursue their education, using on-field counselors to help missionaries with their struggles while they are in them rather than waiting until they return several years later to the sending country, and providing better training for field administrators who are in a position to monitor the interpersonal functioning of missionaries.

We need to expand our investment in assessing gifts and personality structure as they relate to placement and job tasks on the field. We need also to increase our concern for psychological aftercare of personnel returning from a short-term assignment or missionaries on home assignment.

The lesson we can learn from Dorothy Carey's story is that attention to the mental health needs of our missionary personnel is not a new or recent luxury but a vital part of our obligation to those who volunteer to serve cross-culturally in obedience to the Great Commission.

Care for the Casualties

Missionaries in our day who return home because of psychological problems often report feeling very much like lepers. Churches and societies often manifest an uncertainty about those who have had psychological problems abroad and a sense of frustration regarding how to help them. All too often the dilemma results in doing nothing or very little to help the returned missionaries. So the embattled missionary who struggles with mental illness soon experiences rejection, a lack of care, or a message of abandonment.

We have grown accustomed to referring to those who return home from missionary service as casualties. This war-related metaphor may not help the returned missionary envision some ongoing ministry in the home country. In fact the returnee may more often sense failure and a lack of future usefulness. Dorothy's story reminds us that we are just as responsible to attend to the struggles of missionaries as we are to rejoice over their victories. We have known from the very beginning of the modern missionary movement that the cost of obeying the Great Commission can be very high. We can learn needed lessons from the example of Dorothy Carey if we renew our commitment to minister to and care for all those who pay the high price of emotional disablement in their service for Christ.

The Hazards of Public Relations

Many mission societies have followed the pattern established by Carey and Fuller. An organization in the sending country recruits financial support from churches and individuals for a team of missionaries serving overseas. A few go; many give. The societies in the home land serve as brokers between those actually doing the cross-cultural ministries and those who are financially underwriting its cost. The sending societies must pay attention to the needs of both its overseas personnel and the supporters. Public relations is an ongoing task for all sending agencies.

In the Carey story we find several examples of important decisions made by both the society and its missionaries with public relations concerns looming large in the decision-making process. Again we may be surprised to realize that some of the very earliest missionary efforts struggled with concerns that continue to challenge us. How do we accurately interpret what is going on overseas for the benefit of our supporters? How do we help supporters see the wisdom of ministry decisions we are making regarding our outreach strategies?

The risk that arises from our necessary attention to matters of our public relations occurs when the needs of our supporting constituency clash with the needs of missionary personnel overseas. At several points in the Carey story we have seen examples of decisions made with the supporting public in mind that came close to colliding with the best interests of the missionaries in India.

For example, a nineteenth-century biographer of Carey described a serious dilemma the society faced when Dorothy was refusing to accompany her husband to India. Culross maintained that Dorothy thought the proposal to go to India was "worse than a fool's errand."

> It was indeed usual for mercantile and military men to leave their families in England, during their absence in the East; but it was felt that this was very undesirable for missionaries, if it could possibly be avoided.[12]

Andrew Fuller, to his great credit, resisted the idea to allow this concern for what the public thought to interfere with Dorothy's important decision to go or not to go. Yet when Thomas and Carey finally persuaded Dorothy to go, Fuller seemed to utter a sigh of relief. "Thus the Lord prevented their departure in the first instance, that Mr. Carey's family might accompany him, and that all reproaches on that score might be prevented."[13] "The additional sum of money now wanted is on account of Carey's family going with him. But this is so desirable an object, that nothing should be thot much of to accomplish it."[14] Admittedly all of those involved in Dorothy's frustrating preference not to go faced the possibility of criticism and public dissatisfaction no matter which direction they pursued.

Carey himself exhibited great concern that the money he was expending, money that faithful supporters had sacrificially given, be used well. At times Carey borders on making poor decisions for his family in preference to pleasing supporters:

> I not only am convinced of the importance of a missionary being like, and living amongst his people, the success of future missions also lies near my heart and I am fearful lest the great expense of sending out my family should be a check upon the zeal of the society. How much more if I should now live upon an European plan and incur greater charges.[15]

We do not know how much of Carey's dogged determination to move his family into the wilderness stemmed from his missiological convictions and how much arose from his renowned tightness with money. In these early months the point is actually moot since he had no money with which to be tight! Nonetheless, Carey himself felt very early in his missionary career compelled to ask himself, "What will people back home think?"

These frustrations that confront us like cul-de-sacs continue to challenge mission administrators. Sometimes no decision looks like a good one; any way we move has its hazards and costs. In the Carey story we do not find examples of undue attention to the whims of the supporting public as much as we see some very early struggles with the dilemmas of trying to meet the needs of many publics. Perhaps the value of these early examples for us resides in the reminder that whenever the expectations of the supporting public clash with the needs of the missionaries, we must decide for the welfare of the supporters first. As tempting as the situation might be to make sacrifices on the side of the missionaries, the hazards and injustice of such decisions are great. The welfare of Dorothy and her children may have all too often have been of second in importance to the demands of supporters.

Our Ongoing Shame

The mental health struggles of missionaries are often a source of embarrassment for us. As much as we proclaim that missionaries are just human, that they have all the weaknesses and vulnerabilities of the rest of us, that we should not put them up on a pedestal, we still seem embarrassed when they struggle. Perhaps we pay lip service to the need to treat them as ordinary persons, but harbor some deep-seated wish that they really could be perfect. Why does the public often demand so much invulnerability and perfection from the missionary task force?

Our shame is projected also onto missionaries. If some wife or husband or child is suffering with the agony of an emotional disorder shame rules the day. The missionary may feel compelled to hide the struggle, even on the annual visit of the mission administrator. Or, the missionary may feel that some pretense for a trip back home is needed. Missionaries often feel, and maybe they are right, that those of us in their supporting networks do not want to hear that they are returning for treatment of some depression or for help with an anorectic daughter. So "needed rest" or "physical exhaustion" becomes the cover under which a missionary family can sneak back into the home country for some undercover efforts to obtain help.

Why do we do such things to ourselves and to those we love? What is the source of this conspiracy of silence and shame? Perhaps we need to re-examine the dynamics of the supporter-missionary relationship. We all know that the support system we most frequently use renders the missionary dependent on the supporters. Perhaps we have not directly faced the awkward feelings that such financial dependency generates in both the giver and the receiver. Do supporters somehow feel that the missionary is humiliated in this exchange and that we need to compensate for this humiliation by raising the missionary up on to some unrealistically high pedestal? And then when the missionary exhibits signs of human frailty and weakness, our game is exposed and we all sink into shame.

Whatever may be the actual reasons for the ongoing sense of shame present within the missionary community regarding mental illness, we need to root it out. Dorothy's story speaks clearly to us on this point. Realistic and face-to-face encounters with normal human weaknesses, both among missionaries and supporters, need to rule the day. We need to put the days of shame, hiding, and game-playing behind us.

Dorothy's Legacy

Above and beyond these lessons that we can learn from Dorothy's story are some legacies she has left us. Chatterjee pays the following tribute to her:

It was really a bold decision of Dorothy who, subdued to the earnest request of her husband William Carey and John Thomas, agreed to accompany them with her four children including an infant baby in their adventurous voyage to a very far off country. She had overcome her fear of a strange country and unknown environment. She had gained the determination to endure the sufferings that might occur to her for the sake of her little children. This bold decision was really an encouraging example to the wives of other missionaries who were not hesitating to accompany their husbands.[16]

Chatterjee reminds us that Dorothy's going to India served to pave the way for other missionary wives to go with their husbands. Gradually wives played an increasing role in the unfolding of the modern missionary movement.[17]

Dorothy was influential not only in her eventual going to the field but in other ways as well. The tragic story of her mental illness was known to other mission agencies. We cannot prove that Dorothy's example forced other missions to pay more attention to the willingness of wives to accompany their husbands, but she may indeed have had just such an influence.

For example, the Wesleyan Missionary Society developed from a 1790 committee appointed by the conference to manage mission affairs in the West Indies. Gradually the mission produced a policy book that gives us a glimpse at how mission administrators envisioned the missionary enterprise. In 1818 the questions asked of missionary candidates did not refer at all to a spouse's willingness. But in 1822 the following three questions appear in the list that all missionary applicants had to answer:

> 15. Does he offer himself to the committee to go out as a married, or a single man?
> 16. If, as a married man, can the person to whom he is engaged be recommended for her piety, prudence, general fitness for the wife of a missionary, and her zeal in the cause of Christ?
> 17. Have the parents of the young woman given their consent?[18]

If a Wesleyan single missionary wished to return home to England to find a "suitable" wife, he could take up to one year to do so before returning to his assigned field with his new bride.[19] If the new applicant was engaged, the examining committee had to examine the suitableness of his wife-to-be. So very early in the developing missionary enterprise, recognition of the crucial place of the wife in the success of a career emerged. Perhaps Dorothy's long struggles in India served to sensitize other sending agencies to the needs of missionary spouses.

We do know that the Baptist Missionary Society almost immediately became more aware of the need for spousal willingness. Andrew Fuller once wrote that Mr. Brunsdon recently had married a Miss Irons "who is willing to go with him." He was not so certain whether the wives of Marshman and Grant were willing.[20] In an earlier letter Fuller discussed several other candidates for service in India. The Reads were rejected even though Mr. Read was suitable:

> His wife and eldest daughter are not willing. And his family is so large that it was a very serious matter on their account as well as on account of the expense. . . . But the unwillingness of his wife, and the consideration that she had formerly been in a very unhappy state of mind, and that you seemed to want active women, were at present an absolute bar.[21]

Fuller seems to be unwilling to allow other zealous candidates to take unwilling spouses overseas. Fuller also appears to refer to some prior mental health problems on the part of Mrs. Read, perhaps the first example of psychological screening.

Another legacy left by Dorothy centers on the changes that occurred in William as a result of her suffering. His second marriage was dramatically different than his first. A major difference between these two marriages stemmed from the very pronounced differences between Dorothy and Charlotte, but we cannot help but wonder if Carey had learned some important interpersonal lessons from his first marriage. Could he have become more attentive and more aware of the needs of his wife? Could he have realized that a happy marriage was often directly related to how much one invests in the relationship? Could the agony of those twelve years have simply equipped him to be a better husband?

Finally, Dorothy played a vital role in making her husband's whole career possible. She gave birth to his children. She accompanied him to India. Her presence there made a trip home to England unnecessary. And the painful suffering in the Carey family circle because of Dorothy's mental illness may have been the hard anvil on which was hammered some of the success of his remarkable career.

An Account of
Mrs. Fuller's Insanity

Dear and Honoured Father—You have heard, I suppose, before now, that my dear companion is no more! For about three months back our afflictions have been extremely heavy. About the beginning of June she was seized with hysterical affections, which, for a time, deprived her of her senses. In about a week, however, she recovered them, and seemed better; but soon relapsed again; and during the months of July and August, a very few intervals excepted, her mind has been constantly deranged. In this unhappy state, her attention has generally been turned upon some one object of distress; sometimes that she had lost her children; sometimes that she should lose me. . . . Sometimes we were her worst enemies, and must not come near her; at other times she would speak to me in the most endearing terms. . . But lately her mind took another turn, which to me was very afflictive. It is true she never ceased to love her husband. "I have had," she would say, "as tender a husband as ever woman had; but you are not my husband!" She seemed for the last month really to have considered me as an imposter, who had entered the house and taken possession of the keys of every place, and of all that belonged to her and her husband. Poor soul! for the last month, as I said, this and other notions of the kind have rendered her more miserable than I am able to describe. She has been fully persuaded that she was *not at home*, but had wandered somewhere from it; had lost herself, and fallen among strangers. She constantly wanted to make her escape, on which account we were obliged to keep the doors locked, and to take away the keys. . . . You may form some conception what must have been my feelings to have been a spectator of all this anguish, and at the same time incapable of affording her the smallest relief.

Though she seemed not to know the children about her, yet she had a keen and lively remembrance of those that were taken away. One day, when I was going out for the air, she went out of the house. The servant missing her, immediately followed, and found her in the graveyard, looking at the graves of her children. She said nothing; but, with a bitterness of soul, pointed the servant's eyes to the wall, where the name of one of them, who was buried in 1783, was cut in the stone. Then turning to the graves of the other children, in an agony, she with her foot struck off the long grass which had grown over the flat stones, and read the inscriptions with silent anguish, alternately looking at the servant and at the stones. . . .

On Thursday, the 25th instant, she was delivered of a daughter, but was all day very restless, full of pain and misery; no return of reason, except that, from an aversion to me which she had so long entertained, she called me "my dear," and twice kissed me; said she "must die"; and "let me die, my dear," said she, "let me die!" Between nine and ten o'clock, as there seemed no immediate sign of a change, and being very weary, I went to rest; but about eleven was called up again, just time enough to witness the convulsive pangs of death, which in about ten minutes carried her off. . . .

To all this I may add, that, perhaps, I have reason to be thankful for her removal. However the dissolution of such a union may affect my present feelings, it may be one of the greatest mercies both to her and to me. Had she continued in the same state of mind, which was not at all improbable, this, to all appearance, would have been a thousand times worse than death.[1]

Summary of Arnold's Diagnostic Categories

Species: Insanity
Genus: Insanity

I. **Ideal**
    1. Phrenetic
        —incessant raving (may be laughing, singing, whistling, weeping, lamenting, praying, shouting, swearing, threatening, attempting violence)
        —symptoms: redness of eyes, quick pulse, heat of the head, white tongue
    2. Incoherent
        a. ardent
        b. flighty
        c. unconnected
        d. stupid
    3. Maniacal
        —very comprehensive, affects whole internal world of ideas
    4. Sensitive
        —erroneous images relative to person's own form, substance, qualities, or content
        —arises from erroneous sensation
II. **Notional**
    5. Delusive
        a. regarding self, grandiosity
        b. regarding existence of soul or body

6. Fanciful
   —incessant talking, frequent sallies of wit, acute observations
7. whimsical
   —whimsical fancies, aversions, fears, scruples, suspicions
8. Impulsive
   —patient impelled to do or say the unreasonable, imprudent, improper, impertinent, ridiculous, or absurd
9. Scheming
   —sees self as the most knowing of all mankind
10. Vain
    —exalted opinion of self, excessive attention to dress that is either solicitously neat or completely ridiculous
11. Hypochondriacal
    —fancies self threatened by imaginary disease
12. Pathetic
    —some one passion predominates and hides or obscures the other passions
    —among the passions that can become excessive are:
    love
    jealousy
    avarice
    misanthropy
    pride
    anger
    aversion
    suspicion
    bashfulness
    irresolution
    timidity
    grief
    distress
    nostalgia
    superstition
    enthusiasm
    despair

Carey's Proposal (1796)

I will now propose to you, what I would recommend to the Society. You will find it similar to what the Moravians do. Seven or eight families can be maintained for nearly the same expense as one, if this method be pursued. I then earnestly entreat the Society to set their faces this way, and send out more missionaries. We ought to be seven or eight families together; and it is absolutely necessary for the wives of missionaries to be as hearty in the work as their husbands. Our families should be considered nurseries for the mission; and among us should be a person capable of teaching school, so as to educate our children. I recommend all living together, in a number of little straw houses, forming a line or square, and that we have nothing of our own; but all the general stock. One or two should be selected stewards to preside over all the management, which should, with respect to eating, drinking, working, worship, learning, preaching, excursions, &c., be reduced to fixed rules. Should converts from amongst the natives join us, all should be considered equal, and all come under the same regulations.

The utility of this community of good in the beginning of the gospel church here, will be obvious, by considering the following things:—

1. Our finances being small, it will be necessary to live economically; but one set of servants will do all the work for the whole, if thus organized, when, if otherwise, every separate family must have the same number as would be necessary for the whole, if united: and, if God converts the natives, they would in time supersede all want of servants, being partakers of the public stock, and therefore bound to labour for the public benefit.

2. Education of our own and converted heathens' children is a very important object, and is what might, if followed by a divine blessing, train up some of them to be useful preachers or other members of the mission themselves.

3. The example of such a number would be a standing witness of the excellence of the gospel, and would contribute

very much to the furtherance of the cause of Christ.

4. Industry being absolutely necessary, every one would have his proper work allotted him, and would be employed at his post; some cultivating land, some instructing, some learning, some preaching, and the women superintending the domestic concerns.

In order to this, I recommend about one or two hundred bigahs to be cultivated for the mission, which would produce most of the articles necessary for them and their cattle; that all these people should not come at one time, but one or two families in a year, or in two years or so. But as brother Thomas, for obvious reasons, could not join this family, and as there is a far greater probability of his being torn from the work than not, we are in immediate want of more, say one family more, of missionaries; and I entreat the Society to send them, as the only way of keeping the mission together: but pray be very careful what stamp missionaries' wives are of.

Should this place be continued to me, I recommend the seat of the mission to be here; and my income and utensils will be immediately thrown into the common stock. Or any part of Bengal would do; though the north is most agreeable, and will produce wheat, a very necessary article: the heat also is more moderate. Should we go south, the neighbourhood of Nuddea is most eligible; but, I fear, too near Calcutta. All provisions also are much cheaper in the north; and by keeping a small boat, which can be bought for thirty rupees, two persons may travel any where at a time. Cultivation, and all except superintendence, must be performed by the natives.

EXPENSE. The number of servants kept would fall under two hundred rupees per month; I think, about a hundred and thirty; and the expenses of clothing and articles of furniture would be near one hundred for the number mentioned. The table might be well supplied, for all above mentioned, for one hundred rupees at furthest: I think, for sixty; but I say the utmost. Now, if eight families were distinct, their monthly expenses could not, with the utmost frugality, come under one thousand rupees per month: the whole of this would only be four hundred, and the produce of the land would go to lessen even that; so that we should receive from the Society for such a number £30 per month, or £360 per annum, till we were able to say we could do with less. It would be a great saving of even this, if the Society were to send £50 a year of this in woolen cloths, light shoes, strong stockings, hats, and garden seeds. This £50 would save the mission about £100 or £150 a year. Having said this much, I recommend it to your serious consideration. The calculations may all be depended upon.[1]

Serampore Compact (1805)

Form of Agreement respecting the great principles upon which the Brethren of the Mission at Serampore think it is their duty to act in the work of instructing the Heathen, agreed upon at a meeting of the Brethren at Serampore, on Monday, October 7, 1805.

The Redeemer, in planting us in the heathen nation, rather than in any other, has imposed upon us the cultivation of peculiar qualifications. We are firmly persuaded that Paul might plant and Apollos water, in vain, in any part of the world, did not God give the increase. We are sure that only those who are ordained to eternal life will believe, and that God alone can add to the church such as shall be saved. Nevertheless we cannot but observe with admiration that Paul, the great champion for the glorious doctrine of free and sovereign grace, was the most conspicuous for his personal zeal in the work of persuading men to be reconciled to God. In this respect he is a noble example for our imitation. Our Lord intimated to those of His apostles who were fishermen, that He would make them fish-ers of men, intimating that in all weathers, and amidst every disappointment they were to aim at drawing men to the shores of eternal life. Solomon says: "He that winneth souls is wise," implying, no doubt, that the work of gaining over men to the side of God, was to be done by winning methods, and that it required the greatest wisdom to do it with success. Upon these points, we think it right to fix our serious and abiding attention.

First. In order to be prepared for our great and solemn work, it is absolutely necessary that we set an infinite value upon immortal souls; that we often endeavour to affect our minds with the dreadful loss sustained by an unconverted soul launched into eternity. It becomes us to fix in our minds the awful doctrine of eternal punishment, and to realize frequently the unconceivably awful conditions of this vast country, lying in the arms of the wicked one. If we have not this awful sense of the value of souls, it is impossible that we can feel aright in any other part of our work, and in this case it had been better for us to have been in any other situation other than in that of a Missionary. Oh! may our hearts bleed over these poor idolaters, and may their case lie with continued weight on our minds, that we may resemble that eminent Missionary, who compared the travail of his soul, on account of the spiritual state of those committed to his charge, to the pains of childbirth. But while we thus mourn over their miserable condition, we should not be discouraged, as though their recovery were impossible. He who raised the Scottish and brutalized Britons to sit in heavenly places in Christ Jesus; can raise these slaves of superstition, purify their hearts by faith, and make them worshipers of the one God in spirit and in truth. The promises are fully sufficient to remove our doubts, and to make us anticipate that not very distant period when He will famish all the gods of India, and cause these very idolaters to cast their idols to the moles and to the bats, and renounce for ever the work of their own hands.

Secondly. It is very important that we should gain all the information we can of the snares and delusions in which these heathen are held. By this means we shall be able to converse with them in an intelligible manner. To know their modes of thinking, their habits, their propensities, their antipathies, the way in which they reason about God, sin, holiness, the way of salvation, and a future state, to be aware of the bewitching nature of their idolatrous worship, feasts, songs, etc., is of the highest consequence, if we would gain their attention to our discourse, and would avoid to be barbarians to them. This knowledge may be easily obtained by conversing with sensible natives, by reading some parts of their works and by attentively observing their manners and customs.

Thirdly. It is necessary, in our intercourse with the Hindoos, that as far as we are able, we abstain from those things which would increase their prejudices against the Gospel. Those parts of English manner which are most offensive to them should be kept out of sight as much as possible. We would also avoid every degree of cruelty to animals. Nor is it advisable, at once to attack their prejudices by exhibiting with acrimony the sins of their gods; neither should we upon any account do violence to their images, nor interrupt their worship. The real conquests of the Gospel are those of love: "And I, if I be lifted up, will draw all men unto me." In this respect, let us be continually fearful else one unguarded word, or one unnecessary display of the difference betwixt us, in manners, etc., should set the natives at a greater distance from us. Paul's readiness to become all things to all men, that he might by any means save some, and his disposition to abstain even from necessary comforts that he might not offend the weak, are circumstances worthy of our particular notice. This line of conduct we may be sure was founded on the wisest principles. Placed amidst a people very much like the hearers of the Apostle, in many respects, we may now perceive the solid wisdom which guided him as a missionary. The mild manners of the Moravians, and also of the Quakers—towards the North American Indians, have, in many instances, gained the affections and confidence of heathens in a wonderful manner. He who is too proud to stoop to others in order to draw them to him, though he may know that they are in many respects inferior to himself, is ill-qualified to become a Missionary. The words of a most successful preacher of a preacher still living, "that he would not care if the people trampled him under their feet, if he might become useful to their souls," are expressive of the very temper we should always cultivate.

Fourthly. It becomes us to watch all opportunities of doing good. A missionary would be highly culpable if he contented himself with preaching two or three times a week to those persons whom he might be able to get together into a place of worship. To carry on conversations with the natives almost every hour in the day, to go from village to village, from market to market, from one assembly to another, to talk to servants, labourers, etc., as often as opportunity offers, and to be instant in season and out of season—this is the life to which we are called in this country. We are apt to relax in these active exertions, especially in a warm climate; but we shall do well always to fix in our minds, that life is short, that all around us are perishing, and that we incur a dreadful woe if we proclaim not the glad tiding of salvation.

Fifthly. In preaching to the heathen, we must keep to the example of St. Paul, and make the greatest subject of our preaching, Christ Crucified. It would be very easy for a missionary to preach nothing but truths, and that for many years together, without any well-grounded hope of becoming useful to one soul. The doctrine of Christ's expiatory death and all-sufficient merits had been, and must ever remain, the great means of conversion. This doctrine, and others immediately connected with it, have constantly nourished and sanctified the church. Oh that these glorious truths ever be the joy and strength of our own souls and then we will not fail to become the matter of our conversation to others. It was the proclaiming of these doctrines that made the Reformation from Popery in the time of Luther spread with such rapidity. It was these truths that filled the sermons of the modern Apostles, Whitefield, Wesley, etc., when the light of the Gospel which had been held up with such glorious effects by the Puritans was almost extinguished in England. It is a well-known fact that the most successful missionaries in the world at the present day make the atonement of Christ their continued theme. We mean the Moravians. They attribute all their success to the preaching of the death of our Saviour. So far as our experience goes in this work, we must freely acknowledge, that every Hindoo among us who has been gained to Christ, has been won by the astonishing and all-constraining love exhibited in our Redeemer's propitiatory death. O then may we resolve to know nothing among Hindoos and Mussulmans but Christ and Him crucified.

Sixthly. It is absolutely necessary that the natives should have an entire confidence in us, and feel quite at home in our company. To gain this confidence we must on all occasions be willing to hear their complaints; we must give them the kindest advice, and we must decide upon everything brought before us in the most open, upright, and impartial manner. We ought to be easy of access, to condescend to them as much as possible, and on all occasions to treat them as our equals. All passionate behaviour will sink our characters exceedingly in their estimation. All force, and everything haughty, reserved and forbidding it becomes us ever to shun with the greatest care. We can never make sacrifices too great, when the eternal salvation of souls is the object except, indeed, we sacrifice the commands of Christ.

Seventhly. Another important part of our work is to build up, and watch over, the souls that may be gathered. In this work we shall do well to simplify our first instructions as much as possible, and to press the great principles of the Gospel upon the minds of the converts till they be thoroughly settled and grounded in the foundation of their hope towards

God. We must be willing to spend some time with them daily, if possible, in this work. We must have much patience with them, though they may grow very slowly in divine knowledge.

We ought also to endeavour as much as possible to form them to habits of industry, and assist them in procuring such employments as may be pursued with the least danger of temptations to evil. Here too we shall have occasion to exercise much tenderness and forbearance, knowing that industrious habits are formed with difficulty by all heathen nations. We ought also to remember that these persons have made no common sacrifices in renouncing their connections, their homes, their former situations and means of support, and that it will be very difficult for them to procure employment with heathen masters. In these circumstances, if we do not sympathize with them in their temporal losses for Christ, we shall be guilty of great cruelty.

As we consider it our duty to honour the civil magistrate, and in every state and country to render him the readiest obedience, whether we be persecuted or protected, it becomes us to instruct our native brethren the same principles. A sense of gratitude too presses this obligation upon us in a peculiar manner in return for the liberal protection we have experienced. It is equally our wisdom and our duty also to show to the civil power, that it has nothing to fear from the progress of Missions, since a real follower of Christ must resist the example of his Great Master, and all the precepts the Bible contains on this subject, before he can become disloyal. Converted heathens, being brought over to the religion of their Christian Governors, if duly instructed, are much more likely to love them, and be united to them, than subjects of a different religion.

To bear the faults of our native brethren, so as to reprove them with tenderness, and set them right in the necessity of a holy conversation, is a very necessary duty. We should remember the gross darkness in which they were so lately involved, having never had any just and adequate ideas of the evil of sin, or its consequences. We should also recollect how backward human nature is in forming spiritual ideas, and entering upon a holy self-denying conversation. We ought not, therefore even after many falls, to give up and cast away a relapsed convert while he manifests the least inclination to be washed from his filthiness.

In walking before native converts, much care and circumspection are absolutely necessary. The falls of Christians in Europe have not such a fatal tendency as they must have in this country, because there the word of God always commands more attention than the conduct of the most exalted Christian. But here those around us, in consequence of their little knowledge of the Scriptures, must necessarily take our conduct as a specimen of what Christ looks for in His disciples. They know only the Saviour and His doctrine as they shine forth in us.

In conversing with the wives of the native converts, and leading them in to the ways of Christ, so that they may be an ornament to the Christian cause, and make known the Gospel to the native women, we hope always to have the assistance of the females who have embarked with us in the mission. We see that in primitive times the Apostles were very much assisted in their great work by several pious females. The great value of female help may easily be appreciated if we consider how much the Asiatic women are shut up from the men, and especially from men of another caste. It behoves (sic) us therefore, to afford to our European sisters all possible assistance in acquiring the language, that they may, in every way which Providence may open to them, become instrumental in promoting the salvation of the millions of native women who are in a great measure excluded from all opportunities of hearing the word from the mouths of European missionaries. A European sister may do much for the cause in this respect, by promoting the holiness, and stirring up the zeal, of the female converts. A real missionary becomes in a sense a father to his people. If he feels all their welfare and company that a father does in the midst of his children, they will feel all that freedom with, and confidence in him which he can desire. He will be wholly unable to lead them on in a regular and happy manner, unless they can be induced to open their minds to him, and unless a sincere and mutual esteem subsist on both sides.

Eighthly. Another part of our work is the forming of our native brethren to usefulness, fostering every kind of genius, and cherishing every gift and grace in them. In this respect we can scarcely be too lavish of our attention to their improvement. It is only by means of native preachers that we can hope for the universal spread of the Gospel throughout this immense continent. Europeans are too few, and their subsistence costs too much for us ever to hope that they can possibly be the instruments of the universal diffusion of the word amongst so many millions of souls spread over such a large portion of the habitable globe. Their incapability of bearing the intense heat of the climate in perpetual itineracies, and the heavy expenses of their journeys, not to say anything of the prejudices of the natives against the very presence of Europeans, and the great difficulty of becoming fluent in their languages, render it absolute duty to cherish native gifts, and to send forth as many native preachers as possible. If the practice of confining the min-

istry of the word to a single individual in a church be once established amongst us, we despair of the Gospel's ever making much progress in India by our means. Let us therefore use every gift, and continually urge on our native brethren to press upon their countrymen the glorious Gospel of the blessed God.

Still further to strengthen the cause of Christ in this country, and, as far as in our power, to give it a permanent establishment, even when the efforts of Europeans may fail, we think it our duty, as soon as possible, to advise the native brethren who may be formed in separate churches, to choose their pastors and deacons from amongst their own countrymen, that the word may be steadily preached, and the ordinances of Christ administered, in each church by the native minister, as much as possible without interference of the missionary of the district who will constantly superintend their affairs, give them advice in cases of order and discipline, and correct any errors into which they may fall, and who joying and beholding their order, and their steadfastness of their faith in Christ, may direct his efforts continually to the planting of new churches in other places, and to the spread of the Gospel throughout his district as much as in his power. By this means the unity of the missionary character will be preserved, all the missionaries will still form one body, each one movable as the good of the cause may require, the different native churches will also naturally have to care and provide for their ministers, for their church expense, the raising of places of worship, etc., and the whole administration will assume a native aspect, by which means the inhabitants will more readily identify the cause as belonging to their own nation, and their prejudices at falling into the hands of Europeans will entirely vanish. It may be hoped too that the pastors of these churches, and the members in general, will feel a new energy in attempting to spread the Gospel, when they shall thus freely enjoy the privileges of the Gospel amongst themselves.

Under the divine blessing, if, in the course of a few years, a number of native churches be thus established, from them the Word of God may sound out even to the extremities of India, and numbers of preachers being raised up and sent forth, may form a body of native missionaries, inured to the climate, acquainted with the customs, language, modes of speech and reasoning of the inhabitants; able to become perfectly familiar with them, to enter their houses, to live upon their food, to sleep with them, or under a tree; and who may travel from one end of the country to the other almost without any expense. These churches will be in no immediate danger of falling into errors of disorders, because the whole of their affairs will be constantly superintended, by a European missionary.

The advantages of this plan are so evident, that to carry it into complete effect ought to be our continued concern. That we may discharge the important obligations of watching over these infant churches when formed, and of urging them to maintain a steady discipline, to hold forth the clear and cheering light of evangelical truth in this region and shadow of death, and to walk in all respects as those who have been called out of the darkness into marvelous light, we should continually go to the Source of all grace and strength for it. If to become the shepherd of one church be a most solemn and weighty charge, what must it be to watch over a number of churches just raised from a state of heathenism, and placed at a distance from each other?

We have thought it our duty not to change the names of native converts, observing from Scripture that the Apostles did not change those of the first Christians turned from heathenism, as the names Epaphroditus, Phebe, Fortunatus, Sylvanus, Apollos, Hermes, Junia, Narcissus, etc., prove. Almost all these names are derived from those of heathen gods. We think the great object which Divine Providence has in view in causing the Gospel to be promulgated in the world, is not the changing of the names, the dress, the food, and the innocent usages of mankind, but to produce a moral and divine change in the hearts and conduct of men. It would not be right to perpetuate the names of heathen gods amongst Christians, neither is it necessary or prudent to give a new name to every man after his conversion, as hereby the economy of families, neighbourhoods, etc., would be needlessly disturbed. In other respects, we think it our duty to lead our brethren by example, by mild persuasion, and by opening and illuminating their minds in a gradual way rather than use authoritative means. By this they learn to see the evil of a custom, and then to despise and forsake it; whereas in cases wherein force is used, though they may leave off that which is wrong while in our presence, yet not having seen the evil of it, they are in danger of using hypocrisy, and of doing that out of our presence which they dare not do in it.

Ninthly. It becomes us also to labour with all our might in forwarding translations of the sacred scriptures in the languages of Hindoostan. The help which God has afforded us already in this work is a loud call to us to "go forward." So far therefore, as God has qualified us to learn those languages which are necessary, we consider it our bounden duty to apply ourselves with unwearied assiduity in acquiring them. We consider the publication of the Divine Word throughout India as an object which we ought never to give up till accomplished, looking to the Fountain of all knowledge and strength to qualify us for this great work, and to carry us through it to the praise of His Holy name.

It becomes us to use all assiduity in explaining and distributing the Divine Word on all occasions, and by every means in our power to excite the attention and the reverence of the natives towards it, as the fountain of eternal truth and the Message of Salvation to men. It is our duty also to distribute, as extensively as possible, the different religious tracts which are published. Considering how much the general diffusion of the knowledge of Christ depends upon a liberal and constant distribution of the Word, and of these tracts, all over the country, we should keep this continually in mind, and watch all opportunities of putting even single tracts into the hands of those persons with whom we occasionally meet. We should endeavour to ascertain where large assemblies of the natives are to be found, that we may attend upon them, and gladden whole villages at once with the tiding of salvation.

The establishment of native free schools is also an object highly important to the future conquests of the Gospel. Of this very pleasing and interesting part of our missionary labours, we should endeavour not to be unmindful. As opportunities are afforded, it becomes us to establish, visit, and encourage these institutions, and to recommend the establishment of them to other Europeans. The progress of divine light is gradual, both as it respects individuals and nations. Whatever therefore tends to increase the body of holy light in these dark regions is 'as bread cast upon the waters to be seen after many days." In many ways the progress of providential events is preparing the Hindoos for casting their idols to the moles and the bats, and for becoming a part of the chosen generations, the royal

priesthood, the holy nation. Some parts of missionary labours very properly tend to present conversion of the heathen, and others to the ushering in the glorious period when "a nation shall be born in a day." Of the latter kind are native free schools.

Tenthly. That which, as a means, is to fit us for the discharge of these laborious and unutterable important labours, is the being instant in prayer, and the cultivation of personal religion. Let us ever have in remembrance the examples of those who have been most eminent in the work of God. Let us often look at Brainerd, in the woods of America, pouring out his very soul before God for the perishing heathen, without whose salvation nothing could make him happy. Prayer secret, fervent, believing prayer, lies at the root of all personal godliness. A competent knowledge of the languages current where a missionary lives, a mild and winning temper, and a heart giving up on closet religion, these, these are the attainments which, more than all knowledge, or all other gifts, will fit us to become the instruments of God in the great work of Human Redemption. Let us then ever be united in prayer at stated seasons whatever distance may separate us, and let each one of us lay it upon his heart that we will seek to be fervent in spirit, wrestling with God, till He famish these idols and cause the heathen to experience the blessedness that is in Christ.

Finally. Let us give ourselves up unreservedly to this glorious cause. Let us never think that our time, our gifts, our strength, our families, or even the clothes we wear, are our own. Let us sanctify ourselves for His work! Let us ever shut out the idea of laying up a dowry for ourselves or our children. If we give up the resolution which was formed on the subject of private trade, when we first united at Serampore, the Mission is from that hour a lost cause. A worldly spirit, quarrels, and every evil work will succeed the moment it is admitted that each brother may do something on his own account. Woe to that man who shall ever make the smallest movement toward such a measure. Let us continually watch against a worldly spirit, and cultivate a Christian indifference towards every indulgence. Rather let us bear hardness as good soldiers of Jesus Christ, and endeavour to learn in every state to be content.

If in this way we are enabled to glorify God, with our bodies and spirit which are His,—our wants will be His care. No private family ever enjoyed a greater portion of happiness, even in the most prosperous gale of worldly prosperity, than we have done since we resolved to have all things in common, and that no one should pursue business for his own exclusive advantage. If we are enabled to persevere in the same principles, we may hope that multitudes of converted souls will have reason to bless God to all eternity for sending His Gospel into this country.

To keep these ideas alive in our minds, we resolve that this Agreement shall be read publically, at every station, at our three annual meetings, vis., on the first Lord's day in January, in May, and October.[1]

Appendix 5

A Most Painful Task

This evening a most painful task fell to me; to speak a word of reproach to Felix. I feel much, my dear Sir, in communicating this; but as I wish to write with the utmost freedom and confidence to you, I think I ought not to withhold anything which tends to give you a just idea of the state of our Ch. (church) and the character of those who compose it, and surely it is not of small importance that you should be able to form a just idea of the persons whom you may be called hereafter to instruct with the power of God and the welfare of his cause. . . .

It is necessary first to say, that owing to Brother Carey's domestic affliction, his perpetual avocations, or perhaps an easiness of the temperament not wholly free from blame, his two eldest sons were left in great measure without control; hence obstinacy and self-will took a very deep root in their minds while, he, like David, never displeased them. I have heard that it was nothing uncommon for them at table to seize a favorite dish and appropriate it themselves without ceremony; if the fr (father) mildly remonstrated they would throw it from them in anger and refuse to taste a morsel. The good man saw and lamented the will but was too mild to apply an effectual remedy. When we were consolidated into our family, they were of course obliged to submit to rule; however their native propensities would sometimes appear and cause us almost to dread the moments when the management of mission would be in their hands. Felix had for some months past addicted himself to so luxurious a way of eating and drinking that at last it quite alarms us both on his own acct and for the sake of the family.

In vain did his father remonstrate, in vain did Bro. Ward, who loves him with peculiar affection, endeavor to restrain him by the most tender reproofs, nothing was produced but a kind of secret determination to persist. I could not see this, without almost trembling for the consequences of such obstinacy in a lad not yet 17. I thot that to refrain longer would be criminal. At our Saturday evening meeting, therefore, I addressed him, in the most earnest manner, telling him that as the admonitions of his father and his almost paternal friend had been ineffectual all my hope of his future usefulness depended upon my being able to make him feel. I then pointed out the certainty of his being ruined as a future missionary unless he governed his appetites, his manner, and threw away his obstinacy: and that if he persisted we had no other mode of preventing the other branches of the family being injured by his example but by begging them to discipline him. I laid before him the sin of disregarding his father's admonitions, that if he however determined to persist, I as a member of the family, could not behold the rules of it trampled on with impunity; nor as a member of the Church see him despise his f's (father's) word without holding him guilty in a high degree. I added, perhaps you may be angry with me for my plainness, but, God forbid I should fear to incur the anger of my person in the world in the cause of God. Brother C. (Carey) and W (Ward) took it up and urged it with much earnestness. Bro. W (Ward) especially telling him, you know how often I have warned you without effect. He then held up to him the example of young Fernandez, who is most amiable in his manners. "If" say he "I were to desire Fernandez to oblige me in anything, he would run with the greatest delight; but you would hardly move from your seat. I beg therefore you will lay these things closely to heart." When we broke up he retired to his room and seemed exceedingly affected. Thus, I have discharged a painful task relating the faults of my young friend. If I have done wrong forgive me and let it do no harm. Should you, or Bro. Fuller at any time write to him, or any of us, on this subject, it may be best to do it in general terms without any reference to this incident. I think scarcely anyone should see this account but you and Mrs. Sutcliff.[1]

Appendix **6**

Robert Hall's Experience
in the Leicester Asylum

Sir, they took away my watch, and confined me in a place which overlooked the ward in which were a number of pauper lunatics, practicing all manner of ludicrous anticks. Sir, this sight was enough to make me ten times worse; they were as mad as March hares. I was at times quite insensible. I don't believe Dr. Arnold was aware how I was treated by a lazy keeper. Do you know, sir, to save himself a little time and trouble, (being winter) the fellow came at five o'clock, and fastened me down upon my bed, where I could not sir either hand or foot, till about eight o'clock the next morning. During this time I had many lucid intervals he had no business to leave me, sir, so long, but it was to enable him to go away sooner. You cannot conceive the honor of my situation, when I found myself perfectly sensible.

Now, sir, I hope, if ever I am taken ill again, you will use all your influence to prevent my being sent there a second time. It is a very mistaken notion, that severity is requisite. Mild treatment, with proper restraint and kindness, is all that is necessary in such cases. There is nothing so beneficial as private confinement, with proper medical attendance, to prevent abuses by unfeeling keepers.[1]

209

Letter of John Thomas

Dearly Beloved Body,

Thou knowest well how much I have lost or expended for thy sake, or why dost thou grumble or resist or scant back whenever I call thee? Had I been strict, or regular, or severe with thee, I should never have had little trouble or none in getting thee to perform thy duty: but now having imprudently indulged thee so long a time, if I venture to call thee from thine ease, thou dost instantly become angry. Now my dear body, I see my ends & resolve to restrain. I am my Master or should have kept thee under or I am now hit or nigh determined to do so. Thou shalt be in subjection or if not I will _____ thee to death. But if thou submit then thou and I like two yokefellows shall go on comfortably and thou shalt have profit and comfort at last.

Dearly Beloved Body
Thine to rule over thee
JT Soul[1]

Appendix **8**

Sources for the Carey Story

In light of all the distortion about Dorothy Carey, how do we go about finding out what really happened? How can we know what is true and what has been fancied in someone's imagination? Our best hope would be to read Dorothy's own descriptions of her thoughts and feelings while all of these momentous events were swirling around her. But, unfortunately, we do not have any surviving letters or journals from her hand. The next best sources are the letters and journals of her contemporaries, people who knew her and her life. For the most part, we can still read these documents in manuscript form. These then become the primary sources for our story. In a few instances we have to rely on nineteenth-century reprintings of the documents in cases where the original manuscripts have not survived.

Our next best sources are properly called secondary sources, those just one step removed from the eyewitness level. With care these information sources can be helpful in fleshing out the events of Dorothy's story.

Nonetheless, we must admit that we simply do not know many of the facts that we would like to know about Dorothy and her life. These gaps in the story can be frustrating. The best we can do in light of this partial information is to speculate what the various options are at these gaps in the story. I have tried to identify each of these instances, and would invite the reader to participate in deciding what explanations are the most probable ones, even though we may never come to absolute confidence about some of these matters.

Regarding sources, we should also recognize some of the limitations in recreating a story based on letters, and missionary letters at that. Early missionaries wrote home only when a ship arrived in Calcutta. They knew it would likely sail within a few weeks and could take mail back to England. So correspondence was often governed more by when a ship was in port than by when a missionary had news to write about. During many of the years we are concerned with, Carey wrote letters to

211

those with whom he was corresponding about once every five or six months. While some letter writers are able to give full and even coverage for most events occurring in a five- or six-month period, most of us are better at writing about recent events or plans for the immediate future. So this sporadic pattern of correspondence may give us an uneven reconstruction of events.

One positive feature of the pattern is that Carey would send off three or four letters with the same ship, thus giving us several versions of the same events with different levels of candor. The candor of Carey's letters, of course, depended on the recipient and Carey's relationship with that person. The letters with the least amount of information about his family tend to be those addressed to the Baptist Missionary Society.[1] Next in level of candor would be his correspondence with personal friends such as Andrew Fuller, John Ryland, and John Sutcliffe. Even though these men were also officials in the sending society, Carey's relationship with them as individuals was close and he was often candid in his letters to them. Sutcliffe was the one friend in England who kept the most contact with Dorothy's family in Piddington and Hackleton. Thus letters to Sutcliffe nearly always mentioned Dorothy.[2]

Carey's letters to his brother Peter and to his father Edmund did contain some information about the family, but it was always cautious and understated. Carey was always concerned for the personal salvation of his father, brother, nephews, and nieces, and so was careful not to say anything to them that might prove a hindrance to their belief in the gospel.[3] Those letters with the most personal information are those to his sisters Mary (Polly) Carey and Ann Hobson.

In the early and uncertain years of their time in Bengal, the missionaries worried that their letters might be opened by the East India Company. England was at war with France, and at times a sense of paranoia about enemy spies prevailed in Calcutta. At one point mission officials in England became concerned when one of the Baptist missionaries in Bengal, John Fountain, made some sharp political comments in his letters home to England.[4] We do not know whether this fear about censorship might have affected what William said about Dorothy's disturbance. Some of her behavior while she was out of touch with reality might have given the East India Company cause for alarm and hence William might have been cautious about what he wrote regarding Dorothy. We cannot know with certainty.

In quotations from William Carey's journal I have taken care to retain the flavor of his original writing as well as to make his entries readable. Thus I have changed capitalization to modern usage and have inserted periods at the completion of his sentences. But I have not changed his spelling or grammar.[5] Carey at times could be careless. After he wrote to England asking that all society materials take care to spell Indian names and terms consistently, Andrew Fuller replied:

> You must allow me again to remind you of your punctuation. I never knew a person of so much knowledge as you profess of other languages, write English so bad (sic). Where your sentence ends you very commonly make only a semicolon instead of a period. If your Bengal New Testament should be thus pointed I should tremble for its fate.[7]

Notes

Introduction

1. Mary Drewery, *William Carey: Shoemaker and Missionary* (London: Hodder and Stoughton, 1978), p. 32.

2. Neil Gunson, "On the Incidence of Alcoholism and Intemperance in Early Pacific Missions," *Journal of Pacific History* 1 (1966): 43–62.

3. For these and other accounts, see Ruth Tucker, *From Jerusalem to Irian Jaya: A Biographical History of Christian Missions* (Grand Rapids: Zondervan, 1983); Ruth Tucker and Walter Liefeld, *Daughters of the Church: Women and Ministry from New Testament Times to the Present* (Grand Rapids: Zondervan, 1987).

4. J. N. Ogilvie, *The Apostles of India* (London: Hodder and Stoughton, 1915), p. 296.

5. Charlotte M. Yonge, *Pioneers and Founders* (Macmillan, 1871), p. 97.

6. T. Wright, *William Carey* (London: Pearce, 1896), p. 5.

7. J. B. Myers, *William Carey: The Shoemaker Who Became the Father and Founder of Modern Missions* (Kilmarnock, Scotland: John Ritchie, 1887), p. 90.

8. J. Culross, *William Carey* (London: Hodder and Stoughton, 1881), p. 13.

9. R. E. Speer, *Some Great Leaders in the World Movement* (New York: Fleming Revell, 1911), p. 61. Speer is incorrect. Dorothy was the sister-in-law of his former employer.

10. Ibid., pp. 61–62.

11. From the unsigned introduction to the 1891 facsimile edition of William Carey, *Enquiry* (London: Hodder and Stoughton, 1792), p. xxii.

12. George Smith, *The Life of William Carey*, 2d ed. (London: John Murray, 1887), pp. 20, 162.

13. See E. Showalter, *The Female Malady: Women, Madness, and English Culture, 1830–1980* (London: Virago Press, 1985). Showalter argues that prejudice against women who were mentally disturbed was even harsher than that against mentally disturbed men.

14. W. Cathcart, ed., *The Baptist Encyclopedia* (Philadelphia: Louis Everts, 1881), p. 182.

15. John Clark Marshman, *The Life and Times of Carey, Marshman, and Ward*, 2 vols. (London: Longman, Brown, Green, Longmans, and Roberts, 1859), 1:6.

16. Speer, *Great Leaders*, p. 62. See also Smith, *William Carey* (1887), p. 162.

17. William Carey, Journal, February 4, 1795 [BMS].

18. Eustace Carey, *Memoir of William Carey, D.D.* (London: Jackson and Walford, 1836), p. 86. In fact, Eustace Carey's treatment was so balanced that he came under the severe criticism of his Victorian contemporaries. For example, John Fenwick wrote: "The work of Eustace Carey is a failure. He seems not only unable to grasp the character of his mighty uncle, but, with a obliquity all his own, he labours to cool down the fame of that great missionary to the tempera-

ture of an ordinary minister of the cross" (cited in William Herbert, *Biographical Notice of the Rev. William Carey, D.D. of Serampore* [Newcastle: T. and J. Hodgson, 1843], p. 1).

19. Marshman, *Life and Times,* 1:53. Marshman overlooked the fact that Dorothy lived in Leicestershire, the county north of Northamptonshire, from 1789 to 1793.

20. S. P. Carey, *William Carey, D.D., Fellow of the Linnean Society,* 8th ed. (London: Carey Press, 1934), p. xii.

21. S. Farrar and J. Roberts, *Where They Are* (Dallas, Tex.: NBC Players, 1988), p. 2.

22. J. Dirkey, "William Carey of India," a transcribed dramatization in the Stories of Great Christians series. While this dramatization contains a significant number of errors, it sometimes errs in the opposite direction in how it portrays Dorothy. For example, the drama portrays her as going through a spiritual renewal just prior to her consent to accompany William. The evidence we have available refutes this portrayal.

23. A burial appears in the parish register [NCRO] of a Lucy Plackett on May 13, 1784. She could have been Dorothy's mother. The register, however, does not identify her husband or her age at the time of death. This Lucy Plackett died three years after Dorothy married William.

24. Letter from Christopher Anderson to John Clark Marshman, December 25, 1834, cited in H. Anderson, *The Life and Letters of Christopher Anderson* (Edinburgh: William P. Kennedy, 1854), p. 313.

25. The term "insanity" is used in this book in a nontechnical manner. Technically, insanity is a legal term and is defined by a court of law. In broader and earlier usage, the term referred to those states of psychological functioning that we refer to today as psychopathology or mental illness. The use of the term in this work is in line with late eighteenth-century medicine. The term "insanity" is to be preferred over two other eighteenth-century terms for emotional disturbance: lunacy and madness. See Thomas Arnold, *Observations on the Nature, Kinds, Causes, and Preventions of Insanity, Lunacy, or Madness* (Leicester: G. Ireland, 1782), 1:14.

26. S. P. Hays, "History and Genealogy: Patterns of Change and Prospects for Cooperation," in *Generations and Change: Genealogical Perspectives in Social History,* ed. R. M. Taylor and R. J. Crandall (Macon, Ga.: Mercer University Press, 1986), p. 34.

27. H. L. McBeth, *The Baptist Heritage* (Nashville, Tenn.: Broadman Press, 1987), p. 186.

Chapter 1

1. The curate who entered the record of this event in the parish register no doubt was more convincing in his blessing given to Daniel and Lucy Plackett than he was accurate in his spelling. He must have spelled phonetically, because Dorothy is entered as "Dority" and Lucy as "Lusi." He did no better in 1763, when he entered the record of Dorothy's younger sister Catherine's baptism. Her name appears as "Kathran," daughter of Daniel and "Luci" [NCRO].

2. R. L. Greenall, *A History of Northamptonshire* (London: Phillimore, 1979), p. 30.

3. J. Gould, *Northamptonshire* (Shire Publications, 1988), p. 5.

4. Ibid., pp. 44–45.

5. Greenall, *Northamptonshire,* p. 80.

6. The situation is now somewhat reversed. A 1935 reorganization took the old hamlet of Hackleton and the old parish village of Piddington and formed the new civil parish of Hackleton.

7. Parish charities are responsible for the survival of these documents. Before the days of government involvement in assistance to the poor, parishes such as Piddington were wholly dependent for welfare funds on legacies from wealthy persons in the vicinity. For example, Judith Willoughby's will of 1704 set up an annuity from lands that she owned for the purpose of apprenticing poor boys who were living in Piddington. Each boy who successfully completed an apprenticeship would receive a respectable sum of money. See W. Whellan, *History, Gazeteer, and Directory of Northamptonshire* (London: Whittaker, 1849).

Two other charities existed in the parish, both of which came about because of enclosure acts. Prior to enclosure in England, all farmers were assigned certain strips of arable land and were given rights to the common or pasture areas of the village. This medieval system was designed to ensure that each farmer would have a proportion of excellent land as well as a share of marginal land. The poor of a village also had the right to graze animals on the common. In Piddington, they also had certain rights to collect wood in the nearby forest. Enclosure ended this ancient system by switching all the arable ground, pasture, and woods of a village to enclosed pieces of land, a farming approach with which we are more familiar. In this process, the poor lost out on some of their privileges and rights. As a consequence many of the parliamentary enclosure acts made provision in the enclosure of parish property for the poor. In Piddington, Parliament provided for the poor in the following manner:

> The poor's Allotment consists of four acres, which was awarded at the inclosure of Salcey Forest, for the use of the poor of this parish, in lieu of their right to take sear and broken wood from the Common. This land has been let for £5 a year. The poor's Allotment for the hamlet of Hackleton consists of 13a. 1r. 28p. awarded to nine trustees on the inclosure of Piddington, to cut the furze and thorns growing thereon, and to distribute the same among the poor inhabitants; and to let the pasturage of the land, and apply the rents in paying the land tax, and other charges affecting the property.

Most often the parish church officials became trustees of these charitable provisions for the poor. For this reason a set of documents regarding the parochial records of Piddington has survived (Whellan, *Northamptonshire*, p. 265). Church officials had to keep all land documents pertaining to the lands they were administering. Apparently some of the land that church officials supervised for charity in the nineteenth century had been the very same land farmed by Dorothy's father, Daniel Plackett.

8. We do not know the date of his death. At the end of his life he was an active dissenter from the Anglican Church, and would probably not have been buried in an Anglican cemetery.

9. Piddington burial register [NCRO].

10. Piddington marriage register [NCRO].

11. R. W. Malcolmson, *Life and Labour in England: 1700–1780* (London: Hutchinson, 1981), p. 62.

12. Ibid., p. 95.

13. "Further Report of the Commissioners for Inquiring Concerning Charity," 1825 [NCRO].

14. Entrance requirements varied greatly. Some were free schools for sons of the parish (such as the one in Daventry, 1576); others were charity schools for the poor (such as the one in Braunston, 1833). Some of the legacies stipulated which subjects were to be taught. The poor boys of Great and Little Preston were to learn reading, writing, and accounts (Preston Capes, 1637). The poor children of Guilsborough were instructed in the Scriptures (1710). Some schools had a tough entrance requirement: Students had to be able to read a chapter of the Bible before they could attend (as in Duddington, 1667). Some schools had boarding facilities. In Finedon, the girls were employed in lace making outside of school hours (one of two Northamptonshire charity schools for girls only, 1714). Some schools had limited enrollments (only six to eight children at a time). The majority of bequests allowed for either boys or girls to attend, but in actual fact most of these schools in 1825 had boys only attending by default (ibid.).

15. Whellan, *Northamptonshire*, p. 265.

16. Malcolmson, *Life and Labour*, p. 17.

17. Ibid., p. 59.

18. Ibid., p. 60.

19. Ibid., p. 61.

20. Sara, daughter of Robert and Priscilla Plackett, was christened April 23, 1758, and buried exactly one year later, on April 23, 1759 (Piddington parish registers [NCRO]).

21. Malcolmson, *Life and Labour*, p. 74.

22. See her document in Eustace Carey, *Memoir of William Carey, D.D.* (London: Jackson and Walford, 1836), pp. 22–37.

23. Cited in J. Taylor, *Biographical and Literary Notices of William Carey, D.D.* (Northampton: Dryden Press, 1886), p. 21. Emphasis is in Taylor's rendition of the letter.

24. Letter from William Carey to Andrew Fuller, August 14, 1804, cited in Carey, *Memoir*, p. 8.

25. See also M. Drewery, *William Carey: Shoemaker and Missionary* (London: Hodder and Stoughton, 1978), who is of the same opinion.

26. D. Tippleston, *William Carey and Hackleton Baptist Church* (Northampton: Billingham and Son, 1956).

27. Greenall, *Northamptonshire*, p. 81.

28. Malcolmson, *Life and Labour*, p. 63.

29. Ibid., p. 64.

30. The Hackleton chapel, not formally organized into a church until 1781, first began meeting in 1767. In 1776 about 200 poor laborers attended—a very large group for such a small population. Hackleton was populated mainly by domestic servants, agricultural laborers, and cordwainers. The majority of people attending the meeting house were probably women. See C. D. Bond, *God's Forgotten People: A History of Carey Baptist Church, Hackleton*, n.d.

31. Greenall, *Northamptonshire*, p. 74.

32. I. Warren, *The Nonconformist Tradition* (Northampton: Northamptonshire Leisure and Libraries, 1987).

33. Parish marriage register [NCRO]. Carey also served as a witness on March 18, 1781, at the marriage of Asher Howes (a relative of Thomas Old) and Martha West. Clearly, Carey was making friends in his new home of Piddington cum Hackleton.

34. We do not know much about Clarke Nichols except that he married Frances Howes on October 10, 1777, in the Piddington church. Nichols was buried just two years later on October 5, 1779, leaving a widow and a 10-week-old son John. Clarke Nichols died intestate. A bond was posted in January 1780 for the administration of the estate and was signed with a mark by his widow, Frances, and Daniel Howes, probably her brother. They swore that the total value of Clarke's estate was less than £200.The family continued to live in the area. Clark Nichols, a grandson, was christened in Piddington on Christmas Day, 1802 [NCRO], and was listed as a beer retailer in 1849 (see Whellan, *Northamptonshire*).

35. Cited in Carey, *Memoir*, p. 27.

36. Malcolmson, *Life and Labour*, p. 68.

37. *The Book of Common Prayer and Administration of the Sacraments, and Other Ceremonies of the Church* (Cambridge: Joseph Bentham, 1759).

Chapter 2

1. The current successor to this church is the Carey Baptist Church of Hackleton. See C. D. Bond, *God's Forgotten People: A History of Carey Baptist Church, Hackleton*, n.d.

2. Ibid., p. 8.

3. Bond (ibid.) states that neither Clarke Nichols nor Thomas Old (the cordwainer to whom William was apprenticed) was a member of the Hackleton meeting. But S. P. Carey (*William Carey, D.D., Fellow of the Linnean Society*, 8th ed. [London: Carey Press, 1934], p. 40) lists Thomas Old as a charter member in the 1781 organization of the Hackleton church.

4. D. Kirby, D. Thomas, and L. Turner, *Northampton Remembers Boot and Shoe* (Northampton: Northampton Borough Council Community Programme, 1988), p. 7.

5. J. Swann, *Shoemaking* (Aylesbury, Bucks: Shire Publications, 1986), pp. 8–11.

6. See the *Northampton Independent*, December 22, 1937; and W. E. Winks, *Lives of Illustrious Shoemakers* (London: Sampson Low, Matston, Searle, and Rivington, 1883).

7. Ibid., p. 15.

8. This fact is stated on the plaque on the front of the Carey Memorial Baptist Chapel in Hackleton. See Bond, *God's Forgotten People*, p. 3.

9. We do not have the exact birth dates for six of the seven Carey children. We have christening dates for both William and Dorothy but only because their parents were Anglicans at the time. Because William and Dorothy objected to the baptism of infants in their newfound dissenting faith, no precise dates near the births of most of their children were recorded.

10. Carey, *William Carey*, 1934, p. 7. A portrait hastily painted in 1793 before Carey sailed for India and now hanging in the library of Regent's Park College in Oxford confirms these eye-witness evaluations of the wig. Carey allegedly threw the wig overboard on the journey to Calcutta.

11. Cited in Eustace Carey, *Memoir of William Carey, D.D.* (London: Jackson and Walford, 1836), p. 30.

12. M. Drewery, *William Carey: Shoemaker and Missionary* (London: Hodder and Stoughton, 1978), pp. 22–23.

13. Letter from William Carey to John Ryland, cited in J. Taylor, *Biographical and Literary Notices of William Carey, D.D.* (Northampton: Dryden Press, 1886), p. 9.

14. Thomas Old had married Elizabeth Plackett, Dorothy's sister, on October 22, 1769. In their marriage of fourteen years, they had had five children, one of whom died during infancy. Old's widow was left with four children from ages 3 to 13. Thomas had made provision for his family in a will, dated in 1782. Each of the four children was to receive £50 upon reaching majority age. Meanwhile the £200 was to be invested so that his widow could live off the interest. A codicil dated four days before his death wills a small cottage he had recently purchased from his mother to his wife. See Will of Thomas Old [NCRO]. Thomas had become so weak at this point that he was unable to sign his name, and made only a mark on the codicil.

15. Drewery, *William Carey*, p. 24.

16. Carey, *Memoir*, p. 44.

17. Taylor, *Notices*, p. 9.

18. Carey, *William Carey*, 1934, p. 42.

19. Excerpt from a speech at the meeting of the Baptist Missionary Society, London, June 1812, cited in Taylor, *Notices*, p. 36.

20. Carey, *William Carey*, 1934, p. 7.

21. H. L. McBeth, *The Baptist Heritage* (Nashville, Tenn.: Broadman Press, 1987).

22. Letter from Andrew Fuller to his father, August 25, 1792, cited in T. E. Fuller, *A Memoir of the Life and Writings of Andrew Fuller* (London: J. Heaton and Son, 1863), p. 76.

23. E. D. Bebb, *Nonconformity and Social and Economic Life: 1660–1800* (London: Epworth Press, 1935), p. 169.

24. This building still stands. Remodelers have converted the six flats into three and moved the entrances to the rear of the building. A commemorative plaque on the street side of the building commemorates the residency there of Dorothy and William.

25. J. B. Myers, *William Carey: The Shoemaker Who Became the Father and Founder of Modern Missions* (Kilmarnock, Scotland: John Ritchie, 1887).

26. M. J. Murphy, *Poverty in Cambridgeshire* (Cambridge: Oleander Press, 1978), p. 10.

27. Ibid., p. 28.

28. Ibid., pp. 14–15.

29. J. E. Palmer, "The Life and Times of William Carey," *Northamptonshire and Bedfordshire Times*, November 26–28, 1982.

30. R. W. Malcolmson, *Life and Labour in England: 1700–1780* (London: Hutchinson, 1981), pp. 14–17.

31. Letter from William Carey to his parents, March 3, 1787 [AL].

32. S. Mitchell, *Not Disobedient: A History of United Baptist Church, Leicester Including Harvey Lane 1760–1845, Belvoir Street 1845–1940 and Charles Street 1831–1940* (Leicester: Author, 1984), p. 24.

33. Cited in Eustace Carey, *Memoir of William Carey, D.D.* (London: Jackson and Walford, 1836), p. 68.

34. Andrew Gunton Fuller, *Andrew Fuller* (London: Hodder and Stoughton, 1882), p. 99.

35. John Newton had been the Anglican rector in Olney and was later to become helpful to Baptists because of his London connections. William Cowper had also lived and written in Olney.

36. Taylor, *Notices*, pp. 1–2.

37. Baptist polity of the day called for a new ordination whenever a pastor assumed a new pastorate.

38. Max Warren, *Social History and Christian Mission* (London: SCM Press, 1967), p. 38.

39. Moulton burial register [NCRO].

40. Letter from William Carey to John Sutcliffe, December 30, 1785, cited in Taylor, *Notices*, p. 36.

41. Ruth Bottoms, interview with author, May 3, 1990.

42. Cited in Taylor, *Notices*, pp. 3–4.

43. Letter from William Carey to his father, June 12, 1788 [AL].

44. Annual report of the Moulton church to the Baptist Association meeting, Kettering, May 27–28, 1788, cited in Taylor, *Notices*, p. 5.

45. Taylor, *Notices*, p. 3.

46. Ibid., p. 7.

47. Letter from William Carey to his father, November 12, 1790 [AL]. In the twentieth century, their Leicester cottage was demolished for a large urban development program in what is now central Leicester.

48. W. Gardiner, *Music and Friends* (London: Longman, Orme, Brown, and Longman, 1838), 1:393.

49. Myers, *William Carey*.

50. Taylor, *Notices*, pp. 6–7.

51. Mitchell, *Not Disobedient*, p. 25.

52. Cited in Carey, *Memoir*, p. 34.

53. Letter from William Carey to his father, November 12, 1790 [William Carey Collection, AL].

54. Drewery, *William Carey*, p. 33.

55. Mitchell, *Not Disobedient*, p. 27.

56. J. Culross, *William Carey* (London: Hodder and Stoughton, 1881), p. 40.

57. J. Nichols, *History and Antiquities of the County of Leicester* (reprint, Menston, Yorkshire: Scholar Press, 1971), 1:524.

58. W. L. Parry-Jones, *The Trade in Lunacy: A Study of Private Mad-Houses in England in the Eighteenth and Nineteenth Centuries* (London: Routledge and Kegan Paul, 1972), p. 78.

59. Peter K. Carpenter, "Thomas Arnold: A Provincial Psychiatrist in Georgian England," *Medical History* 33 (1989): 199–216.

60. Thomas Arnold, *Observations on the Nature, Kinds, Causes, and Preventions of Insanity, Lunacy, or Madness*, 2 vols. (Leicester: G. Ireland, 1782, 1786).

61. *Psychiatry and Mental Health in Britain: A Historical Exhibition, 1963* (London: Wellcome Historical Medical Library, 1963), p. 5.

62. E. R. Frizelle and J. D. Martin, *The Leicester Royal Infirmary, 1771–1971* (Leicester: Raithley, Lawrence, 1971), p. 82.

63. E. R. Frizelle, *The Life and Times of the Royal Infirmary at Leicester: The Making of a Teaching Hospital, 1766–1980* (Leicester: Leicester Medical Society, 1988), p. 189.

Chapter 3

1. Sutcliffe gave Carey a Latin grammar. See L. and M. Williams, eds., *Serampore Letters: Being the Unpublished Correspondence of William Carey and Others with John Williams, 1800–1816* (New York: G. P. Putnam's Sons, 1892), p. 6.

2. J. Culross, *William Carey* (London: Hodder and Stoughton, 1881).

3. E. A. Payne, "Two Dutch Translations by Carey: An Angus Library Find," *Baptist Quarterly* New Series 11 (1942): 35.

4. F. Deauville Walker, *William Carey: Missionary Pioneer and Statesman* (reprint, Chicago: Moody Press, 1980), demonstrates how the Northampton press greatly influenced Carey.

5. No public lending library existed in Northampton during the time Carey held a pastorate in Moulton. See T. M. Anstey, *A History of Libraries in Northampton from the Middle Ages until 1910* (Northampton: Northampton Central Library, 1971). Carey must have relished the comparatively rich access to books that he enjoyed in his next pastorate at Leicester.

6. G. W. Hughes, *Robert Hall* (London: Carey Press, 1943), p. 19.

7. Robert Hall, *Help to Zion's Travellers: Being an Attempt to Remove Various Stumbling Blocks out of the Way Relating to Doctrinal, Experimental, and Practical Religion* (London: Book Society, 1781).

8. Letter from William Carey to Andrew Fuller, August 14, 1804, cited in M. Drewery, *William Carey: Shoemaker and Missionary* (London: Hodder and Stoughton, 1978), p. 23.

9. *One Hundred Years After: A Sermon and Addresses, London, October, 1934* (London: Carey Press, 1934).

10. F. D. Walker, *William Carey: Missionary Pioneer and Statesman* (London: Student Christian Movement, 1926), p. 25.

11. See M. K. Beddie, ed., *Bibliography of Captain James Cook* (Sydney: University of New South Wales, 1970); and S. A. Spence, comp., *Captain James Cook: A Bibliography* (Mitcham, Surrey: Compiler, 1960).

12. A. G. Price, ed., *The Explorations of Captain James Cook in the Pacific As Told by Selections of His Own Journals 1768–1779* (Sydney: Angus and Robertson, 1969), p. 286.

13. *Encyclopaedia Britannica*, 15th ed., s.v. "Cook, James."

14. J. K. Munford, ed., *John Ludyard's Journal of Captain Cook's Last Voyage* (Corvallis, Oreg.: Oregon State University Press, 1963).

15. J. C. Beaglehole, "Cook the Man," in *Captain Cook: Navigator and Scientist*, ed. G. M. Badger (London: C. Hurst, 1970), p. 28.

16. T. and C. Stamp, *James Cook: Maritime Scientist* (Whitby, England: Caedmon of Whitby, 1978), pp. 148–49.

17. A. Villiers, *Captain Cook, The Seaman's Seaman: A Study of the Great Discoverer* (London: Hodder and Stoughton, 1967), p. 92.

18. Ibid., pp. 144–45.

19. We do know that groups of Moravians met for worship and fellowship in the Northampton area. See *A Short Sketch of the Work Carried on by the Ancient Protestant Episcopal Moravian Church in Northamptonshire* (London: Hazell, Watson, and Viney, 1886).

20. *Periodical Accounts Relating to the Missions of the Church of the United Brethren Established Among the Heathen* (1790), 1(1):6.

21. Ibid., 1(3):52.

22. Ibid., 1(4):62.

23. Ibid., p. 76.

24. Ibid., p. 77.

25. Ibid., pp. 78–79.

26. Ibid., 1(6):119.

27. Ibid., 1(7):129.

28. Among the books about Eliot available in England were J. Eliot and T. Mayhew, *Tears of Repentance or a Further Narrative of the Progress of the Gospel Amongst the Indians in New England* (London: n.p., 1653); J. Eliot, *A Brief Narrative of the Progress of the Gospel Amongst the Indians in New England in the Year 1670* (London: J. Allen, 1671); and Thomas Shepard, *The Clear Sunshine of the Gospel Breaking Forth Upon the Indians in New England* (London: R. Cotes, 1648).

29. Walker, *William Carey*. John Taylor (*Biographical and Literary Notices of William Carey, D.D.* [Northampton: Dryden Press, 1886], p. 30) wrote: "In the collection of Mr. Sheffield of Earl's Barton is a copy of The Life of Mr. David Brainerd; Published by Jonathan Edwards. Edinburgh, 1798. On the title page is the autograph of W. Carey."

30. David Brainerd, *An Abridgement of Mr. David Brainerd's Journal Among the Indians or the Rise and Progress of a Remarkable Work of Grace Among a Number of the Indians in the Provinces of New Jersey and Pennsylvania* (London: John Oswald, 1748), p. 23.

31. Ibid., p. 37.

32. Carey was also a great admirer of Edwards. On November 11, 1806, Carey wrote a letter to John Ryland telling of a unique experience in India: "A tall gentleman was one night introduced to me after preaching, whom I found to be Timothy Edwards, son of Timothy, son of President Edwards. You may guess at my feelings on that occasion. He is a very steady man, talked little, but I hope from his conversation he loves the truth. He attends our preaching here, but being master of a ship will soon go from us" [NYCRO].

33. Jonathan Edwards, *An Account of the Life of the Late Reverend Mr. David Brainerd* (Edinburgh: John Gray and Gavin Alston, 1765), p. v.

34. S. P. Carey, *William Carey, D.D., Fellow of the Linnean Society*, 8th ed. (London: Carey Press, 1934), p. 43.

35. Ibid., p. 57.

36. Jonathan Edwards, *An Humble Attempt to Promote Explicit Agreement and Visible Union of God's People in Extraordinary Prayer* (reprint, Northampton, Old England: T. Dicey, 1789).

37. "One Hundred and Fiftieth Anniversary," *Baptist Times*, June 14, 1984, p. 1.

38. Ernest A. Payne, *The Prayer Call of 1784* (London: Baptist Laymen's Missionary Movement, 1941).

39. These prayer groups spread to other denominations and were still meeting as late as 1816. See J. W. Morris, *Memoirs of the Life and Writings of the Rev. Andrew Fuller* (London: Author, 1816), p. 94.

40. Carey, *William Carey*, p. 54.

41. Ibid.

42. See Ernest A. Payne's introduction to the 1961 facsimile edition of the *Enquiry*.

43. Carey read a draft of his *Enquiry* to his friends who had gathered in Leicester on May 24, 1791, for his ordination to the pastorate at Harvey Lane Baptist Church.

44. Max Warren, *The Missionary Movement from Britain in Modern History* (London: SCM Press, 1965), p. 21.

45. Kenneth Scott Latourette, *A History of the Expansion of Christianity*, vol. 4 (London: Eyre and Spottiswoode, 1941).

46. Ernest A. Payne, "Carey's 'Enquiry': An Essay for the Ter-Jubilee," *International Review of Missions* 31(1942): 185.

47. Ibid.

48. One London shopkeeper who sold the *Enquiry* was Joseph Johnson of St. Paul's Churchyard. He also published the radical *Vindication of the Rights of Women* by Mary Wollstonecraft. Ibid.

49. William Carey, *An Enquiry into the Obligations of Christians to Use Means for the Conversion of the Heathens* (Leicester: Ann Ireland, 1792), p. 38.

50. Ibid., pp. 62–63.

51. Ibid., p. 64.

52. He also felt that Isaiah 60:9 ("Surely the islands look to me; in the lead are the ships of Tarshish, bringing your sons from afar, with their silver and gold, to the honor of the Lord your God, the Holy One of Israel, for he has endowed you with splendor") was a prophecy that missions would follow in the wake of commerce. Ibid., p. 67. Thus the East India Company, to Carey, would become a Cyrus, not a Pharaoh.

53. Ibid., p. 68.

54. Ibid., p. 72.

55. Ibid., p. 73.

56. Carey was here referring to slavery. Ibid., p. 86.

57. Warren, *Missionary Movement*, p. 22.

58. Letters [AL].

59. Williams, *Serampore Letters*, p. 11.

Chapter 4

1. J. Culross, *William Carey* (London: Hodder and Stoughton, 1881), p. 50.

2. C. B. Lewis, *The Life of John Thomas* (London: Macmillan, 1873), p. 11.

3. M. Siddiq Khan ("William Carey and the Serampore Books [1800–1834]," *Libri* 11 [1961]:208) states that Thomas "got into monetary difficulties through investing in , among other things, the great Calcutta Lottery."

4. See Appendix 7 for an undated letter from Thomas's soul to his body [BMS].

5. John Clark Marshman, *The Life and Times of Carey, Marshman, and Ward* (London: Longman, Brown, Green, Longmans, and Roberts, 1859), 1:30. However, the Victoria County History for Gloucestershire does not list a medical school for that county. Thus we cannot establish the quantity or quality of Thomas's medical training.

6. M. H. Khan, "History of Printing in Bengali Characters up to 1866" (Ph.D. diss, School of Oriental and African Studies, University of London, 1976), p. 213.

7. Ibid.

8. S. P. Carey, *William Carey, D.D., Fellow of the Linnean Society*, 8th ed. (London: Carey Press, 1934), p. 105.

9. Letter from Andrew Fuller to William Steadman, cited in T. Steadman, *Memoir of the Rev. William Steadman, D.D.* (London: Thomas Ward, 1838), p. 117.

10. John Ryland, *Life and Death of the Rev. Andrew Fuller* (London: Button and Son, 1818), pp. 151–52. The society urged Carey to cease his school teaching so that more time could be dedicated to necessary preparations. The society paid him the income that he lost as a result of this decision.

11. T. E. Fuller, *A Memoir of the Life and Writings of Andrew Fuller* (London: J. Heaton and Son, 1863), p. 70. See Appendix 1 for a description of Mrs. Fuller's mental illness.

12. Carey, *William Carey*, p. 111.

13. Letter from Andrew Fuller to William Steadman, in Steadman, *Memoir*, pp. 116–17.

14. Marshman, *Life and Times*, p. 53.

15. P. E. C. Manson-Bahr and F. I. C. Apted, *Manson's Tropical Diseases*, 18th ed. (London: Balliere Tindall, 1982), p. 13.

16. Earlier the company had been much more tolerant. John Kiernanader, a Swede sent by the Danish Missionary Board, had entered India without any opposition. The change in company attitude occurred around 1790. See J. Richter, *A History of Missions in India* (Edinburgh: Oliphant, Anderson and Ferrier, 1980).

17. C. H. Philips, *The East India Company, 1784–1834* (Manchester: University Press, 1961), p. 158.

18. J. N. Ogilvie, *Our Empire's Debt to Missions* (London: Hodder and Stoughton, 1924).

19. The charter of the East India Company was subject to renewal by Parliament every twenty years.

20. David Brainerd, *An Abridgement of Mr. David Brainerd's Journal Among the Indians or the Rise and Progress of a Remarkable Work of Grace Among a Number of the Indians in the Provinces of New Jersey and Pennsylvania* (London: John Oswald, 1748), pp. 57–58.

21. M. Drewery, *William Carey: Shoemaker and Missionary* (London: Hodder and Stoughton, 1978), p. 45.

22. C. D. Bond, *God's Forgotten People: A History of Carey Baptist Church, Hackleton*, n.d.

23. Drewery, *William Carey*, p. 44.

24. J. Hunter, *The Gospel of Gentility: American Women Missionaries in Turn-of-the-Century China* (New Haven: Yale University Press, 1984), p. 90.

25. F. D. Walker, *William Carey: Missionary Pioneer and Statesman* (London: Student Christian Movement, 1926).

26. Carey, *William Carey*, p. 114.

27. Ibid., p. 115.

28. Letter from William Carey to his father, January 17, 1793, cited in ibid., p. 110.

29. Eustace Carey, *Memoir of William Carey, D.D.* (London: Jackson and Walford, 1836), p. 77.

30. J. B. Myers, *William Carey: The Shoemaker Who Became the Father and Founder of Modern Missions* (Kilmarnock, Scotland: John Ritchie, 1887).

31. "Extracts from the Late Rev. A. Fuller's Correspondence with the Late Rev. Mr. Stevens, of Colchester," *Baptist Magazine* 8 (1816): 452–53.

32. Carey, *Memoir*, p. 86.

33. Carey, *William Carey*, p. 114.

34. Ibid., p. 122.

35. E. A. Payne, "Carey and His Biographers," *Baptist Quarterly* 19 (1961): 8.

36. B. R. Pearn, "Felix Carey and the English Baptist Mission in Burma," *Journal of the Burma Research Society* 28 (1938): 2.

37. Carey, *William Carey*, p. 110.

38. Lewis, *John Thomas*, p. 234. Lewis also mentioned "Mr. Thomas' black boy Andrew," although we know nothing more about him (ibid., p. 237).

39. Letter from William Carey to his sisters, April 25, 1793 [William Carey Collection, AL].

40. Ibid.

41. Letter from William Carey to his father, May 2, 1793 [William Carey Collection, AL].

42. Myers, *William Carey*, p. 33; John Taylor, *Biographical and Literary Notices of William Carey, D.D.* (Northampton: Dryden Press, 1886), p. 37.

43. Among the expenditures of the first year of the Baptist Society for Propagating the Gospel Among the Heathen was £17, s15, d0 given "to Mrs. Carey during her residence at Piddington, according to agreement, in case she had not gone with Mr. Carey, one quarter in advance and five guineas for expence attending her lying in" (Taylor, *Notices*, pp. 31–32).

44. Letter from John Thomas to Andrew Fuller, March 10, 1794 [BMS].

45. Carey, *Memoir*, p. 36.

46. Letter from John Thomas to Andrew Fuller, March 10, 1794 [BMS].

47. Ibid.

48. The sale of their property netted £18, 10s (Marshman, *Life and Times*, vol. 1).

49. Letter from William Carey to John Sutcliffe, May 24, 1793 [BMS].

50. Letter from Andrew Fuller to Rev. J. Saffrey, May 30, 1793 [Wittaker gift per B. Grey Griffiths, BMS].

51. Unsigned statement in *Brief Narrative of the Baptist Mission in India*, 5th ed. (Bristol: J. G. Fuller, 1819), p. 8.

Chapter 5

1. Unsigned note [BMS]. Three people could have written it: William, Dorothy, or Kitty. The salutation might suggest either Dorothy or Kitty. But we do not have samples of Dorothy's handwriting, and the only extant samples of Kitty's handwriting are dated 1808. The handwriting on the note is quite similar to William's. If he wrote the note, he obviously was in a hurry, because the date on the note is incorrect. Their sailing date was June 13, not June 14. Perhaps William called his father-in-law "father."

2. John Thomas, Journal [BMS].

3. S. K. Chatterjee, *Missions in India: A Catalogue of the Carey Library* (Serampore: Council of Serampore College, 1980).

4. William Carey, Journal, June 13, 1793 [BMS].

5. Eustace Carey, *Memoir of William Carey, D.D.* (London: Jackson and Walford, 1836), p. 118.

6. Letter from William Carey to the Baptist Missionary Society, cited in ibid., p. 118.

7. Ibid., p. 122.

8. Letter from John Thomas to an unknown addressee, October 26, 1793, cited in ibid., p. 100.

9. Journal, July 23–August 2 [BMS]. In a letter to Andrew Fuller dated January 2, 1794, Carey says that he wants a third son to learn Chinese. "And if God should hereafter bless them with his grace, this may fit them for a mission to any part of Persia, India, or China" [NYCRO].

10. Letter of John Thomas, October 26, 1793, in Carey, *Memoir*, p. 100.

11. Journal, September 20, 1793 [BMS].

12. Letter from Andrew Fuller to William Carey and John Thomas, March 25, 1794 [AL].

13. Journal, November 9, 1793.

14. The shortage of cash that soon developed for the missionary team in Calcutta may not have been due only to Thomas's financial irresponsibility. The original planning had been for only two people. Now six members of the Carey family needed food and shelter. Mrs. Thomas had to borrow money to live in Calcutta during the weeks that she waited for her husband to arrive. See C. B. Lewis, *The Life of John Thomas* (London: Macmillan, 1873), pp. 257–61.

15. Journal, January 13, 1794 [BMS].

16. Letter from William Carey to Andrew Fuller, December 26, 1793, entry dated January 2, 1794 [NYCRO].

17. Journal, November 9, 1793 [BMS].

18. E. D. Potts, *British Baptist Missionaries in India, 1793–1837: The History of Serampore and Its Missions* (Cambridge: University Press, 1967), p. 14.

19. Letter from William Carey to his father, November 25, 1793 [AL]. Carey detested West Indian sugar because of the use of slaves to grow the sugarcane.

20. Dating the onset of their illness is difficult. On January 3, 1794, Carey said that his wife had been ill for one month (letter from William Carey to John Sutcliffe, January 3, 1794, cited in Carey, *Memoir*, pp. 137–38). On August 9, 1794, Carey said his wife had been ill for eight months (letter from William Carey to John Sutcliffe, August 9, 1794, cited in ibid., p. 193). On November 13, 1794, he wrote that his family was well (Journal, November 11–13, 1794 [BMS]). Carey calculated that his wife was ill for a total of twelve months (letter from William Carey to Richard Brewin, March 12, 1795 [BMS]). Hence she must have contracted dystentery soon after landing in Calcutta. J. B. Myers dates the onset somewhat later, in Bandel (*William Carey: The Shoemaker Who Became the Father and Founder of Modern Missions* [Kilmarnock, Scotland: John Ritchie, 1887]).

21. Letter from William Carey to Andrew Fuller, November 14, 1793, cited in Carey, *Memoir*, p. 121.

22. O. P. Jaggi, *Western Medicine in India: Epidemics and Other Tropical Diseases* (Delhi: Atma Ram and Sons, 1979), p. 226. The presence of pus led observers to suspect the involvement of the liver. See Charles Curtis, *An Account of the Diseases of India as They Appeared in the English Fleet and in the Naval Hospital at Madras in 1782 and 1783*, cited in ibid., pp. 223–24.

23. Carey was aware of this theory and agreed with it: "My wife and two children have been very ill indeed because of the Bloody Flux I believe occasioned by the cold nights, succeeding to hot days. The thermometer differing about 15 or 20 degrees between day and night" (letter from William Carey to Andrew Fuller, February 15, 1794, cited in L. and M. Williams, eds., *Serampore Letters: Being the Unpublished Correspondence of William Carey and Others with John Williams, 1800–1816* [New York: G. P. Putnam's Sons, 1892], p. 43).

24. The main symptom of dystentery is diarrhea with blood and pus. See B. Maegraith, *Clinical Tropical Diseases*, 8th ed. (Oxford: Blackwell Scientific Publications, 1984), p. 60. The disease is contracted by consuming food or water contaminated by infected human feces. The spread of the disease is often related to the poor hygiene of a food handler.

25. A. W. Woodruff and S. Bell, *A Synopsis of Infectious and Tropical Diseases*, 2d ed. (Bristol: John Wright and Sons, 1978), p. 29.

26. Jaggi, *Western Medicine*, p. 228.

27. Waltraud Ernst, "The Rise of the European Lunatic Asylum in Colonial India (1750–1858)," *Bulletin of the Indian Institute of History of Medicine* 17 (1987): 100.

28. Interview with Dr. Denis Leigh, The Maudsley Hospital, Denmark Hill, London, June 12, 1990.

29. Journal, January 13, 1793 [BMS].

30. Letter from William Carey to his sisters, December 4, 1793 [AL].

31. Ibid.

32. C. B. Lewis, *The Life of John Thomas* (London: Macmillan, 1873), p. 253.

33. Ibid.

34. Letter from William Carey to John Sutcliffe, January 3, 1794 [BMS].

35. Journal, January 13, 1794 [BMS].

36. J. Culross, *William Carey* (London: Hodder and Stoughton, 1881), p. 62.

37. Letter from William Carey to John Sutcliffe, January 3, 1794 [BMS].

38. Journal, January 13, 1794 [BMS].

39. Ibid.

40. Letter from William Carey to John Sutcliffe, January 3, 1794, cited in Carey, *Memoir*, p. 138.

41. Rice was not cultivated in England. Rice was available there only as an imported food, perhaps from Italy. Dorothy may never even have tasted rice before her departure for India. Rice, although a grain, does not make good bread.

42. Some authors (such as Drewery and Middlebrook) date the beginning of Dorothy's mental illness at this point in the story. Two facts, however, discount this possibility: (1) both Dorothy and her sister Kitty were upset in Manicktullo, but no one has ever suggested that Kitty was also mentally ill; and (2) complaining and arguing, as disruptive as they may be to family life, are not the equivalents of mental illness.

43. Journal, January 15–16, 1794 [BMS]. Carey's reference here to groundless fears raises the possibility of a phobic state. But the evidence is not strong enough for us to diagnose such a condition at this point. Carey's ability to separate realistic from groundless fears was not astute enough for us to be able to rely on his observations on this detail.

44. Letter from William Carey to John Sutcliffe, January 3, 1794 [BMS].

45. Journal, January 17, 1794 [BMS].

46. Letter from William Carey to Andrew Fuller, January 2, 1794 [NYCRO].

47. Culross, *William Carey*, p. 66.

48. Lewis (*John Thomas*) states that Carey had received money from John Thomas after arriving in India for the purchase of items that they were unable to bring with them in the haste of leaving (shoes, dishes, furniture, etc.).

49. Journal, February 5, 1794 [BMS].

50. Letter from William Carey to John Sutcliffe, August 9, 1794 [BMS].

51. S. P. Carey, *William Carey, D.D., Fellow of the Linnean Society*, 8th ed. (London: Hodder and Stoughton, 1934), p. 251.

52. Potts, *British Baptist Missionaries*, p. 14.

53. Carey, *William Carey*, p. 251.

54. George Udney's brother and sister-in-law, Mr. and Mrs. Robert Udney, had drowned in a night accident on the Hooghly River (Carey, *William Carey*, p. 155).

55. M. Drewery, *William Carey: Shoemaker and Missionary* (London: Hodder and Stoughton, 1978), p. 76.

56. Journal, March 2–4, 1794 [BMS].

57. Lewis, *John Thomas*, p. 263.

58. Culross, *William Carey*, p. 66.

59. M. A. Sherring, *The History of Protestant Missions in India* (London: Trubner, 1875), p. 134.

60. Lewis, *John Thomas*, p. 284. Carey and Thomas were able to obtain such permits because of their employment with Udney so that from 1797 to 1802 they were legally in company territory.

61. Journal [BMS].

62. Journal, April 8–10, 1794 [BMS].

63. Journal, March 31, 1794. The society wisely disregarded Carey's impetuous request.

64. Kitty Plackett and Charles Short were married on November 15, 1794 (Lewis, *John Thomas*, p. 267) after a properly chaperoned period of engagement (Carey, *William Carey*, p. 158).

65. One day later Andrew Fuller in England finally heard that the ship on which the Careys had sailed had arrived safely in India (entry dated May 24, 1794, in a letter from Andrew Fuller to John Thomas and William Carey begun March 25, 1794 [AL]).

66. Journal, May 23, 1794 [BMS].

67. Journal [BMS].

68. Journal, June 25–26, 1794 [BMS].

69. Letter from William Carey to his father, October 5, 1795 [AL].

70. Ibid.

71. Ibid.

72. Journal, July 5, 1794 [BMS].

73. Journal, August 11–15, 1794 [BMS].

74. Journal, August 5–7, 1794 [BMS].

75. Journal [BMS].

76. Journal, September 1–October 11, 1794 [BMS].

77. Ibid.

78. Letter from William Carey to his father, August 8, 1794 [AL].

79. Journal, September 1–October 11, 1794 [BMS]. Carey's description of Peter's symptoms does not help us pinpoint the cause of death. A two-week illness of this sort could have been either bacillary or amoebic dystentery. A very sudden and brief illness resulting in death would probably have been cholera (interview with Denis Leigh).

80. Journal, ibid.

81. Carey, *Memoir*.

82. Years later the issue of caring for the deceased was still a problem for missionaries. When Carey's son Jabez had to bury a young daughter in 1819, he encountered the same problems his parents did in 1794 (letter from Jabez Carey to William Carey, January 25, 1819 [AL]). Jabez and his wife Eliza had to bury their daughter in a trunk they were using on that trip. Similar frustrations occurred when John Chamberlain had to bury his wife at Cutwa (S. K. Chatterjee, *Hannah Marshman: The First Woman Missionary in India* [Hooghly, India: S. S. Chatterjee, 1987], p. 55).

83. Journal, September 1–October 11, 1794 [BMS].

84. Letter of Jabez Carey to William Carey, January 25, 1819 [AL].

85. Journal, September 1–October 11, 1794 [BMS].

86. Ibid.

87. Ibid.

Chapter 6

1. Journal, October 28, 1794 [BMS].
2. Journal, December 5, 1794 [BMS].
3. Journal, December 22–31, 1794 [BMS].
4. Journal, January 18, 1795 [BMS].
5. Journal, January 1–15, 1795 [BMS].
6. Letter from John Thomas to Andrew Fuller, January 11, 1796 [BMS].
7. Journal, January 1–15, 1795 [BMS].
8. Letter from John Thomas to Andrew Fuller, January 11, 1796 [BMS]. Some biographers (such as A. Dakin, *William Carey: Shoemaker, Linguist, Missionary* [London: Carey Press, 1942]; and C. B. Lewis, *The Life of John Thomas* [London: Macmillan, 1873]) appear to have known the true nature of Dorothy's mental illness. Perhaps they chose not to publish these details because a frank discussion of emotional difficulties was taboo in their society. S. P. Carey knew of the Thomas letter to Fuller but apparently found the material after he had completed his biography of Carey.
9. *Diagnostic and Statistical Manual of Mental Disorders*, 3d rev. ed. (Washington, D.C.: American Psychiatric Association, 1987), pp. 199–203.
10. Letter from William Carey to Andrew Fuller, April 23, 1796 [NYCRO].
11. Letter from John Thomas to William Carey, n.d. [BMS].
12. The resulting year-long silence about Dorothy did raise some suspicion in England. Samuel Pearce of Birmingham wrote on August 27, 1795: "How is it we hear nothing about Mrs. C., Mrs. T. or your children, except in the note from Mr. T. in which he says you have lost a son?" (letter from Samuel Pearce to William Carey, August 27, 1795, cited in *Missionary Correspondence: Containing Extracts of Letters from the Late Mr. Samuel Pearce to the Missionaries in India, Between the Years 1794–1798 and From Mr. John Thomas From 1798–1800* (London: T. Gardiner and Son, 1814).
13. Letter from William Carey to his sisters, October 5, 1795 [AL]. Carey's reference to his friends must refer to the Thomases, Powells, and Udneys. But we know that fifteen to sixteen other Europeans lived in the area (see the letter from William Carey to his sisters, March 11, 1795 [William Carey Collection, AL]). If Dorothy had accused some of these women, the circle of knowledge about her problems would have extended beyond the immediate mission family.
14. Letter from William Carey to Andrew Fuller, June 17, 1796, cited in Eustace Carey, *Memoir of William Carey, D.D.* (London: Jackson and Walford, 1836), p. 268.
15. [BMS].
16. Letter from William Carey to Andrew Fuller, June 17, 1796 [BMS].
17. Dr. Arnold also maintained a close relationship with the society back in England, perhaps as a financial supporter. See letter from Andrew Fuller to Samuel Pearce, October 31, 1795 [BMS].
18. Letter from John Thomas to Andrew Fuller, January 11, 1796 [BMS].
19. Letter from William Carey to his sisters, October 5, 1795 [AL].
20. Letter from John Thomas to Andrew Fuller, January 11, 1796 [BMS].
21. Journal, March 22, 1794 [BMS].
22. Ibid.
23. Letter from William Carey to his sisters, October 5, 1795 [AL].
24. M. Donnelly, *Managing the Mind: A Study of Medical Psychology in Early Nineteenth-Century Britain* (London: Tavistock, 1983), p. 115.
25. Thomas Arnold, *Observations on the Nature, Kinds, Causes, and Preventions of Insanity, Lunacy or Madness* (Leicester: G. Ireland, 1782), 1:72–74. Contemporaries did not adopt Arnold's classification scheme—not even his former Edinburgh professor. See R. Hunter and I. Macalpine, *Three Hundred Years of Psychiatry, 1535–1860* (New York: Carlisle Publishing, 1982), p. 479. See Appendix 2 for Arnold's diagnostic scheme.

26. After Carey read Arnold, he concluded that Dorothy was suffering from Ideal Insanity. Thomas felt she had Notional Insanity. Thomas was more correct since Arnold placed jealous delusions under the notional category. This confusion is yet one example of the major problem with Arnold's classification scheme.

27. Letter from John Thomas to William Carey, n.d. [BMS].

28. Carey wrote: "I long for their deliverance from their miserable state on two accounts, principally because I see God daily dishonoured, and them drowned in sensuality, ignorance and superstition, and likewise because I think that news of the conversion of some of them would much encourage the society, and excite them to double their efforts in other places for the propagation of the glorious gospel" (Journal, February 23, 1795 [BMS]).

29. We know that Carey and Thomas got together on several occasions during this time period. On February 26, 1795, Carey traveled to Moypaldiggy to see Thomas, perhaps after Carey had received Thomas's letter telling of Dorothy's secret missive. On March 2–7 of the same year, Mr. Udney, John Thomas, and two others came to Mudnabatti. In the third week of March 1795 Mr. and Mrs. Thomas came on a Saturday and left the following Wednesday. These visitors may have come in an effort to reason with Dorothy. See Carey's Journal, February 26–March 29, 1795 [BMS].

30. Letter from John Thomas to Andrew Fuller, January 11, 1796 [BMS].

31. H. G. Orme and W. H. Brock, *Leicestershire's Lunatics: The Institutional Care of Leicestershire Lunatics During the Nineteenth Century* (Leicester: Leicestershire Museums, Art Galleries and Records Service, 1987), p. 6. See also E. Showalter, *The Female Malady: Women, Madness, and English Culture, 1830–1980* (London: Virago Press, 1985), for a description of sexuality as the presumed cause of mental illness in women in the nineteenth century.

32. In an April 10, 1796, letter to his sisters [AL], Carey said that Jonathan was born in January. But in a January 18, 1798, letter to his father [William Carey Collection, AL], he said that "Mrs. Carey was delivered of a son in Feb 1796." In a June 23, 1803, letter to John Ryland [NYCRO] Carey admitted that "I cannot recollect the exact ages of my sons."

33. Many theorists viewed the entire sexual development cycle as filled with danger for women. Mental illness could arise during any phase, leading to the frequent suggestion that mental illness was passed along in families through the female line. See V. Skultans, *Madness and Morals: Ideas on Insanity in the Nineteenth Century* (London: Routledge and Kegan Paul, 1975).

34. Ibid.

35. Friends and family in England were writing letters throughout this two-year period, but war conditions had made mail delivery very erratic. The problem continued. In 1798 Carey wrote, "This has been a year of uncommon neglect in our friends in England, not a magazine . . . or a publication arrived, and scarcely a letter. This is discouraging. But I know all my friends too well to suspect them" (letter from William Carey to John Sutcliffe, January 16, 1798 [BMS]).

36. In 1800, when the Careys and other Baptist missionaries lived in Serampore, a straitjacket was available for use on John Thomas when he became mentally ill in December (letter from William Carey to John Sutcliffe, December 18, 1800 [BMS]). We do not know if the straitjacket was a homemade device designed just for this occasion or if they had obtained it from elsewhere. We also do not know if this jacket was ever used on Dorothy.

37. Letter from John Thomas to Andrew Fuller, January 11, 1796 [BMS].

38. Hunter and Macalpine, *Psychiatry*, p. 468.

39. A. Digby, *Madness, Morality and Medicine: A Study of the York Retreat, 1796–1914* (Cambridge: Cambridge University Press, 1985), p. 5.

40. Apart from his nonspecific journal entries, we do not know how Carey felt about confinement. Thirty years later, however, when his son Jabez was having marital difficulties, Carey wrote, "Never yield in the smallest degree to Eliza's violence but if she plays the mad-woman keep her under proper restraint" (letter from William Carey to Jabez Carey, October 11, 1826 [AL]).

41. Letter from William Carey to his sisters, April 10, 1796 [William Carey Collection, AL].

42. Journal [BMS].

43. Letter from Andrew Fuller to William Carey, May 2, 1796 [BMS]. The letter Fuller refers to here is undoubtedly Carey's October 15, 1795, letter to his sisters.

44. Letter from John Thomas to Andrew Fuller, January 11, 1796 [BMS].

45. Letter from William Carey to his sisters, October 5, 1795 [William Carey Collection, AL].

46. Interview with Denis Leigh.

47. The ever-present threat of physical disease or its presence might predispose a person to the development of a "mental disorder of a somatic nature" (Waltraud Ernst, "The Rise of the European Lunatic Asylum in Colonial India [1750–1858]," *Bulletin of the Indian Institute of History of Medicine* 17 (1987): 101. Dorothy's paranoia, however, was not a somatic disorder.

48. R. L. Sibelrud, "The Relationship Between Mercury from Dental Amalgam and Mental Health," *American Journal of Psychotherapy* 43 (1989): 575–87.

49. The medical literature suggests that certain endocrine disorders can trigger paranoid reactions. Graves' disease, a condition of hyperthyroidism, can trigger delusions as can hyperparathyroidism. However, we will never know if Dorothy was afflicted by one of these endocrine disorders. See S. H. Kamlana and L. Holms, "Paranoid Reaction and Underlying Thyrotoxicosis," *British Journal of Psychiatry* 149 (1986): 376–77; R. S. Brown, A. Feschman, and C. R. Showalter, "Primary Hyperparathyroidism, Hypercalcemia, Paranoid Delusions, Homicide, and Attempted Murder," *Journal of Forensic Sciences* 32 (1987): 1460–63.

50. William did, however, describe various medications, including mercury, which he used during his illnesses.

51. The stress on a European living in the tropics is a widely acknowledged difficulty. See C. R. M. Wilson, "Psychiatry in the Tropics," in *Medicine in the Tropics,* ed. A. W. Woodruff (Edinburgh: Churchill Livingstone, 1979), p. 584.

52. P. E. C. Manson-Bahr and F. I. C. Apted, *Manson's Tropical Diseases,* 18th ed. (London: Balliere Tindall, 1982), p. 14.

53. Ibid.

54. Another mental illness found in the tropics is *amok,* a condition that drives its victims to blind fury and to murder without reason. Running *amok* was common among the Malays. Although Dorothy could be violent, her pattern of behavior does not match the standard description of *amok.* See ibid., p. 15.

55. "No information is available regarding the familial pattern of Delusional Disorder itself. However, there is limited evidence that cases of Avoidant and Paranoid Personality Disorders may be especially common among first-degree biologic relatives with Delusional Disorder" (*Diagnostic and Statistical Manual,* p. 201). We do not know of any such condition among Dorothy's first-degree relatives.

56. B. R. Pearn, "Felix Carey and the English Baptist Mission in Burma," *Journal of the Burma Research Society* 28 (1938): 7.

57. M. S. Kahn, "Felix Carey: A Prisoner of Hope," *Libri* 16 (1966): 240. He translated *Pilgrim's Progress, The Vicar of Wakefield,* and portions of the Bible. See *Dictionary of National Biography,* s.v. "Carey, Felix."

58. Khan, "Felix Carey," p. 243.

59. Pearn, "Felix Carey," p. 21.

60. Letter from William Carey to Jabez Carey, November 25, 1814 [AL].

61. Letter from William Carey to Andrew Fuller, May 17, 1815 [BMS].

62. Letter from William Carey to Jabez Carey, n.d. (but probably between October and December 1818) [AL].

63. Letter from William Carey to his sister, January 28, 1817 [AL].

64. Pearn, "Felix Carey," p. 72.

65. Ibid., p. 81.

66. S. K. Chatterjee disagrees that Felix was wandering aimlessly at this point in his life. See S. K. Chatterjee, *Felix Carey: A Tiger Tamed* (Calcutta: Author, 1991).

67. John Clark Marshman, *The Life and Times of Carey, Marshman, and Ward* (London: Longman, Brown, Green, Longmans, and Roberts, 1958), p. 160.

68. M. Drewery, *William Carey: Shoemaker and Missionary* (London: Hodder and Stoughton, 1978), p. 146.

69. W. W. Meissner, *The Paranoid Process* (New York: Jason Aronson, 1978), p. 125.

70. Interview with S. K. Chatterjee, June 30, 1987.

71. Letter from William Carey to John Sutcliffe, November 27, 1800 [BMS].

72. Arnold, *Observations*, 2:424–28.

73. H. Maudsley, *The Pathology of Mind: A Study of Its Distempers, Deformities, and Disorders* (reprint, London: Julian Friedmann Publishers, 1979), p. 237.

74. Arnold reportedly was able to devise a creative cure for one man's delusion. "A patient . . . imagined that he had a leg of mutton hanging from his nose, and walked nearly double to prevent the dangling joint from hitting against his knees. The cure was simple; he was taken into a dark room, where a person was stationed with the reality, and on just cutting off the tip of his nose, the mutton was let fall on the floor. On opening the window-shutters the patient was convinced that he had got rid of his load, and walked in an upright posture ever afterwards" (William Gardiner, *Music and Friends* [Leicester: Crossley and Clarke, 1853], p. 409). Arnold would have been hard-pressed, however, to come up with such a creative cure for Dorothy's delusion.

75. J. Colaizzi, *Homicidal Insanity, 1800–1985* (Tuscaloosa: University of Alabama Press, 1989), p. 7.

76. *Diagnostic and Statistical Manual*, p. 201.

77. Hubert Tellenbach, "On the Nature of Jealousy," *Journal of Phenomenological Psychology* 4 (1974): 464.

Chapter 7

1. T. E. Fuller, *A Memoir of the Life and Writings of Andrew Fuller* (London: J. Heaton and Son, 1863), p. 68.

2. C. D. Bond, *God's Forgotten People: A History of Carey Baptist Church, Hackleton*, n.d., p. 7.

3. Letter from Andrew Fuller to John Thomas and William Carey, March 25, 1794 [BMS].

4. M. S. Guttmacher, *America's Last King: An Interpretation of the Madness of George III* (New York: Charles Scribner's Sons, 1941).

5. R. Hunter and I. Macalpine, *George III and the Mad-Business* (London: Allen Lane, 1969).

6. J. Greene, *Reminiscences of the Rev. Robert Hall, A.M.* (London: Westley and Davis, 1832), p. 45.

7. See Appendix 6 for a more complete account.

8. O. Gregory, "Memoir," in *The Miscellaneous Works and Remains of the Rev. Robert Hall* (London: Henry G. Bohn, 1846).

9. Letter from William Carey to Jabez Carey, August 25, 1819 [AL].

10. J. C. Marshman, *The Life and Times of Carey, Marshman, and Ward* (London: Longman, Brown, Green, Longmans, and Roberts, 1859), 2:473.

11. S. P. Carey, *William Carey, D.D., Fellow of the Linnean Society*, 8th ed. (London: Carey Press, 1934), p. 142.

12. Letter from Andrew Fuller to John Sutcliffe, March 13, 1795 [BMS].

13. Letter from Andrew Fuller to John Thomas and William Carey, March 1795, cited in Fuller, *Memoir*.

14. Letter from William Carey to his brother, December 20, 1796 [William Carey Collection, AL]. The actual situation was the opposite of information on the rumor mill. Funds and supplies Thomas and Carey were to sell for income were slow in arriving. One shipment of cutlery sat

in a Cripplegate, England, warehouse for two years before the mistake was discovered. The minute book of the society reads: "And if they had not engaged in business for their own support, they must long ago have perished for want" (Fuller, *Memoir*, p. 102).

15. Mary Drewery, *William Carey: Shoemaker and Missionary* (London: Hodder and Stoughton, 1978), p. 187.

16. Journal, January 15–16, 1794 [BMS].

17. Letter from William Carey to John Sutcliffe, January 3, 1794 [BMS].

18. Marshman, *Life and Times*, 2:475.

19. Ibid., p. 478.

20. F. D. Walker, *William Carey: Missionary Pioneer and Statesman* (London: Student Christian Movement, 1926), p. 220.

21. K. Ingham, *Reformers in India, 1793–1833: An Account of the Work of Christian Missionaries on Behalf of Social Reform* (Cambridge: University Press, 1956), p. 7.

22. Journal, January 13, 1794 [BMS].

23. Letters from William Carey to Jabez Carey, July 25, 1815, March 9, 1819 [AL].

24. Marshman, *Life and Times*, 2:479.

25. Letter from William Carey to Andrew Fuller, August 14, 1804 [BMS]. Carey asked that Fuller not publish this self-evaluation until after his death: "The less said about me the better."

26. Journal, January 24, 1794 [BMS].

27. Letter from William Carey to Jabez Carey, January 20, 1816 [AL].

28. Letter from William Carey to Jabez Carey, January 18, 1822 [AL].

29. Letter from William Carey to his sisters, February 16, 1822 [William Carey Collection, AL].

30. Letter from William Carey to Mr. Burls, October 5, 1821, cited in Eustace Carey, *Memoir of William Carey, D.D.* (London: Jackson and Walford, 1836), p. 546.

31. Cited in J.·N. Ogilvie, *Our Empire's Debt to Missions* (London: Hodder and Stoughton, 1924), p. 124.

32. J. Macheath, "William Carey's Secret," in *One Hundred Years After: A Sermon and Addresses, London, October, 1934* (London: Carey Press, 1934), pp. 11–28.

33. Max Warren, *The Missionary Movement from Britain in Modern History* (London: SCM Press, 1965), p. 107.

34. Carey, *William Carey*, p. 7.

35. William Carey, *An Enquiry into the Obligations of Christians to Use Means for the Conversion of the Heathens* (Leicester: Ann Ireland, 1792), p. 79.

36. Letter from William Carey, November 15, 1803, cited in L. and M. Williams, eds., *Serampore Letters: Being the Unpublished Correspondence of William Carey and Others with John Williams, 1800–1816* (New York: G. P. Putnam's Sons, 1892), p. 87.

37. M. A. Sherring, *The History of Protestant Missions in India* (London: Trubner, 1875), pp. 75–76.

38. D. B. Forrester, *Caste and Christianity: Attitudes and Policies on Caste of Anglo-Saxon Protestant Missions in India* (London: Curzon Press, 1980), pp. 25–28.

39. Ingham, *Reformers*, p. 26.

40. Neil Gunson, *Messengers of Grace: Evangelical Missionaries in the South Seas, 1797–1860* (Melbourne: Oxford University Press, 1978).

41. Letter from William Carey to John Sutcliffe, January 1, 1806 [BMS].

42. Letter from William Carey to Jabez Carey, September 17, 1816 [AL].

43. Letter from William Carey to Andrew Fuller, October 14, 1809 [BMS].

44. Wiser heads prevailed. William Ward wrote to Andrew Fuller on November 26, 1810 [BMS]: "If you have not sent out a young woman to be married to Felix you had better not do

it for our brother Chater begins to think that European women can not live in Burma. Felix, I suppose, will try to fit himself in that country."

45. Letter from William Carey to Jabez Carey, January 24, 1814 [AL].

46. Esther Carey, *Eustace Carey: A Missionary in India* (London: Pewtress, 1857), p. 26.

47. Ingham, *Reformers*, pp. 84–95.

48. S. Mitchell, *Not Disobedient: A History of United Baptist Church, Leicester Including Harvey Lane 1760–1845, Belvoir Street 1845–1940 and Charles Street 1831–1940* (Leicester: Author, 1984), p. 25.

49. *One Hundred Years After*, p. 104.

50. Letter from William Carey to his father, July 11, 1805 [AL].

51. Marshman, *Life and Times*, 2:479.

52. See Appendix 5 for details of their "most painful task."

53. Letter from Joshua Marshman to John Sutcliffe, June 5, 1802 [BMS]. Many biographers attribute the authorship of the "most painful task" piece to Hannah Marshman, although it is not clear whether Felix was given this tongue-lashing by Joshua or Hannah. The account sounds like a reconstruction of events after a parental-like loss of temper over the behavior of a very rowdy young man.

54. The rare reference Carey makes to enjoying time with his family is in his journal, where he recounts instructing them in religion on the Sabbath.

55. In December 1800 when a missionary named Burnsdon was ill "We called in the Danish physicians belonging to the settlement who administered several remedies but he got no better" (letter from William Carey to John Sutcliffe, November 27, 1800 [BMS]).

56. Carey, *Memoir*, p. 504; Carey, *William Carey*, p. 333.

57. Drewery, *William Carey*, p. 162.

58. In 1823 Carey slipped and injured his hip. In two days' time 110 leeches were applied to reduce the inflammation (Carey, *William Carey*, p. 377). In 1806 he thought he was suffering from a hepatic infection: "I have begun a course of Mercury, and as the disease is but just perceptible, I hope it will soon give way to it" (letter from William Carey to John Ryland, July 17, 1806 [NYCRO]). On another occasion he wrote: "I am now mercifully recovering from a very severe bilious fever which brought me exceedingly low, my mouth now suffers severely from the vast quantities of mercury which the doctor rubbed in and gave in other forms" (letter from William Carey to Jabez Carey, November 23, 1816 [AL]).

59. Letter from William Carey to his father, September 11, 1804 [William Carey Collection, AL]. On many occasions Carey said in his letters that he had never been healthier in his entire life: "I have in general enjoyed better health than in England" (letter from William Carey to Mr. Yates, March 16, 1795 [BMS]); "Everything in this country is now as familiar to me as if it were my native country" (letter from William Carey to his father, December 1, 1802 [AL]). He wondered if he could possibly endure an English winter, because he had become so acclimatized to the tropics (letter from William Carey to his sisters, December 31, 1805 [AL]). Perhaps he was consciously or subconsciously justifying his decision not to return to England, even though many had urged him to do so.

60. Letter from William Carey to his father, September 11, 1804 [William Carey Collection, AL].

61. See Appendix 6 for his account.

62. E. Showalter, *The Female Malady: Women, Madness, and English Culture, 1830–1980* (London: Virago Press, 1985).

63. Waltraud Ernst, "Psychiatry and Colonialism: Lunatic Asylums in British India, 1800–1858," *The Society for the Social History of Medicine Bulletin* 39 (1986): 27–31.

64. Letter from William Carey to Andrew Fuller, October 25, 1809 [BMS].

65. Letter from William Carey to John Sutcliffe, January 3, 1794 [BMS].

66. See Appendix 3 for his complete proposal.

67. Cited in Carey, *Memoir*, p. 37.

Chapter 8

1. Mary Drewery, *William Carey: Shoemaker and Missionary* (London: Hodder and Stoughton, 1978), p. 100.

2. Letter from William Carey to Andrew Fuller, November 16, 1796 [BMS].

3. Letter from William Carey to Andrew Fuller, March 23, 1797 [BMS].

4. Letter from William Carey to John Sutcliffe, January 16, 1798 [BMS].

5. Letter from William Carey to his sisters, January 18, 1798 [AL].

6. Jonathan's stability as an adult and his success in the civil service of India suggest that Dorothy was a good caregiver in spite of her derangement. Admittedly, this conclusion is speculative. Eustace Carey (*Memoir of William Carey, D.D.* [London: Jackson and Walford, 1836], p. 181) said that "Mrs. Carey's indisposition so increased upon her, that she was quite incapable of regulating domestic economy." He gives no evidence for this assessment, however.

7. Letter from William Carey to his father, November 9, 1799 [William Carey Collection, AL].

8. Letter from William Carey to his father, January 18, 1798 [William Carey Collection, AL].

9. Letter from William Carey to his father, November 9, 1799 [William Carey Collection, AL].

10. Ibid.

11. Letter from William Carey to his sister, January 18, 1798 [AL].

12. Letter from William Carey to the Baptist Missionary Society, December 28, 1796 [BMS].

13. Letter from William Carey to John Sutcliffe, January 16, 1798 [BMS].

14. Letter from William Carey to his father, April 10, 1796 [William Carey Collection, AL].

15. Drewery, *William Carey*, p. 84.

16. Letter from William Carey to his father, November 9, 1799 [William Carey Collection, AL].

17. Letter from William Carey to Samuel Pearce, October 2, 1795 [BMS].

18. C. B. Lewis, *The Life of John Thomas* (London: Macmillan, 1873), p. 302.

19. Letter from William Carey to the Baptist Missionary Society, January 12, 1796 [BMS].

20. John Taylor, *Biographical and Literary Notices of William Carey, D.D.* (Northampton: Dryden Press, 1886), p. 8.

21. F. D. Walker, *William Carey: Missionary Pioneer and Statesman* (London: Student Christian Movement, 1926).

22. Lewis, *John Thomas*, p. 338. Thomas apparently made the switch from indigo to sugarcane sometime in 1798 or 1799. See letter from Claudius Buchanan, December 30, 1800 [India Office Library].

23. B. Chaudhuri, "Eastern India, II," in *The Cambridge Economic History of India*, vol. 2, c. 1757–c. 1970, ed. D. Kumar (Cambridge: Cambridge University Press, 1983), p. 316.

24. Letter from William Carey to his sisters, November 30, 1799 [AL].

25. Letter from William Carey to Andrew Fuller, October 27, 1799 [BMS].

26. Letter from William Carey to his father, November 9, 1799 [William Carey Collection, AL].

27. Council of Serampore College, *The Story of Serampore and Its College*, p. 2.

28. In his journal William Ward indicates that he and Carey left Mudnabatti on a quick survey trip of surrounding areas only to meet Mrs. Carey and the children later in Malda. Dorothy and her children traveled the first leg of their journey alone. She was apparently stable enough to undertake this task. Ward writes: "On our return the boats had arrived with the goods, Mrs. Carey and the children. We dined, and then went on board" (Journal, December 31, 1799 [BMS]).

29. The missionaries were not the only ones seeking refuge from the British in Serampore. The colony was also a haven for debtors seeking to escape their creditors (letter from William Carey to John Ryland, January 17, 1800 [NYCRO]).

30. Walker, *William Carey*. A similar British occupation occurred in 1808–15 until the peace after Waterloo restored normal diplomatic relationships between the two countries.

31. William Ward, Journal, June 22, 1800 [BMS].

32. Letter from William Carey to John Sutcliffe, December 29, 1800 [BMS].

33. Letter from William Carey to John Sutcliffe, April 8, 1801 [BMS].

34. Letter from William Carey to John Ryland, June 15, 1801 [NYCRO].

35. Letter from William Carey to his sisters, November 23, 1801 [AL].

36. Letter from William Carey to his father, November 23, 1801 [William Carey Collection, AL]. Carey's language ("confined to her room") does not help us determine if they simply restricted her movement to her room only or if they also restricted her movement within the room.

37. By August 17, 1800, the community numbered nineteen: five men, five women, and nine children (letter from Joshua Marshman to his father [BMS]). By 1804 the community employed sixty attendants (Hannah Marshman, cited in Drewery, *William Carey*, p. 117).

38. Although modern therapies have low success rates with paranoias of this severity, tranquilizers relieve this kind of intense distress. No such medication was available in 1801.

39. John Clark Marshman, *The Life and Times of Carey, Marshman, and Ward* (London: Longman, Brown, Green, Longmans, and Roberts, 1859), 1:301–2.

40. Archival material in Copenhagen, Denmark, and government documents from Fredericksnagore (Serampore) from this period reveal no official judgments about Dorothy. The recommendations made by the Serampore police to Carey may have been unofficial or informal.

41. Several authors have noted a double triumvirate in the Carey story: one in India (Carey, Marshman, Ward) and one in England (Fuller, Sutcliffe, Ryland). See E. A. Payne, "Carey and His Biographers," *Baptist Quarterly* 19 (1961): 3. The Serampore trio worked together for twenty-three years until Ward's death. Carey and Marshman carried on together for an additional eleven years until Carey died in 1834.

42. They planned to read the compact publicly when each mission station held business meetings in January, May, and October. See Appendix 4 for the Serampore Compact.

43. Cited in James Culross, *William Carey* (London: Hodder and Stoughton, 1881), p. 82.

44. Carey referred to some initial "womanish differences" among some wives in the Serampore community that had been resolved by January 1801 (letter from William Carey to John Ryland, January 30, 1801 [NYCRO]).

45. S. K. Chatterjee, *Hannah Marshman: The First Woman Missionary in India* (Hooghly, India: S. S. Chatterjee, 1987).

46. E. D. Potts called her domineering, but admitted that she was the "only missionary wife who took a constantly active part in the Mission's work" (*British Baptist Missionaries in India, 1793–1837: The History of Serampore and Its Missions* [Cambridge: University Press, 1967], p. 21).

47. Journal, June 22, 1800 [BMS].

48. Walker, *William Carey*.

49. Letter from William Carey to John Sutcliffe, December 29, 1800 [BMS].

50. George Smith, *The Life of William Carey*. 2d ed. (London: John Murray, 1887), p. 119.

51. Lewis, *John Thomas*.

52. Press list of public department records, December 30, 1800, 17:557 [India Office Library and Records].

53. Letter from William Carey to John Ryland, January 30, 1801 [BMS].

54. Letter from William Carey to his father, November 23, 1801 [William Carey Collection, AL].

55. Letter from William Carey to John Sutcliffe, November 27, 1800 [BMS].

56. Letter from William Carey to John Ryland, June 15, 1801, cited in Carey, *William Carey*, p. 455.

57. Ingham, *Reformers*, p. 58.

58. K. W. Jones, *The New Cambridge History of India* (Cambridge: Cambridge University Press, 1989), III.1.26.

59. M. M. Ali, *The Bengali Reaction to Christian Missionary Activities: 1833–1857* (Chittagong: Mehrub Publications, 1965), p. 3.

60. M. S. Khan, "William Carey and the Serampore Books (1800–1834)," *Libri* 11 (1961): 233.

61. Carey deposited all income from Fort William College into the common fund, as did the Marshmans, who earned a considerable amount of income from operating their schools.

62. Letter from William Carey to his father, December 1, 1802 [AL].

63. Marshman, *Life and Times*, 2:478. Two different sets entitled *Universal History* were printed in England during the period 1779–84. One was eighteen volumes and the other was forty-two volumes. Whichever Carey read, he did a lot of reading in a bumpy coach!

64. Letter from William Carey to John Sutcliffe, March 17, 1802 [NYCRO].

65. William Ward, Journal, March 28, 1802 [BMS].

66. Letter from William Carey to John Ryland, June 29, 1802 [NYCRO].

67. Letter from William Carey to his father, December 1, 1802 [AL].

68. Letter from William Carey to his sisters, December 2, 1802 [William Carey Collection, AL].

69. Letter from William Carey to John Sutcliffe, March 17, 1802 [BMS].

70. Williams, *Serampore Letters*, p. 18.

71. Taylor, *Notices*, pp. 20–21.

72. Letter from William Carey to his sisters, August 24, 1803 [William Carey Collection, AL].

73. Letter from William Carey to John Ryland, December 14, 1803 [NYCRO].

74. Letter from William Carey to Andrew Fuller, February 27, 1804 [BMS].

75. Letter from William Carey to his sisters, March 9, 1804 [William Carey Collection, AL].

76. Letter from William Carey to his sister, August 23, 1804 [William Carey Collection, AL].

77. A. H. Oussoren, *William Carey: Especially His Missionary Principles* (Leiden: A. W. Sijthoff, 1945), p. 86.

78. Claudius Buchanan, *The College of Fort William in Bengal* (London: T. Cadell, 1805), p. 126.

79. Letter from William Carey to his sisters, July 7, 1805 [AL].

80. Letter from William Carey to his father, July 11, 1805 [William Carey Collection, AL].

81. Letter from William Carey to his sisters, December 31, 1805 [AL].

82. Letter from William Carey to John Sutcliffe, January 1, 1806 [BMS].

83. Letter from William Carey to John Sutcliffe, July 29, 1806 [BMS].

84. H. Pearson, *Memoirs of the Life and Writings of the Rev. Claudius Buchanan* (Oxford: University Press, 1817), 1:386.

85. Letter from William Carey to Andrew Fuller, May 15, 1806 [AL].

86. Letter from William Carey to his father, February 7, 1807 [AL].

87. Letter from William Carey to his sisters, February 25, 1807 [AL].

88. Letter from William Carey to his brother, March 3, 1807 [William Carey Collection, AL].

89. Letter from William Carey to his sisters, October 1, 1807 [William Carey Collection, AL].

90. Letter from Martha L. Mitchell, archivist, John Hay Library, Brown University, June 27, 1990.

91. Journal, November 27, December 2, December 8, December 9, 1807 [BMS].

92. George Smith, *The Life of William Carey*, 2d ed. (London: John Murray, 1887), p. 163.

93. *Periodical Accounts Relative to the Baptist Missionary Society* 3 (1808): 416.

94. From T. E. Brown, "To Chalse in Heaven," in S. P. Carey, *William Carey, D.D., Fellow of the Linnean Society* (London: Hodder and Stoughton, 1923), p. 270. In the 8th ed. of his book (1934), Carey edited the last two lines of the poem to read "And appointed her her station / Before and near His throne."

Chapter 9

1. Ernest A. Payne, "Carey and His Biographers," *Baptist Quarterly* 19 (1961): 9.

2. K. Ingham, *Reformers in India, 1793–1833: An Account of the Work of Christian Missionaries on Behalf of Social Reform* (Cambridge: University Press, 1956), p. 7. An even more ironic event occurred when the East India Company—the very company that had harassed missionaries—later recruited and hired William's son Jabez as a teacher at a government school (p. 60).

3. Letter from Kitty Short to William Carey, 1808 [BMS].

4. Letter from Andrew Fuller to William Carey, September 5, 1808 [BMS].

5. Letter from William Carey to his sisters, January 20, 1808 [AL]. Most Carey biographers misquote this letter to read "affectionate attendance which the sisters paid," assuming that Carey was referring to the missionary wives who no doubt helped care for Dorothy. The original letter, however, clearly reads "sons."

6. Charlotte took an immediate interest in Carey's family. On May 4, 1808, she included a "Dear Father" letter with William's letter to Edmund Carey (letter from William Carey to his father, May 4, 1808 [William Carey Collection, AL]).

7. "The Governor-General, writing light-heartedly to his wife of the event, describes Carey as a 'learned & very pious' man marrying a Danish countess 'whom he had converted from a Christian to a Baptist' by 'very near drowning her in the ceremony of baptism . . . performed in that sect'!" (Mary Drewery, *William Carey: Shoemaker and Missionary* [London: Hodder and Stoughton, 1978], p. 147).

8. Letter from William Carey to an unidentified recipient, March 11, 1812, cited in Eustace Carey, *Memoir of William Carey, D.D.* (London: Jackson and Walford, 1836), p. 520.

9. Letter from William Carey to the Marshmans, n.d. [BMS].

10. Letter from William Carey to his sisters, February 16, 1822 [William Carey Collection, AL].

11. Letter from William Ward to Andrew Fuller, January 1, 1811 [BMS].

12. Payne, "Carey and His Biographers," p. 8.

13. E. D. Potts, *British Baptist Missionaries in India, 1793–1837: The History of Serampore and Its Missions* (Cambridge: University Press, 1967).

14. George Smith, *Carey in the Evangelical Succession, Third Series* (Edinburgh: Macniven and Wallace, 1884), p. 203.

15. S. P. Carey, *William Carey, D.D., Fellow of the Linnean Society*, 8th ed. (London: Carey Press, 1934), p. 352.

16. Drewery, *William Carey*, p. 194.

17. L. and M. Williams, eds., *Serampore Letters: Being the Unpublished Correspondence of William Carey and Others with John Williams, 1800–1816* (New York: G. P. Putnam's Sons, 1892), p. 69.

18. H. Anderson, *The Life and Letters of Christopher Anderson* (Edinburgh: William P. Kennedy, 1854), pp. 183, 201.

19. Payne, "Carey and His Biographers," p. 1.

20. M. M. Ali, *The Bengali Reaction to Christian Missionary Activities: 1833–1857* (Chittagong: Mehrub Publications, 1965), p. 3.

21. K. Kripalani, "Modern Literature," in *A Cultural History of India*, ed. A. L. Baham (Delhi: Oxford University Press, 1975), p. 409.

22. P. J. Marshall, *The New Cambridge History of India: Bengal, the British Bridgehead* (Cambridge: Cambridge University Press, 1987), p. 176.

23. J. B. Myers, *William Carey: The Shoemaker Who Became the Father and Founder of Modern Missions* (Kilmarnock, Scotland: John Ritchie, 1887).

24. F. Robinson, ed., *The Cambridge Encyclopedia of India, Pakistan, Bangladesh, Sri Lanka, Nepal, Bhutan, and the Maldives* (Cambridge: Cambridge University Press, 1989).

25. *One Hundred Years After: A Sermon and Addresses, London, October, 1934* (London: Carey Press, 1934), p. 67.

26. J. Richter, *A History of Missions in India* (Edinburgh: Oliphant, Anderson, and Ferrier, 1980), p. 140.

27. W. Stewart, *The Plan and the Sequel: The Missionary Purpose and Legacy of William Carey and Alexander Duff* (Serampore: Council of Serampore College, 1980), p. 13.

28. Payne, "Carey and His Biographers," p. 4.

29. S. K. Chatterjee, *William Carey and Serampore* (Serampore: Kartik Dutta Banik, n.d.).

30. M. Siddiq Khan, "William Carey and the Serampore Books (1800–1834)," *Libri* 11 (1961): 258.

31. Drewery, *William Carey*, p. 154.

32. F. D. Walker, *William Carey: Missionary Pioneer and Statesman* (reprint, Chicago: Moody Press, 1980).

33. R. Coupland, *Britain and India, 1600–1941* (London: Longmans, Green, 1941), pp. 25–26.

34. S. C. Raychoudhary, *Social, Cultural, and Economic History of India* (Delhi: Surjeet Publications, 1980). The law was not totally successful. In 1844 ten wives and 300 concubines perished on a Sikh nobleman's funeral pyre (Coupland, *Britain and India*, p. 26).

35. Letter from William Carey to John Sutcliffe, September 16, 1807 [NYCRO].

36. R. Coupland, *Wilberforce*, 2d ed. (London: Collins, 1945), pp. 316–17.

37. F. Watson, *A Concise History of India* (London: Thames and Hudson, 1974), p. 137.

38. J. N. Ogilvie, *Our Empire's Debt to Missions* (London: Hodder and Stoughton, 1924).

39. Letter from William Carey to Jabez Carey, September 10, 1814 [AL].

40. A. Mayhew, *Christianity and the Government of India* (London: Faber and Gwyer, 1929).

41. K. Ingham, *Reformers in India, 1793–1833: An Account of the Work of Christian Missionaries on Behalf of Social Reform* (Cambridge: University Press, 1956), p. 118.

42. Ibid., p. 121.

43. The Rev. William Carey, D.D., of Serampore Bengal is listed as a member every year from 1823 to 1834. See *List of Members, 1805–1839* (London: Linnean Society, 1939).

44. John Clark Marshman, *The Life and Times of Carey, Marshman, and Ward* (London: Longman, Brown, Green, Longmans, and Roberts, 1859), 2:288.

45. William Herbert, *Biographical Notice of the Rev. William Carey, D.D. of Serampore* (Newcastle: T. and J. Hodgson, 1843).

46. J. Sims, "Dr. Carey's Crinum," *Curtis's Botanical Magazine* 51 (1854): 2466–67.

47. *Catalogue of the Printed Books and Pamphlets in the Library of the Linnean Society of London* (London: Longmans, Green, 1925).

48. Robert Home (1752–1834) was an accomplished Calcutta portrait artist. Carey appears in the portrait with his pundit; both are at work on translation. The original now hangs at Regent's Park College, Oxford. See M. Archer, *India and British Portraiture, 1770–1825* (London: Sotheby Parke Bernet, 1979), p. 313.

49. Carey, *William Carey*, p. 386.

50. Letter from William Carey to his sisters, September 25, 1833 [William Carey Collection, AL].

51. Letter from William Carey to his sisters, October 3, 1833 [William Carey Collection, AL].

52. Payne, "Carey and His Biographers," p. 1.

53. S. K. Chatterjee, *William Carey and Serampore* (Serampore: Kartik Dutta Banik, n.d.), p. 20.

Conclusion

1. S. P. Carey, *William Carey, D.D., Fellow of the Linnean Society*, 8th ed. (London: Hodder and Stoughton, 1934), p. 288, wrote of Carey: "He was begged and bidden by the local authorities to put her away, but his Leicester friend, Dr. Arnold, had filled him with dread of the then average asylum." The very opposite is more likely to have been the case. Arnold was a great advocate of the asylum for the treatment of the violent insane, especially his own asylum, of course. But the Calcutta Asylum for Lunatics was also known for its state-of-the-art treatment. See Waltraud Ernst, "Psychiatry and Colonialism: Lunatic Asylums in British India, 1800–1858," *The Society for the Social History of Medicine Bulletin* 39 (1986): 27–31; and "The Rise of the European Lunatic Asylum in Colonial India (1750–1858)," *Bulletin of the Indian Institute of History of Medicine* 17 (1987): 94–107. Arnold would have encouraged Dorothy's hospitalization.

2. W. L. Parry-Jones, *The Trade in Lunacy: A Study of Private Mad-Houses in England in the Eighteenth and Nineteenth Centuries* (London: Routledge and Kegan Paul, 1972), p. 44.

3. Ibid., p. 86.

4. Ibid., p. 175.

5. Letter from William Carey to his sisters, December 22, 1796 [AL].

6. Letter from William Carey to his father, December 1, 1802 [AL].

7. Letter from William Carey to his father, August 8, 1794 [William Carey Collection, AL].

8. Letter from William Carey to his sisters, March 9, 1804 [AL].

9. Letter from William Carey to his sisters, August 23, 1804 [AL].

10. Robert Hall, *Help to Zion's Travellers: Being an Attempt to Remove Various Stumbling Blocks out of the Way Relating to Doctrinal, Experimental, and Practical Religion* (London: Book Society, 1781), pp. 183–84.

11. Ibid., p. 184.

12. James Culross, *William Carey* (London: Hodder and Stoughton, 1881), p. 52.

13. Cited in Eustace Carey, *Memoir of William Carey, D.D.* (London: Jackson and Walford, 1836), p. 77.

14. Letter from Andrew Fuller to Rev. J. Saffrey, May 30, 1793 [AL].

15. Journal, January 13, 1794 [BMS].

16. S. K. Chatterjee, *Hannah Marshman* (Hooghly, India: S. Chatterjee, 1987), p. 100.

17. R. Pierce Beaver (*American Protestant Women in World Mission: History of the First Feminist Movement in North America* [Grand Rapids: Eerdmans, 1980]) chronicles the role of missionary wives in North American mission endeavors. British missionary wives played a similar role in mission outreach from England.

18. W. Peirce, *The Ecclesiastical Principles and Polity of the Wesleyan Methodists* (London: Hamilton, Adams, 1854), pp. 607–8.

19. Ibid.

20. Letter from Andrew Fuller to Rev. Mr. Saffrey, May 1, 1799 [BMS].

21. Letter from Andrew Fuller to William Carey, September 6, 1797 [BMS].

Appendix 1

1. T. E. Fuller, *A Memoir of the Life and Writings of Andrew Fuller* (London: J. Heaton and Son, 1863), pp. 70–75.

Appendix 3

1. C. B. Lewis, *The Life of John Thomas* (London: Macmillan, 1873), pp. 339–41.

Appendix 4

1. A. H. Oussoren, *William Carey: Especially His Missionary Principles* (Leiden: A. W. Sijthoff, 1945), pp. 274–84.

Appendix 5

1. Letter from Joshua Marshman to John Sutcliffe, June 5, 1802 [BMS].

Appendix 6

1. J. Greene, *Reminiscences of the Rev. Robert Hall, A.M.* (London: Westley and Davis, 1832), p. 48.

Appendix 7

1. Letter of John Thomas, n.d. [BMS].

Appendix 8

1. Very early in the modern missionary movement societies realized that letters to supporters at home could be a problem. See W. Peirce, *The Ecclesiastical Principles and Polity of the Wesleyan Methodists* (London: Hamilton, Adams, 1854), pp. 618–23, for instructions to missionaries. One reads: "VIII. It is *peremptorily required* of every Missionary in our Connexion to keep a Journal, and to send home frequently such copious abstracts of it as may give a full and particular account of his labours, success, and prospects. He is also required to give such details of a religious kind as may be generally interesting to the friends of Missions at home; particularly, accounts of conversions. Only, we recommend to you, not to allow yourselves, under the influence of religious joy, to give any *high colouring* of facts; but always write such accounts as you would not object to see return in print to the place where the facts reported may have occurred."

2. In letters from William Carey to John Sutcliffe [BMS] are the following statements: "My love to Mrs. Carey's relations" (December 29, 1800); "Love to Mrs. Carey's friends" (April 8, 1801); "Give my love to Mrs. Carey's friends when you see them" (January 1, 1805).

3. Letter from William Carey to his sisters, February 25, 1807 [AL].

4. Mary Drewery, *William Carey: Shoemaker and Missionary* (London: Hodder and Stoughton, 1978), p. 100.

5. When biographers mention Dorothy's illiteracy and then correct William's grammar and spelling, they create the impression of an even greater educational gap between the two than actually did exist.

6. Letter from William Carey to John Ryland, November 26, 1796 [NYCRO].

7. Letter from Andrew Fuller to William Carey, September 6, 1797 [BMS].

Bibliography

Manuscripts

Angus Library (AL), Regent's Park College, Oxford, England.

    Carey, Jabez. Letters to William Carey.

    Carey, William. Letters to Jabez Carey.

    ———. Letters. New MS.

    ———. Letters.

    ———. Letters. FPC E. 18 (16).

    ———. Letters to family members. William Carey Collection.

    Fuller, Andrew. Letters.

Baptist Missionary Society Archives (BMS). Housed at the Angus Library, Regent's Park College, Oxford, England.

    Carey, William. Journal, June 1793–June 1795. Transcription by Chesterman, 1961.

    ———. Letters to the Baptist Missionary Society, Andrew Fuller, the Marshmans, miscellaneous persons, and John Sutcliffe.

    Chamberlain, John. Letter to John Ryland.

    Fountain, John. Letter to Andrew Fuller.

    Marshman, Joshua and Hannah. Letters and journal.

    Short, Catherine. Letter to William Carey.

    Thomas, John. Letters and journal.

    Ward, William. Letters and journal, 1799–1811. Journal transcription by E. Daniel Potts.

India Office and Library (IOL), British Library, London, England.

    Buchanan, Claudius. Letter, December 30, 1800.

    Press List of Public Documents, Bengal, 10, 11, 12. Imperial Records Department.

Northampton County Record Office (NCRO), Northampton, England.
   Parish registers of christenings, marriages, and burials.
   MSS of leases and mortgages.
North Yorkshire County Record Office (NYCRO), Northallerton, Yorkshire,
   England.
   Marshman, Joshua and Hannah. Letters and journals. Part of the Have-
   lock Papers.

Other Unpublished Materials

Bottoms, R. E. Interview with author. Northampton, England, May 3, 1990.

Chatterjee, S. K. Interview with author. Serampore, India, June 1987.

Dirkey, J. "William Carey of India." Transcribed dramatization for radio, Stories of Great Christians series.

Drewery, M. Interview with author. Pulborough, Sussex, England, April 27,
   1990.

————. Letter to author. May 21, 1990.

Elliot, W. J. Interview with author. Northampton, England, May 3, 1990.

India House Library and Records, British Library, London, England. Index of
   christenings, marriages, burials: Bengal.

Khan, M. H. "History of Printing in Bengali Characters up to 1866." Ph.D.
   diss., School of African and Oriental Studies, University of London,
   1976.

Leigh, D. Interview with author. Denmark Hill, London, England, June 12,
   1990.

Mitchell, M. L. Letter to author. June 27, 1990.

Murray, J. "Anglican and Protestant Missionary Societies in Britain: Their
   Use of Women as Missionaries from the Late Eighteenth to the Late
   Nineteenth Century." Paper presented at Femmes en Mission, France,
   August 26–31, 1990.

Westminster Abbey. Lectern Inscription.

Published Materials

Ali, M. M. The Bengali Reaction to Christian Missionary Activities:
   1833–1857. Chittagong: Mehrub Publications, 1965.

Anderson, H. *The Life and Letters of Christopher Anderson*. Edinburgh: William
   P. Kennedy, 1854.

Anstey, T. M. *A History of Libraries in Northampton from the Middle Ages
   until 1910*. Northampton: Northampton Central Library, 1971.

Archer, M. *India and British Portraiture, 1770–1825*. London: Sotheby Parke Bernet, 1979.

Arnold, T. *Observations on the Nature, Kinds, Causes, and Preventions of Insanity, Lunacy, or Madness*. 2 vols. Leicester: G. Ireland, 1782, 1786.

———. *Observations on the Management of the Insane; and Particularly on the Agency of and Importance of Humane and Kind Treatment in Effecting Their Cure*. London: Richard Phillips, 1809.

———. Obituary. *Gentleman's Magazine* 86ii(1816): 378.

Beaglehole, J. C. "Cook the Man." In *Captain Cook: Navigator and Scientist*, ed. G. M. Badger, 11–29. London: C. Hurst, 1970.

Beaver, R. P. *American Protestant Women in World Mission: History of the First Feminist Movement in North America*. Grand Rapids: Eerdmans, 1980.

Bebb, E. D. *Nonconformity and Social and Economic Life: 1660–1800*. London: Epworth Press, 1935.

Beddie, M. K., ed. *Bibliography of Captain James Cook*. Sydney: University of New South Wales, 1970.

Bond, C. D. *God's Forgotten People: A History of Carey Baptist Church, Hackleton*, n.d.

The Book of Common Prayer and Administration of the Sacraments, and Other Ceremonies of the Church. Cambridge: Joseph Bentham, 1759.

Brainerd, D. *An Abridgement of Mr. David Brainerd's Journal Among the Indians or the Rise and Progress of a Remarkable Work of Grace Among a Number of the Indians in the Provinces of New Jersey and Pennsylvania*. London: John Oswald, 1748.

Brief Narrative of the Baptist Mission in India. 5th ed. Bristol: J. G. Fuller, 1819.

Brown, R. S., A. Fischman, and C. R. Showalter. "Primary Hyperparathyroidism, Hypercalcemia, Paranoid Delusions, Homicide, and Attempted Murder." *Journal of Forensic Sciences* 32(1987): 1460–63.

Buchanan, C. *The College of Fort William in Bengal*. London: T. Cadell, 1805.

Carey, Esther. *Eustace Carey: A Missionary in India*. London: Pewtress, 1857.

Carey, Eustace. *Memoir of William Carey, D.D*. London: Jackson and Walford, 1836.

"Carey Memorial Unveiled." *Northampton Independent*, June 24, 1922.

Carey, S. P. *William Carey, D.D., Fellow of the Linnean Society*. London: Hodder and Stoughton, 1923.

———. *William Carey, D.D., Fellow of the Linnean Society*. 8th ed. London: Carey Press, 1934.

Carey, W. *An Enquiry into the Obligations of Christians to Use Means for the Conversion of the Heathens.* Leicester: Ann Ireland, 1792.

Carpenter, P. K. "Thomas Arnold: A Provincial Psychiatrist in Georgian England." *Medical History* 33(1989): 199–216.

Catalogue of the Printed Books and Pamphlets in the Library of the Linnean Society of London. London: Longmans, Green, 1925.

Cathcart, W., ed. *The Baptist Encyclopedia.* Philadelphia: Louis Everts, 1881, s.v. "William Carey."

Chatterjee, S. K. *Missions in India: A Catalogue of the Carey Library.* Serampore: Council of Serampore College, 1980.

———. *Hannah Marshman: The First Woman Missionary in India.* Hooghly, India: S. S. Chatterjee, 1987.

———. *Felix Carey: A Tiger Tamed.* Calcutta: Author, 1991.

———. *William Carey and Serampore.* Serampore: Kartik Dutta Banik, n.d.

Colaizzi, J. *Homicidal Insanity, 1800–1985.* Tuscaloosa: University of Alabama Press, 1989.

Coupland, R. *Britain and India, 1600–1941.* London: Longmans, Green, 1941.

———. *Wilberforce.* 2d ed. London: Collins, 1945.

Culross, J. *William Carey.* London: Hodder and Stoughton, 1881.

Dakin, A. *William Carey: Shoemaker, Linguist, Missionary.* London: Carey Press, 1942.

Dale, M. K. "Piddington and Hackleton." In *The Victoria History of the Counties of England: Northampton,* vol. 4, ed. L. F. Salzman. London: University of London, 1937.

Digby, A. *Madness, Morality and Medicine: A Study of the York Retreat, 1796–1914.* Cambridge: Cambridge University Press, 1985.

Donnelly, M. *Managing the Mind: A Study of Medical Psychology in Early Nineteenth-Century Britain.* London: Tavistock, 1983.

Drewery, M. *William Carey: Shoemaker and Missionary.* London: Hodder and Stoughton, 1978.

Edwards, J. *An Humble Attempt to Promote Explicit Agreement and Visible Union of God's People in Extraordinary Prayer.* 1747. Reprint, Northampton, Old England: T. Dicey, 1789.

———. *An Account of the Life of the Late Reverend Mr. David Brainerd.* Edinburgh: John Gray and Gavin Alston, 1765.

Eliot, J. *A Brief Narrative of the Progress of the Gospel Amongst the Indians in New England in the Year 1670.* London: J. Allen, 1671.

Eliot, J., and Mayhew. *Tears of Repentance or a Further Narrative of the Progress of the Gospel Amongst the Indians in New England.* London: n.p., 1653.

Encyclopaedia Britannica. 15th ed., s.v. "James Cook."

Ernst, W. "Psychiatry and Colonialism: Lunatic Asylums in British India, 1800–1858." *The Society for the Social History of Medicine Bulletin* 39(1986): 27–31.

———. "The Rise of the European Lunatic Asylum in Colonial India (1750–1858)." *Bulletin of the Indian Institute of History of Medicine* 17(1987): 94–107.

Ewens, G. F. W. *Insanity in India: Its Symptoms and Diagnosis with Reference to the Relation of Crime and Insanity.* Calcutta: Thacker, Spink, 1908.

"Extracts from the Late Rev. A. Fuller's Correspondence with the late Rev. Mr. Stevens, of Colchester." *Baptist Magazine* 8(1816).

Farrar, S., and J. Roberts. *Where They Are.* Dallas, Tex.: NBC Players, 1988.

Forrester, D. B. *Caste and Christianity: Attitudes and Policies on Caste of Anglo-Saxon Protestant Missions in India.* London: Curzon Press, 1980.

Frizelle, E. R. *The Life and Times of the Royal Infirmary at Leicester: The Making of a Teaching Hospital, 1766–1980.* Leicester: Leicester Medical Society, 1988.

Frizelle, E. R., and J. D. Martin. *The Leicester Royal Infirmary, 1771–1971.* Leicester: Raithley, Lawrence, 1971.

Fuller, A. G. *Andrew Fuller.* London: Hodder and Stoughton, 1882.

Fuller, T. E. *A Memoir of the Life and Writings of Andrew Fuller.* London: J. Heaton and Son, 1863.

Gardiner, W. *Music and Friends.* Vol. 1. London: Longman, Orme, Brown, and Longman, 1838.

Gould, J. *Northamptonshire.* Shire Publications, 1988.

Greenall, R. L. *A History of Northamptonshire.* London: Phillimore, 1979.

Greene, J. *Reminiscences of the Rev. Robert Hall, A.M.* London: Westley and Davis, 1832.

Gregory, O. "Memoir." In *The Miscellaneous Works and Remains of the Rev. Robert Hall.* London: Henry G. Bohn, 1846.

Gunson, N. "On the Incidence of Alcoholism and Intemperance in Early Pacific Missions." *Journal of Pacific History* 1(1966): 43–62.

———. *Messengers of Grace: Evangelical Missionaries in the South Seas, 1797–1860.* Melbourne: Oxford University Press, 1978.

Guttmacher, M. S. *America's Last King: An Interpretation of the Madness of George III.* New York: Charles Scribner's Sons, 1941.

Hall, R. *Help to Zion's Travellers: Being an Attempt to Remove Various Stumbling Blocks out of the Way Relating to Doctrinal, Experimental, and Practical Religion.* London: Book Society, 1781.

Hays, S. P. "History and Genealogy: Patterns of Change and Prospects for Cooperation." In *Generations and Change: Genealogical Perspectives in Social History,* ed. R. M. Taylor and R. J. Crandall. Macon, Ga.: Mercer University Press, 1986.

Herbert, W. *Biographical Notice of the Rev. William Carey, D.D. of Serampore.* Newcastle: T. and J. Hodgson, 1843.

Hughes, G. W. *Robert Hall.* London: Carey Press, 1943.

Hunter, J. *The Gospel of Gentility: American Women Missionaries in Turn-of-the-Century China.* New Haven: Yale University Press, 1984.

Hunter, R., and I. Macalpine. *Three Hundred Years of Psychiatry, 1535–1860.* New York: Carlisle Publishing, 1982.

Ingham, K. *Reformers in India, 1793–1833: An Account of the Work of Christian Missionaries on Behalf of Social Reform.* Cambridge: University Press, 1956.

Jaggi, O. P. *Western Medicine in India: Epidemics and Other Tropical Diseases.* Delhi: Atma Ram and Sons, 1979.

Johnson, T. F. *Glimpses of Ancient Leicester.* Leicester, 1891.

Jones, K. W. *The New Cambridge History of India, III.1: Socio-Religious Reform Movements in British India.* Cambridge: Cambridge University Press, 1989.

Kamlana, S. H., and L. Holms. "Paranoid Reaction and Underlying Thyrotoxicosis." *British Journal of Psychiatry.* 149(1986): 376–77.

Khan, M. S. "William Carey and the Serampore Books (1800–1834)." *Libri* 11(1961): 197–280.

———. "Felix Carey: A Prisoner of Hope." *Libri* 16(1966): 237–68.

Kirby, D., D. Thomas, and L. Turner. *Northampton Remembers Boot and Shoe.* Northampton: Northampton Borough Council Community Programme, 1988.

Kripalani, K. "Modern Literature." In *A Cultural History of India,* ed. A. L. Baham. Delhi: Oxford University Press, 1975.

Latourette, K. S. *A History of the Expansion of Christianity.* 7 vols. London: Eyre and Spottiswoode, 1938–45.

Leigh, D. *The Historical Development of British Psychiatry, vol. 1, 18th and 19th Century.* Oxford: Pergamon Press, 1961.

Lewis, C. B. *The Life of John Thomas.* London: Macmillan, 1873.

Linnean Society of London. *List of Members, 1805–1939.* London: Linnean Society, 1939.

Macalpine, I., and R. Hunter. *George III and the Mad-Business*. London: Allen Lane, 1969.

McBeth, H. L. *The Baptist Heritage*. Nashville, Tenn.: Broadman Press, 1987.

Madge, S. Letter to the Editor. *Northampton Mercury*, August 29, 1895.

Maegraith, B. *Clinical Tropical Diseases*. 8th ed. Oxford: Blackwell Scientific Publications, 1984.

Malcolmson, R. W. *Life and Labour in England: 1700–1780*. London: Hutchinson, 1981.

Manson-Bahr, P. E. C., and F. I. C. Apted. *Manson's Tropical Diseases*. 18th ed. London: Balliere Tindall, 1982.

Marshall, P. J. *The New Cambridge History of India: Bengal, The British Bridge-head*. Cambridge: Cambridge University Press, 1987.

Marshman, J. C. *The Life and Times of Carey, Marshman, and Ward*. 2 vols. London: Longman, Brown, Green, Longmans, and Roberts, 1859.

Maudsley, H. *The Pathology of Mind: A Study of Its Distempers, Deformities, and Disorders*. 1895. Reprint, London: Julian Friedmann Publishers, 1979.

Mayhew, A. *Christianity and the Government of India*. London: Faber and Gwyer, 1929.

Meissner, W. W. *The Paranoid Process*. New York: Jason Aronson, 1978.

Middlebrook, J. B. *William Carey*. London: Carey Kingsgate Press, 1961.

Missionary Correspondence: Containing Extracts of Letters from the Late Mr. Samuel Pearce to the Missionaries in India, Between the Years 1794–1798 and From Mr. John Thomas From 1798–1800. London: T. Gardiner and Son, 1814.

Mitchell, S. *Not Disobedient: A History of United Baptist Church, Leicester Including Harvey Lane 1760–1845, Belvoir Street 1845–1940 and Charles Street 1831–1940*. Leicester: Author, 1984.

Morris, J. W. *Memoirs of the Life and Writings of the Rev. Andrew Fuller*. London: Author, 1816.

Morrison, J. H. *William Carey: Cobbler and Pioneer*. London: Hodder and Stoughton, 1924.

Munford, J. K., ed. *John Ludyard's Journal of Captain Cook's Last Voyage*. Corvallis, Oreg.: Oregon State University Press, 1963.

Murphy, M. J. *Poverty in Cambridgeshire*. Cambridge: Oleander Press, 1978.

Myers, J. B. *William Carey: The Shoemaker Who Became the Father and Founder of Modern Missions*. Kilmarnock, Scotland: John Ritchie, 1887.

Neill, S. *Colonizing and Christian Missions*. London: Lutterworth Press, 1966.

Nichols, J. *History and Antiquities of the County of Leicester*. 4 vols., 1815. Reprint, Menston, Yorkshire: Scholar Press, 1971.

Ogilvie, J. N. *The Apostles of India*. London: Hodder and Stoughton, 1915.

———. *Our Empire's Debt to Missions*. London: Hodder and Stoughton, 1924.

"One Hundred and Fiftieth Anniversary." *Baptist Times,* June 14, 1984.

One Hundred Years After: A Sermon and Addresses, London, October, 1934. London: Carey Press, 1934.

Orme, H. G., and W. H. Brock. *Leicestershire's Lunatics: The Institutional Care of Leicestershire Lunatics During the Nineteenth Century.* Leicester: Leicestershire Museums, Art Galleries and Records Service, 1987.

Oussoren, A. H. *William Carey: Especially His Missionary Principles.* Leiden: A. W. Sijthoff, 1945.

Palmer, J. E. "The Life and Times of William Carey." *Northamptonshire and Bedfordshire Times,* November 26–28, 1982.

Parry-Jones, W. L. *The Trade in Lunacy: A Study of Private Mad-Houses in England in the Eighteenth and Nineteenth Centuries.* London: Routledge and Kegan Paul, 1972.

Payne, E. A. *The Prayer Call of 1784.* London: Baptist Laymen's Missionary Movement, 1941.

———. "Carey's 'Enquiry': An Essay for the Ter-Jubilee." *International Review of Missions* 31(1942): 180–86.

———. "Two Dutch Translations by Carey: An Angus Library Find." *Baptist Quarterly* New Series 11(1942): 33–38.

———. "Carey and His Biographers." *Baptist Quarterly* 19(1961): 1–9.

Pearn, B. R. "Felix Carey and the English Baptist Mission in Burma." *Journal of the Burma Research Society* 28(1938): 1–91.

Pearson, H. *Memoirs of the Life and Writings of the Rev. Claudius Buchanan.* 2 vols. Oxford: University Press, 1817.

Peirce, W. *The Ecclesiastical Principles and Polity of the Wesleyan Methodists.* London: Hamilton, Adams, 1854.

Periodical Accounts Relative to the Baptist Missionary Society 3(1808).

Periodical Accounts Relating to the Missions of the Church of the United Brethren Established Among the Heathen 1(1790–92).

Petersen, W. J. *Martin Luther Had a Wife, Harriet Beecher Stowe Had a Husband.* Wheaton, Ill.: Tyndale House, 1983.

Philips, C. H. *The East India Company, 1784–1834.* Manchester: University Press, 1961.

Potts, E. D. *British Baptist Missionaries in India, 1793–1837: The History of Serampore and Its Missions.* Cambridge: University Press, 1967.

Price, A. G., ed. *The Explorations of Captain James Cook in the Pacific As Told by Selections of His Own Journals 1768–1779*. Sydney: Angus and Robertson, 1969.

Psychiatry and Mental Health in Britain: A Historical Exhibition, 1963. London: Wellcome Historical Medical Library, 1963.

Raychoudhary, S. C. *Social, Cultural and Economic History of India*. Delhi: Surjeet Publications, 1980.

Richter, J. *A History of Missions in India*. Edinburgh: Oliphant, Anderson and Ferrier, 1980.

Robinson, F., ed. *The Cambridge Encyclopedia of India, Pakistan, Bangladesh, Sri Lanka, Nepal, Bhutan, and the Maldives*. Cambridge: Cambridge University Press, 1989.

Ryland, J. *Life and Death of the Rev. Andrew Fuller*. London: Button and Son, 1818.

Shepard, T. *The Clear Sunshine of the Gospel Breaking Forth Upon the Indians in New England*. London: R. Cotes, 1648.

Sherring, M. A. *The History of Protestant Missions in India*. London: Trubner, 1875.

A Short Sketch of the Work Carried on by the Ancient Protestant Episcopal Moravian Church in Northamptonshire. London: Hazell, Watson, and Viney, 1886.

Showalter, E. *The Female Malady: Women, Madness, and English Culture, 1830–1980*. London: Virago Press, 1985.

Sibelrud, R. L. "The Relationship Between Mercury from Dental Amalgam and Mental Health." *American Journal of Psychotherapy* 43(1989): 575–87.

Sims, J. "Dr. Carey's Crinum." *Curtis's Botanical Magazine* 51(1854): 2466–67.

Skultans, V. *Madness and Morals: Ideas on Insanity in the Nineteenth Century*. London: Routledge and Kegan Paul, 1975.

Smith, G. *Carey in the Evangelical Succession, Third Series*. Edinburgh: Macniven and Wallace, 1884.

———. *The Life of William Carey, D.D.: Shoemaker and Missionary*. London: John Murray, 1885.

———. *The Life of William Carey*. 2d ed. London: John Murray, 1887.

Spear, P. *The Oxford History of Modern India, 1740–1975*. 2d ed. Delhi: Oxford University Press, 1978.

Speer, R. E. *Some Great Leaders in the World Movement*. New York: Fleming Revell, 1911.

Spence, S. A., comp. *Captain James Cook: A Bibliography.* Mitcham, Surrey: Compiler, 1960.

Stamp, T. and C. *James Cook: Maritime Scientist.* Whitby, England: Caedmon of Whitby, 1978.

Steadman, T. *Memoir of the Rev. William Steadman, D.D.* London: Thomas Ward, 1838.

Stephen, L., and S. Lee. *The Dictionary of National Biography.* London: Oxford University Press, 1917.

Stewart, W. *The Plan and the Sequel: The Missionary Purpose and Legacy of William Carey and Alexander Duff.* Serampore: Council of Serampore College, 1980.

Swann, J. *Shoemaking.* Aylesbury, Bucks: Shire Publications, 1986.

Taylor, J. *Biographical and Literary Notices of William Carey, D.D.* Northampton: Dryden Press, 1886.

Tellenbach, H. "On the Nature of Jealousy." *Journal of Phenomenological Psychology* 4(1974): 461–68.

Tippleston, D. *William Carey and Hackleton Baptist Church.* Northampton: Billingham and Son, 1956.

Tucker, R. A. *From Jerusalem to Irian Jaya: A Biographical History of Christian Missions.* Grand Rapids: Zondervan, 1983.

Tucker, R. A., and W. L. Liefeld. *Daughters of the Church: Women and Ministry from New Testament Times to the Present.* Grand Rapids: Zondervan, 1987.

Villiers, A. *Captain Cook, The Seaman's Seaman: A Study of the Great Discoverer.* London: Hodder and Stoughton, 1967.

Walker, F. D. *William Carey: Missionary Pioneer and Statesman.* London: Student Christian Movement, 1926. Reprint, Chicago: Moody Press, 1980.

Warren, I. *The Nonconformist Tradition.* Northampton: Northamptonshire Leisure and Libraries, 1987.

Warren, M. *The Missionary Movement from Britain in Modern History.* London: SCM Press, 1965.

———. *Social History and Christian Mission.* London: SCM Press, 1967.

Watson, F. *A Concise History of India.* London: Thames and Hudson, 1974.

Whellan, W. *History, Gazeteer, and Directory of Northamptonshire.* London: Whittaker, 1849.

Williams, L. and M., eds. *Serampore Letters: Being the Unpublished Correspondence of William Carey and Others with John Williams, 1800–1816.* New York: G. P. Putnam's Sons, 1892.

Wilson, C. R. M. "Psychiatry in the Tropics." In *Medicine in the Tropics,* ed. A. W. Woodruff. Edinburgh: Churchill Livingstone, 1979.

Winks, W. E. *Lives of Illustrious Shoemakers.* London: Sampson Low, Marston, Searle, and Rivington, 1883.

Woodruff, A. W., and S. Bell. *A Synopsis of Infectious and Tropical Diseases.* 2d ed. Bristol: John Wright and Sons, 1978.

Wright, T. *William Carey.* London: Pearce, 1896.

Yonge, C. M. *Pioneers and Founders.* Macmillan, 1871.

Index